EXPLORING RACE IN PREDOMINANTLY WHITE CLASSROOMS

Although multicultural education has made significant gains in recent years, with many courses specifically devoted to the topic in both undergraduate and graduate education programs, and more scholars of color teaching in these programs, these victories bring with them a number of pedagogic dilemmas. Most students in these programs are not themselves students of color, meaning the topics and the faculty teaching them are often faced with groups of students whose backgrounds and perspectives may be decidedly different – even hostile – to multicultural pedagogy and curricula. This edited collection brings together an interdisciplinary group of scholars of color to critically examine what it is like to explore race in predominantly White classrooms. It delves into the challenges academics face while dealing with the wide range of responses from both White students and students of color, and provides a powerful overview of how teachers of color highlight the continued importance and existence of race and racism. *Exploring Race in Predominately White Classrooms* is an essential resource for any educator interested in exploring race within the context of today's classrooms.

George Yancy is Professor of Philosophy at Duquesne University.

Maria del Guadalupe Davidson is Assistant Professor of Business Communication and Co-Director of the Center for Social Justice at the University of Oklahoma.

The Critical Social Thought Series

Edited by Michael W. Apple
University of Wisconsin–Madison

Radical Possibilities
Public Policy, Urban Education, and a New Social Movement
Jean Anyon

Race, Identity, and Representation in Education (2nd ed.)
Cameron McCarthy, Warren Crichlow, Greg Dimitriadis, and Nadine Dolby (Eds.)

Could it be Otherwise? Parents and the Inequities of Public School Choice
Lois André-Bechely

Reading and Writing the World with Mathematics
Towards a Pedagogy for Social Justice
Eric Gustein

Market Movements
African American Involvement in School Voucher Reform
Thomas C. Pedroni

Rightist Multiculturalism
Core Lessons on Neoconservative School Reform
Kristen L. Buras

Unequal by Design
High-Stakes Testing and the Standardization of Inequality
Wayne Au

Black Literate Lives
Historical and Contemporary Perspectives
Maisha T. Fisher

Hidden Markets
The New Education Privatization
Patricia Burch

Critical Perspectives on bell hooks
Maria del Guadalupe Davidson and George Yancy (Eds.)

Advocacy Leadership
Toward a Post-Reform Agenda in Education
Gary L. Anderson

Race, Whiteness, and Education
Zeus Leonardo

Controversy in the Classroom
The Democratic Power of Discussion
Diana E. Hess

The New Political Economy of Urban Education
Neoliberalism, Race, and the Right to the City
Pauline Lipman

Critical Curriculum Studies
Education, Consciousness, and the Politics of Knowing
Wayne Au

Learning to Liberate
Community-Based Solutions to the Crisis in Urban Education
Vajra Watson

Act Your Age! A Cultural Construction of Adolescence (2nd ed.)
Nancy Lesko

Critical Pedagogy and Social Change
Critical Analysis on the Language of Possibility
Seehwa Cho

Educating Activist Allies
Social Justice Pedagogy with the Suburban and Urban Elite
Katy Swalwell

EXPLORING RACE IN PREDOMINANTLY WHITE CLASSROOMS

Scholars of Color Reflect

Edited by
George Yancy and
Maria del Guadalupe Davidson

NEW YORK AND LONDON

First published 2014
by Routledge
711 Third Avenue, New York, NY 10017

and by Routledge
2 Park Square, Milton Park, Abingdon, Oxon OX14 4RN

Routledge is an imprint of the Taylor & Francis Group, an informa business

Library of Congress Cataloging-in-Publication Data
Exploring race in predominantly white classrooms : scholars of color reflect /
[edited by] George Yancy, Maria del Guadalupe Davidson.
     pages cm. — (Critical social thought)
   Includes bibliographical references and index.
   Multicultural education. 2. Racism — Study and teaching — United States.
   3. Race relations — Study and teaching (Higher) — United States.
   4. Education, Higher — Social aspects — United States. 5. United States —
   Race relations — Study and teaching (Higher)   I. Yancy, George.
   II. Davidson, Maria del Guadalupe.
   LC1099.3.E98 2014
   370.117—dc23

                                                                    2013039566

ISBN: 978-0-415-83668-5 (hbk)
ISBN: 978-0-415-83669-2 (pbk)
ISBN: 978-0-203-41671-6 (ebk)

Typeset in Bembo
by RefineCatch Limited, Bungay, Suffolk, UK

To my wife Susan Hadley for all the critical intellectual energy and work that she brings to bear upon her own field of expertise

George Yancy

To Dr. Barry Gan—master teacher, champion of justice, comforter of souls

Maria del Guadalupe Davidson

CONTENTS

SERIES EDITOR'S INTRODUCTION

Michael W. Apple

There has deservedly been a growing interest in the political and pedagogical processes through which "race" and racializing practices and identities are understood, performed, and especially interrupted.[1] Indeed, I can think of few areas as important as this. Take the field of critical education as but one example. The influences of, and debates about, critical race theory, about whiteness, about what the curriculum and pedagogy of a truly critical education surrounding issues of "race" actually look like, and many more issues of theory and practice are increasingly central to the entire field.[2] I personally am not alone in saying that my own work has been strongly influenced by these debates and by the powerful and eloquent voices of scholars of color.[3]

One of the major challenges facing the gains that have been made in a truly critical discussion of, and education about, "race" is actually the result of victories. Many more courses specifically devoted to race are now offered and often required in undergraduate education and in graduate programs. In addition, many more scholars of color are now teaching in these undergraduate and graduate programs, not only here in the United States but in other nations as well. While this represents only a partial victory after years of cultural struggles over what should count as "legitimate knowledge,"[4] there can be no doubt that at predominantly "White" institutions gains have been made indeed.

While these are indeed gains, they have brought with them a number of very real political, personal, and pedagogic dilemmas and conflicts. Most of the students in these undergraduate and graduate programs are not themselves persons of color. This means that both the topics and the faculty teaching them are often faced with groups of students whose backgrounds and perspectives may be decidedly different—and sometimes even overtly hostile to the substantive and serious pedagogy and curriculum so necessary to challenge the dominant understandings of race and to displace whiteness as the prevailing commonsense.

To give just one example, at the University of Wisconsin, Madison—the highly rated university where I personally teach—we have an undergraduate teacher education program that is specifically aimed at critically reflexive understandings of, and action on, the ways in which race and racializing policies and practices work in and through education. Yet, of over a hundred students whom we have admitted this year to the elementary teacher education program, only a very few students are themselves persons of color. This has a major effect on what we do.

Of course, the word "we" is a crucial one. Who is the "we"? Who is included and excluded in such a category? Who is seen as the "human ordinary," as the unmarked and unraced one? What does it mean to be marked as the "other"? For faculty and students of color at universities, these questions cannot be avoided.

George Yancy and Maria del Guadalupe Davidson's book, *Exploring Race in Predominantly White Classrooms: Scholars of Color Reflect*, is both an insightful treatment of the problems that faculty members of color face in dealing with this complex situation and a very thoughtful examination of what they do when they teach their students. It examines teaching in multiple kinds of settings and programs in ways that illuminate the limits and possibilities of teaching about race in predominantly White classrooms. But it goes further. It also examines the experiences and positions that are occupied by students of color in these very same classrooms and programs.

The authors included here come from varied kinds of institutions. This is a very good element in a book such as this, since a large portion of students in undergraduate and graduate programs in this nation and others are in colleges and universities of different kinds—from high-status universities to institutions that engage primarily in an education that aims at different populations and goals. Because of this, the book speaks to a wide audience.

Exploring Race in Predominantly White Classrooms: Scholars of Color Reflect is characterized by a clear and compelling narrative style. Yancy and Davidson have chosen well, with a focus that is theoretically and politically powerful. But the emphasis of the book is less on theory—although it does contain some insightful theoretical material—and more on reflections on what actually happens in real situations and what might be done about this.

These reflections are of crucial significance not "only" in terms of how scholars of color reflect on how educators can engage in an education that challenges dominance and can provide a classroom environment that enables this to go on. The compelling narratives included in Yancy and Davidson's collection continually remind us of what is at stake if we don't engage in such challenging pedagogic work in *all* fields and disciplines.

Take the field of philosophy and social theory as one example. In his now classic text, *The Racial Contract*, Charles Mills engages in a detailed analysis of the history of some of the most influential social and political theories that have established much of the foundation of our ideas about rights and the visions of rationality that underpin them. If I were to speak very generally about what is Mills' much more detailed argument, he illuminates how these ideas are grounded in the construction of what might be called an "irrational Other"—a constitutive outside that is closely related to the history of racialization in the West.[5]

Thus, when faculties of color deal with the dilemmas, identities, and dominant understandings of students, they have to face not only the struggles with their own identities and the politics of who they are and what they need to do. They also have to confront some of the most deep-seated and all-too-often disembodied assumptions about what it means to know, how such knowledge functions, and who this society pictures as a knower. Raising substantive questions about this often means confronting core elements of students' identities, their sense of history and of their place in it, and what a just society should look like. This is hard educational, political, and personal work. The authors included here display an honesty and a courage about what this means to them, to their students, and to a society in need of such honesty and courage.

Michael W. Apple
John Bascom Professor of Curriculum and Instruction
and Educational Policy Studies
University of Wisconsin–Madison

Notes

1 I have purposely put the word "race" in quotation marks to remind us that race is not a biological but a social category. It is a construction, a category that has had a very complex conceptual and political history.
2 To name just a few, see, for example: Edward Taylor, David Gillborn, and Gloria Ladson-Billings (Eds.) (2009), *Foundations of Critical Race Theory*. New York: Routledge; Zeus Leonardo (2009), *Race, Whiteness, and Education*. New York: Routledge; Maria del Guadalupe Davidson and George Yancy (Eds.) (2009), *Critical Perspectives on bell hooks*. New York: Routledge; Michael W. Apple, Wayne Au, and Luis Armando Gandin (Eds.) (2009), *The Routledge International Handbook of Critical Education*. New York: Routledge; Zeus Leonardo and W. Norton Grubb (2013), *Education and Racism*. New York: Routledge; and Marvin Lynn and Adrienne D. Dixson (Eds.) (2013), *Handbook of Critical Race Theory in Education*. New York: Routledge.
3 See Michael W. Apple (2013), *Can Education Change Society?* New York: Routledge.
4 For further discussion of the history and struggles over what counts as legitimate or official knowledge, see Michael W. Apple (2014), *Official Knowledge*, 3rd edn. New York: Routledge.
5 Charles Mills (1997), *The Racial Contract*. Ithaca, NY: Cornell University Press.

ACKNOWLEDGMENTS

Yancy: I would like to thank the contributors to this significant volume, especially for their bravery and conviction to address an under-theorized topic within academia. Without your pedagogical insights, this project would not have gotten off the proverbial ground. I would also like to thank our Critical Social Thought series editor Michael W. Apple for his support of this project. As a leading critical educational theorist, I am honored by his delight in this volume. I would also like to thank Allison Bush, Senior Editorial Assistant at Routledge, for her guidance and diligence. I would also like to thank Lupe, my friend, colleague, and co-editor, who continues to inspire rich conceptual possibilities that are designed to make a difference in the world we all inhabit. Thanks to James Swindal, Professor of Philosophy and Dean of the McAnulty College and Graduate School of Liberal Arts, who has continued to support my work with such vigor. Thanks to James Spady and Charles Johnson for all of your wisdom, support, and groundbreaking work. The intellectual standard that you've set will always keep my mind and body engaged in intellectual excellence. I would also like to thank Janine Jones for her philosophical insights and for pushing me to think with greater intensity, and to rethink my concept of gift-giving, especially in ways that avoid offering mere outwardly beautiful packages that can't be opened. I would also like to thank Barbara Applebaum for her work on White complicity pedagogy; Bridget M. Newell for the incredible work that she does within the context of critically engaging issues of diversity; Claudia Ruitenberg for taking the time to establish links between my early work and my more recent work; the late Joel Olson for his important work on democracy and whiteness; and the late John Warren, whose work in pedagogy and whiteness continues to impact all of us.

Davidson: First, I would like to thank my friend George Yancy for inviting me to be a part of this project. George, I appreciate your unwavering support over the years. I would like to acknowledge my colleagues in the Marketing and Supply Chain Management Division of the Price College of Business, University of Oklahoma, especially Dr. Daniel Emery, Dr. Rajiv Dant, and Professor Ron Davidson. Thank you for being so welcoming. I would also like to thank Dr. Michele Eodice, Dr. Jill Irvine, Dr. Diane Perpich, Dr. Ben Kepple, Dr. Meta Carstarphen, and Professor Renae Butler King for their friendship and support. And, I would like to acknowledge my former students: George Lee, Rashid Campbell, Dominique Baker, Natalie Dickson, Alex Francisco, Lindsey Vanderventer, and Matt Bruenig. You are the best students a professor could ever ask for. Thank you for being lights of pure joy in my life. I would like to thank *mi amigo* Dr. Steve Martinot—a warrior in the struggle to eradicate whiteness. Finally, I would like to thank Scott Davidson for his companionship and love.

INTRODUCTION

White Crisis and the Value of *Losing One's Way*

George Yancy

> The fact that we notice such arrivals tells us more about what is already in place than it does about "the who" that arrives.[1]
>
> *Sara Ahmed*

The above epigraph speaks to the *lived* reality of academics of color who teach at predominantly White universities, and powerfully captures the phenomenological predicament of the critical cadre of scholars of color within the important text—*Exploring Race in Predominantly White Classrooms: Scholars of Color Reflect*—that you hold before you. We walk into classrooms where our bodies are always already marked, where White racist normative assumptions truncate who we are and what we are deemed "capable" of teaching. Within this "sea of whiteness," we move against the tide of White gazes that attempt to fix us according to iterative frames of reference that have become normalized and naturalized ways of making sense of the social world. "To see" a body of color in the capacity of professor/teacher is "to know" a priori about that body. This is a situation where perception and knowledge are collapsed, where "to know" bodies of color is "to see" bodies of color, and where, conversely, "to see" bodies of color is "to know" bodies of color. We are seen as "inferior," as intellectually "inadequate" in relationship to our White colleagues, as somehow "out of place." We are also marked as pseudo-scholars who often teach subjects that are specific to an identity politics gone awry. White gazes surround us. We feel their penetrating curiosity, their wonderment. While unspoken, their White gazes are interrogative: "Just who do you think you are?" "Are you really qualified?" "Are you sure you have the right classroom?" And even after their initial skepticism has subsided, and as the semester progresses, their White gazes, bodily postures, styles of questioning, innuendoes, hubris, and interrogations create a space that is unwelcoming, a space that is hermeneutically hostile to our self-understanding as experts in our various academic fields. Within the context of White philosophical academic spaces, Linda Alcoff writes:

> As a Latina in the academic world of North American philosophy, I regularly feel that, indeed, I have lost, or am in the process of losing, my marbles. Neither my general lived experience, nor my reference points in argumentation, nor my routine affective responses to events, nor my philosophical intuitions are shared with most people in my immediate milieu.[2]

Alcoff's point here is that she seems to occupy a different life-world, a different epistemic and affective geography.

Both predominantly White academic institutions and White classrooms convey White territoriality. It is as if one has entered a neighborhood governed and controlled by a White covenant that bespeaks your desired absence. Within this space, it feels as if one's presence is being policed as stoppable; where the social skin of the classroom does not call out to you with dialectical smoothness—that is, where you don't move within that space in such a way that it claims you as desirable, as someone "fit" *to be* in that space. Academic bodies of color within such White spaces "could be described in terms of the bodily and social experience of restriction, uncertainty, and blockage."[3]

Linking themes of (a) claiming intellectual space with ease/difficulty, (b) the complexities and difficulties of identity formation within the predominantly White field of philosophy, and (c) the ways in which the field of philosophy signifies a space of whiteness that thereby specifically places under erasure Black women as *lovers of wisdom*, Donna-Dale Marcano writes:

> This was brought home to me as I walked into [an] Introduction to Philosophy class and many others, consisting in my case of mostly young White boys, and realized that their ability to take up the position of the philosopher occurred with relative ease. Whether they accept or reject philosophy they are able to articulate their positions as knowers. But then again, they also are known by philosophy.[4]

To apply Marcano's point more broadly, one might argue that White bodies are always already sanctioned as "knowers" and are always already known as being at home within disciplinary matrixes of knowledge production. As a Black female philosopher, as someone who constitutes the quintessence of philosophical iconographic tension in relationship to the history of White philosophical assumptions, Marcano's body is stressed, noticed, even deemed oxymoronic. As Sara Ahmed writes, "White bodies are habitual insofar as they 'trail behind' actions: they do not get 'stressed' in their encounters with objects or others, as their whiteness 'goes unnoticed.'"[5]

Unlike our White colleagues, it is said that we fail, because of our *raced bodies*, to appreciate universality, objectivity, and neutrality. In short, it is assumed that we can't do theory without it being "sullied" by our value-laden assumptions, by our ontological particularity. Our nonwhite skin color is marked as different or deviant, where our "raced" bodies become the foreground vis-à-vis an invisible background of whiteness qua normative. In other cases, our accents are deemed unintelligible, a sure sign of being alien and unlike those who speak "standard" American (White) English.

There are other times when we are seen as criminals who have somehow invaded the "sanctity" of White spaces, spaces where we are (must be) watched with suspicion. We have also been mistaken for the custodial help. And while working in this capacity on college campuses is not to be labeled ersatz, bodies of color, through the White gaze, fall "naturally" within the category of "the help." We have also been sexualized in problematic ways. Women of color academics, for example, endure forms of oppressive multiplicity; they are deemed inferior as women and as hypersexual vis-à-vis their "exotic" features. At the end of the day, they are considered sexual playthings that are not to be taken seriously as academics, as persons who think and publish and do so with tremendous productivity, creativity, and rigor. Often entering within a broader intellectual tradition that already valorizes "mind" over "body," "cognition" over "context," the content of "knowledge claims" over "lived autobiography," women of color academics—and academics of color, more generally—are reduced to their bodies, and their "academic" work is deemed idiosyncratic, hermetic, and biased.

Sara Ahmed's epigraph above, though, shifts the gaze away from, in this case, academic bodies of color. It is not about "us"; that is, bodies of color who *arrive*. Rather, it is about "them"; that is, White bodies, White institutional norms, White dominated spaces, White ways of being-in-the-world, and White power and hegemony that are *already in place*. And while reframing the problem does not rid us of the lived or phenomenological pain that we undergo as we enter such White dominated spaces, we are able to locate the source of our pain in problematic forms of White interpellation/hailing. We understand how the meaning that we give our embodied selves is "confiscated" and challenged through White gazes that return us to ourselves in ways that render us foreign to our self-understanding. Indeed, we are able to render such processes visible. Rendering such processes visible empowers us to militate against the ways in which White gazes may install forms of double consciousness that can result in profound expressions of epistemological violence.

So, when we walk into predominantly White classrooms, it is not about the ways in which we are problem bodies qua problem bodies. Our arrival is rendered hyper-visible because of how various social spaces—the classroom being one—are constituted as an enveloping White racial integument that holds together

White bodies and that installs those White bodies as familiar and "familial"; a social skin that calls to those bodies as wanted and as desirable. As a result, then, academics of color actually "intrude" upon a preexisting social intelligibility not because they are intrusive bodies as such, but because there already exists a form of White normative sedimentation that is operatively exclusionary. In short, it is the White bodies that inhabit those White spaces that constitute the conditions in terms of which academic bodies of color are deemed problematic.

As scholars of color who teach courses that critically engage questions of race and whiteness, we know all too well the specific challenges that we encourage White students to face. Moreover, we are witnesses to their resistance, anger, obfuscation, denial, and bad faith. In fact, we are often targets of their resentment. We are recipients of such resentment not simply because the conceptual content is so incredibly challenging to their place in the world and their White identities, but because of our embodiment as scholars of color. Our bodies function as texts that White students deploy against us, suggesting that we possess and express *personal* forms of animosity toward them *because they are White*.

In a course that I regularly teach entitled Race Matters: Literary and Philosophical Perspectives, a White undergraduate student shared with me that he was buying books for that course when confronted by another White student. "So, you're taking a course with Dr. Yancy. You know he hates White people." My student was bemused. During another time when teaching this course, a White student shared with the class that he told his father that we had been critically discussing the concept of whiteness, and his father said, "Be careful of Dr. Yancy. He is trying to get you to feel White guilt." I immediately shared with the class how the "advice" of his father had not only misconstrued (indeed, distorted) the aims of my course, but that such defensive responses help to reinforce psychological barriers to growth and to preclude risk. His father may have thought that he was helping his son; protecting his son against my insidious efforts to get his son to feel guilty about what he had no part in creating—like the history of American slavery or the history of lynching Black bodies. Yet, it is my sense that he failed his son. Many of our White students already wear reactionary armor to protect them from engaging in critical forms of self-reflection on their whiteness, especially from the likes of us. You know, those academics of color that use their classroom spaces to guilt White students, and to leave them crying at the end of the day about being encased in White skin. Our classrooms are believed to function as cathartic spaces where we—finally—get even. His father reinforced his armor of resistance. Luckily, this one White student appeared to be aware of the dangerous implications of his father's "advice."

Yet, the courses that we, academics of color, teach that address the issue of race are designed to speak dangerously and courageously to various forms of White hegemony that oppress and marginalize people of color along the axis of race.[6] Teaching courses that critically engage race—specifically, whiteness—not only disrupt forms of White complacency, privilege, and power within the classroom, but within the larger White academic institution itself and the society at large that is predicated upon White nation building. Yet, as many of us know, the violence has already been done to our White students before we face that sea of whiteness within our classrooms. This is a point to which I will return.

A philosophy graduate student shared with me recently that a fellow White philosophy graduate student said to her that he is *not* prepared to take any of my courses as he is *not* ready to face those parts of himself—yet. But of what is he afraid? While there are other graduate philosophy courses that I teach, two of those courses have been very challenging not only to my White students, but to me as well. My course Critical Whiteness Studies engages the historical dimensions of whiteness as a site of White bonding and collective identity formation. This identity formation is theorized as parasitic upon the nonwhite body. In fact, we engage the issue of whether or not White identity is anything other than a site of parasitism, which raises the possibility that White identity is empty except for its historical and current exercises of power, colonialism, and privilege. As the transcendental norm, whiteness defines nonwhiteness as "different" while it, whiteness, remains the same across a field of difference. Without its dependency on "difference," though, we also explore the issue of the limits of whiteness and its possible vacuity. Within this course, White students are encouraged to think about whiteness within the context of the history of philosophy, and to think about ways in which their identities as White students of philosophy (many of whom will become professional White philosophers) have been subjected to processes of interpellation. As we engage issues of whiteness and philosophy, many if not all of them are struck by the fact that they are entangled within power relationships of which they were *not* previously cognizant. I have noticed that, for them, the experience can be existentially jolting; indeed, threatening to their sense of self, autonomy, and agency.

The other course that I teach is entitled Phenomenology of Race. In this course, we examine race through the lens of phenomenology, where we critically engage such themes as *Erlebnis*, race and social motility, whiteness as a lived site of spatial latitude, racial embodiment and forms of bodily malediction, whiteness and the social/spatial world as ready-to-hand, the White gaze and ontological truncation, the reduction of the body of color to its surface epidermis, the ontic dimensions of race vis-à-vis its socially constructed and intersubjective dimensions, etc. We also explore the ways in which White bodies are "at home" within philosophy departments, philosophy conferences, and such mundane spaces as philosophy department lounges, and how that *feeling* of being at home is a function of an assemblage of philosophical practices enacted by White, typically male, bodies, bodies that have become reified as the paragon of philosophical performance.

So, within that course, we collectively remove the veil that hides the fact that the category of "White philosopher" is a social construction that is embedded within historically contingent norms, norms that masquerade as natural. The point here is that the White philosopher is not only historically positioned within a critical space where his/her philosophical assumptions are shown to be embedded within social-epistemic *White ways* of theorizing the world, but we think critically about the ways in which the White philosopher is always already part of a larger space of historical and institutional hegemony that *excludes* other (nonwhite) ways of knowing, being, valuing. In this way, my White philosophy graduates begin to think about the ways in which they are subjected to White racist technologies that underwrite who they are and what they deem philosophically of value.

In short, both of my courses are dangerous as they demand that my White students refuse to be silent about the quotidian operations of race in their lives, their philosophical lives, even as they attempt to separate the two. By "dangerous," I don't mean that White students (or any students) are exposed to physical danger. While I do make it clear to my White students that university classrooms, more generally, flirt too much with simulacra and fail to dwell with the existential funk of everyday life, physical safety is an unquestioned given.

From the above, it is clear to me what the one White graduate student feared/ fears. He is afraid to give an account of himself, to critique his whiteness, and to begin to reimagine himself in ways that counter White normative and imaginative limits. By implication, then, in the other philosophy courses that he takes—those that don't explore race and where the professors look like him, even when they don't share his gender or sexual orientation—he is at peace with his identity as a White male, he is able to be fully in the space of the classroom in the mode of mythical self-possession. Those courses, presumably, don't force him to recognize how his White embodiment is constituted within that space as a philosophical ally. He does not recognize how his presence helps to constitute those philosophical spaces as normative. I am not suggesting that he should not take those courses. My point is that he needs to be honest; philosophy needs to be honest. If my courses encourage him to engage his philosophical White identity critically as a site that is complicit with White racism and he begins to see this connection, whereas those other courses apparently normalize his philosophical White identity and worldview as they seemingly engage racially neutral concepts formulated by apparently transracial abstract minds, then it is his responsibility to begin to challenge the ways in which, as I would put it, he is a racist. After all, he will more than likely be one of those White philosophy graduate students, along with other White scholars, who, for example, only study White male philosophers or White female philosophers from Europe. It will be incumbent upon him to identify (or certainly try to identify) the procrustean limits of his knowledge, interests, and focus—and, of course, reveal himself as racist. Critically engaging his whiteness, he will begin to enter those courses that are filled with White bodies, mostly White *male* student bodies, that are also taught by White professional philosophers (again, mostly White and male) prepared to call into question not only the ways in which

White bodies easily occupy the spaces within those classrooms, but he will also challenge the limited and value-laden epistemological assumptions that prevail within the conceptual space of that course or other courses.

This raises the fact that such spaces are also violent spaces, especially in terms of what they communicate to nonwhite bodies. Those spaces monochromatically speak to nonwhite bodies as unwanted; and communicate to nonwhite bodies that their epistemic experiences are nugatory. As a person of color, one undergoes experiences of alienation vis-à-vis an imposed and deceitful universality. As a Black philosopher, I have often gotten the sense that students of color within my courses breathe a sigh of relief not only because I speak to the entire class with fearless speech (or parrhesia) about the realities of race/racism, but because my bodily presence reflects back to them their own "raced" embodied selves. Given this, I would argue that my presence provides for them a sense of sanity. My discursive challenges, and the challenges of my embodied presence, communicate to them (a) that they have been correct about so many of those instances of subtle racism and (b) that, despite the domination of White academic bodies within academic spaces, they can become professional academics of color.

I have given talks about race on so many university campuses where the student body is predominantly White. And, almost always, I have been told by students of color, the few that are there, that they are in need of my fearless speech about race; that they are in need of scholars of color. In fact, many faculty of color will also make it clear, though often quietly, that the university has failed them, that the university is afraid to engage race seriously and openly. I have even been told by faculty of color that publishing within the area of race, especially where whiteness is critiqued, can threaten their careers, possibly blocking tenure and promotion. I have been told that they stand in fear of the repercussions; that they are scared. I have no reason to doubt this. As such, scholars of color who critically engage race and who attempt to disclose the ways in which whiteness continues in 2013 to usurp power and control bodies of color and curricula, and who face departments and academic administrators who attempt to derail forms of critical scholarship regarding race, might be said to be fighting behind enemy lines. Within such spaces, academics of color suffer; many may even kowtow and relinquish their academic projects, their passions for racial justice, and perhaps dumb down their intellectual criticality. Others may stand and fight and face the consequences. Many predominantly White universities will accommodate critical voices of color. Of course, as scholars of color who see it as our mission to engage in "radical scholarship," more generally, we owe it to ourselves to think critically about the price of that accommodation.

There are other scholars of color who are not afraid to voice their predicaments, or, perhaps, who do so indirectly, posing questions as opposed to making direct accusations against their home universities. This is telling. I gave a talk at a predominantly White university where I argued that Black people, because of their epistemic social locations, are able to see whiteness in ways that Whites miss or obfuscate.[7] I concluded that Black people possess a *gift* of insight into White ways of being and that Black people are thereby necessary for installing what I call a form of White double consciousness, where Whites see themselves through the eyes of Black people. One Black female faculty member attending my public talk raised a very powerful point. She wanted me to address what she judged to be a problematic implication of my view. She argued that, based upon my view, White people would then be dependent upon Black people for the former's liberation. She saw this as a form of White dependency and control. In short, Black people would be placed in the position of serving White people. While I argued that this was not what I had in mind, she had a point. Was I not arguing that Black scholars—and, perhaps I might add, scholars of color more generally—must function both as objects of White racist vitriol and as liberators of White people, liberating them from their racism? I must admit that this is a very peculiar place to occupy and a fecund issue that needs to be addressed.

My initial response was that, if she did not want to take on that role, she ought to leave the university. This response, though, communicated more than I desired. My aim, or so I believe, was to bring attention to the reality of the degree of White racism on *that* campus. "If this place is racist, and it certainly sounds like it is, then leave." "If it is hostile to academics of color, then leave. No one needs to work in such a racially toxic space." After much thought, I have come to think differently about this. Imagine a woman complaining about sexual harassment on the job and the best that we can offer her is the advice: "Just leave!" We will have failed her. After all, where are Black women to teach in academia where whiteness is absent? And where are women to work without the presence of male power? Within the context of this discussion regarding race in the classroom, it is my sense that we must hold accountable predominantly White universities and colleges to do all that they can to make the places where we, as scholars and academics of color, are not working alone as liberators of White students/people. While I believe that Black people are necessary to the project of "undoing" whiteness, as Whites may not be able to do it themselves, I am not arguing that Black people or people of color must bear the sole responsibility to change White people.

White people who have come to understand many of the complexities involved in the deep socio-structural and psychic dimensions of whiteness will prove essential for helping other Whites to face the problems of whiteness. To argue that Black people and people of color shoulder this responsibility alone only adds insult to injury. So, unlike what Joy A. James and João Costa Vargas brilliantly theorize as the "Black cyborg," which is "a modified, improved human whose increased ethical, spiritual, and physical capabilities generate unusual strength, omniscience, and boundless love,"[8] I would argue that Black people are not angelic *Übermenschen*, slavish gift-givers whose sole telos it is to liberate White people from their racism. Whiteness is not an ontological ineradicable feature of human existence. It is, on this score, contingent. It had a beginning and therefore, logically, it can have an end. And while whiteness, as an ideological and historical process, is structurally anti-Black, there is the hope that it can and will be undone. The price to be paid is unknown.

I would argue that *Exploring Race in Predominantly White Classrooms: Scholars of Color Reflect* functions for scholars of color as a site of safety and sanity, driving home the reality that they are not alone. The text provides a space for validating shared experiences of the complexities, challenges, and difficulties of pedagogically engaging the theme of race in predominantly White academic spaces, classrooms in particular. As such, then, for scholars of color, the text helps to militate against the voices of those who deny the epistemic integrity of the experiences that scholars of color endure within such classrooms. The text speaks to those White scholars who also engage race within their classrooms, communicating to them that, as scholars of color, we face very different challenges when we engage race within our classrooms. Knowledge of this difference can help White academics to think critically about how their White bodies may go racially unmarked within such spaces and what the pedagogical implications of this might entail. This does not deny, however, that students of color, and some of our fellow colleagues of color, have not been accustomed to seeing the world through what Joe R. Feagin calls the "White racial frame." According to Feagin:

> For centuries, to the present day, the dominant [White] racial frame has sharply defined inferior and superior racial groups and authoritatively rationalized and structured the great inequalities of this society. In a White-washing process, and most especially today, this dominant framing has shoved aside, ignored, or treated as incidental numerous racial issues, including the realities of persisting racial discrimination and racial inequality.[9]

There have been times, though few, when students of color—specifically, my African American students—have denied White skin privilege and have embraced a colorblind liberalism, who have argued that the world is different now in terms of race relations. In moments like these, I am reminded that, just because there are students of color in my classrooms, it doesn't mean that I am preaching to the choir. Students of color are also in need of critical discourses about race, discourses that fearlessly engage the subtle and overt racist dynamics in White America. Yet, unlike their fellow White classmates, not having available such a critical framework can cost them their lives.

I recall giving a lecture once where a Black female student defended tooth and nail that the view that I had provided of White racist America did not apply to her. My sense is that she saw herself as a young, productive, and smart undergraduate, someone whose "racial" identity did not matter. She seemed terribly offended when I said that White America sees her and me as "Niggers" despite our successes. However, she persisted. The air was tense. I even felt as if I was being too strong. Yet, I pushed the narrative that the color of her skin diminished her *in the eyes of White America*. Not that *she* was any less, but that White America saw her as less. I could see that she was angry and deeply uncomfortable. Other students of color in the audience, through nods of agreement, supported my narrative. However, it wasn't a victory for me. Rather, I saw it as an important message that needed to be communicated to both that young Black female student and to the other students of color who were present. I provided a realistic, though deeply unfortunate, conceptualization of White America; it was a racial narrative that might, one day, preserve her sanity or perhaps save her life. It is important that, as scholars of color, we don't forget that our students of color (indeed, even many of our colleagues of color) have come "to see the world wrongly."[10] Hence, not only has violence been done to White students within our classrooms, but violence has also been done to students of color.

Thus, I return to the claim I made earlier—that violence has already been done to our White students before we face them in classrooms in which we are excited about critically engaging race and dispelling ignorance about the realities of racism. My point here is that my White students have already been lied to; the strength and force of distortion has already taken hold. There are forms of "violence" that are subtle, quiet, and that don't bring attention to their enactment. Yet, they exist. The social matrix within which this violence takes place can be a place as familiar and as benign as one's home, where White children are told that racism is something of the past; and where, when it does raise its ugly head, they are told that such instances are only minor and anomalous. They have been taught to see themselves as unraced, as persons qua persons. Many of them come to my classes believing in the Horatio Alger narrative and the promises of meritocracy without any knowledge of how their whiteness has functioned, and continues to function, to elevate them over similarly situated people of color. They live according to a philosophical anthropology where they see themselves as autonomous subjects who move through history with absolute freedom and as a law unto themselves. They see themselves as liberal subjects extricated from effective history, especially the effective history of White racism. Like being born from the head of Zeus, they begin their lives as if "full grown," without having *become* White, without being *complicit* with whiteness, especially where that whiteness forms the site from which they have come *to think* and *to feel* about the world as they do.

As Barbara Applebaum writes:

> Most significantly, this notion of White complicity is grounded in the belief that one cannot transcend the social system that frames how one makes meaning of oneself and the social world within which one is embedded.[11]

In short, the lie of non-complicity has already taken hold. They have already been given over to whiteness; to live in bad faith and denial about the ways in which they are free from complicity vis-à-vis White racism. After all, the threshold for perpetuating White racism is very low; all that is necessary is for White people to do nothing at all. Yet, in doing nothing at all, one makes a contribution. One still chooses and that choice produces results or sustains results. There is no "outside," as it were, in terms of which Whites escape processes of White interpellation. By the time White students have arrived to our classrooms, they have already been shaped by White ways of being-in-the-world, White ways of avoiding the issue of White privilege, White ways of constructing nonwhite bodies as "different," White ways of seeing themselves as "innocent" of White racism, and White ways of taking up space and moving through that space in the capacity of ownership and possession. Of course, these White ways of being-in-the-world have profound implications for people of color, implications that our White students have come to find effective ways to deny. It is this denial that is dialectically linked to the preservation of White students' sense of moral character. As Applebaum writes:

> White people contribute to the perpetuation of systemic racism through benefitting from a perpetuating and systemically induced ignorance, a relentless readiness to deny, ignore and dismiss what victims who experience the effects of racism are saying in order that White people can maintain their moral innocence.[12]

I have argued elsewhere[13] that Whites are *embedded* within the history of White racism. In short, my White students are implicated in a complex network of racist power relationships. On this score, White racism constitutes a heteronomous web of White practices to which they, as Whites, are linked as both beneficiaries of such a web and as co-contributors to the web's continual function. White racial oppression, power, and privilege can be conceptualized, though not exclusively so, as uneventful acts of being White, like walking into a store and not being followed. In this way, White racial oppression, power, and privilege are linked to ways of being White in the world. My White students have difficulty accepting what I call the "conception of the embedded White racist." In my view, though, this conception of the embedded White racist self helps them come to terms with, though not without tremendous resistance, the ways in which they have been lied to about the social ontologically robust ways in which they are *not* self-identical substances moving through space and time, fully self-present and fully autonomous. Exploring the ways in which they are embedded within a preexisting social matrix of White power—one that is fundamentally constitutive, though not deterministic—my White students are encouraged to think critically about ways in which they are *not* sites of complete self-possession, but sites of dispossession. This concept of dispossession is theorized in ways that challenge my White students' assumption that it is through a sincere act of introspection that the limits of their racism can be ascertained. On this score, my White students have difficulty accepting what I refer to as the "conception of the opaque White racist."

My White students assume that if they "look" deep enough and shine the light of consciousness brightly and for long enough they will be able to determine the full extent of their racism. Indeed, they assume that the process of ascertaining the limits of one's White racism is guaranteed by an "all-knowing" consciousness that is capable of peeling back, as it were, various levels of internalized racism and at once discovering a nonracist innocent White core. In this view, my White students presume that, when it comes to ascertaining the complexity and depth of their own racism, they possess the capacity for absolute epistemic clarity, and that the self is transparent, fully open to inspection. However, as one embarks upon the process of giving an account of one's "racist limits," the White racist self has already "gotten done" by White racism in fundamentally and profoundly constitutive ways, ways that are densely complex. The White self that attempts to "ascertain such limits" has already arrived too late[14] to determine the complex and insidious ways in which White racism has become embedded within one's White embodied self. It is not that there is no transparency at all, that one is incapable of identifying various aspects of one's racist/nonracist White self. Rather, the reality of the sheer depth of White racialization is far too opaque.

The important point here is that our White students arrive in our classrooms already dispossessed. The assumption that they are in full possession of themselves, unencumbered by White racist sociohistorical and psychic processes that are constitutive of who they are as White, provides them with a sense of coherence and tranquility. It provides them with a sense of being at home in the world. To attempt to chip away at that feeling of being at home, that sense of cognition, of knowing one's place in the world, creates trauma for my White students.

As we neared the end of the semester in my Phenomenology of Race course—a course where, as mentioned above, we had discussed whiteness and the social/spatial world as ready to hand[15]—a graduate student argued that we must "put whiteness in crisis."[16] This, it seems to me, is just right. In fact, it occurs to me that this is what many scholars of color who teach race within predominantly White classrooms do. We create spaces where whiteness is put into crisis. This is certainly my effort. By theorizing the ways in which my White students are embedded within White racism, both historically and psychically, they begin to feel disoriented. Not all will benefit from that cognitive and emotive disorientation, that sense of phenomenological or lived uncertainty about what they "know" and "feel" about themselves, as Whites, and their whitewashed world. After all, we meet for only one semester, a few hours a week. Yet, there are some who undergo that sense of vertigo, even if only while in class. The very notion of dispossession is itself unnerving. This is partly why I make a point of sharing with *all* of my students that we are finite and destined for the grave. Faith aside, I want to instill in them that death awaits us, and that we may never cross this way again; that *this moment* in human existence, this moment of our awareness may never repeat itself in the history of the universe. I want them to feel the weight of dispossession; the reality that we have already been claimed by death through the contingency of our birth. The experience is profoundly humbling.

My effort is to cultivate a space where White students can experience crisis. In therapeutic terms, "crisis" is typically something that we want to mitigate and possibly medicate. By crisis, I don't only mean that sense of losing one's footing, of *losing one's way*, but the etymological sense (from Greek *krisis*; i.e., decision) where one is faced with the need to make *a decision*. Within the context of whiteness, where a single action or intention does not "undo" whiteness, the concept of *deciding* denotes a life of commitment to "undo," over and over again, the complex ways in which one is embedded in whiteness; it involves, as Clevis Headley argues, "a continuously affirmed refusal to prolong the ontological and existential project of whiteness."[17] Hence, the concept of crisis within this context is suggestive of an iterative process that is to be sustained. It is demanding as it will require an iterative process of *losing one's way* vis-à-vis one's whiteness, especially as White social norms militate against this process. Yet, one must *tarry* not only with the feeling of loss, but with the pain and suffering that people of color endure because of the effects of the historical sedimentation of White supremacy and its continued subtle and not so subtle manifestations. One must be prepared to linger, to remain, with the truth about one's White self and the truth about how whiteness has structured and continues to structure forms of relationality that are oppressive to people of color. Of course, White people will typically flee such situations by denying the ways in which whiteness privileges them, and, thereby, the ways in which they need to begin to take forms of responsibility for confronting whiteness. As Applebaum writes, "White students often resist this knowledge because the only message they can hear is 'you are to blame.'"[18]

The point here, though, is not to blame or to instill immobilizing guilt, but to nurture responsibility. Yet, for academics of color who face White students in whom the violence has already taken place, where they already see themselves as autonomous and immune to interpellative forces, more is needed in order to cultivate vulnerability in them. They must be prepared to be *wounded*, to be touched. As Erinn Gilson writes:

> Taken in this way, as a fundamental state, vulnerability is a condition of potential that makes possible other conditions. Being vulnerable makes it possible for us to suffer, to fall prey to violence and be harmed, but also to fall in love, to learn, to take pleasure and to find comfort in the presence of others, and to experience the simultaneity of these feelings. Vulner*ability* is not just a condition that limits us, but also one that can *enable* us. As potential, vulnerability is a condition of openness, openness to being affected and affecting in turn.[19]

It is this vulner*ability* that enables White students to see that whiteness is held together by lies, and that, once they begin to question those lies, they begin to lose their way; that is, they begin to inhabit the world and move through the world in ways that are *oblique*. It is at this point that they begin to question ways of being that they have taken for granted, ways that communicate to them that their lives are innocent and untouched by whiteness. Returning to my Phenomenology of Race course, I recall a White male student of mine who asked me how it was possible that he was negatively impacting his White daughter of only 11 months in ways that are racist. I explained to him that, even as she is young and innocent, she is nevertheless raced as White. As such, I explained that her whiteness has implications for where she will live, how long she might live, how others will treat her and respond to her. Yet, he was skeptical about his own direct influence on her vis-à-vis White racism. *This was one relationship that for him was exempt from the influence of whiteness.* He made motions of rocking her in his arms, making note of her innocence and sweetness. He continued to wonder just how he, especially given the way in which she is protected from anything as harsh as White racism, could possibly be communicating to his child the ugliness of racism. It was at this point that I said, "But will she ever feel safe in *Black arms*?"[20] I could see a clear change of expression on his face. Tarrying with this new insight, he went on to mention, in private, the fact that his daughter is only held by his parents and his wife's parents, all of whom are White. He recognized the weight of this moment; he was wounded by the realization that his daughter does not know (or has not known) the security of Black arms, that her life is filled with White people only, White bonding, White social and White familial spaces. Through such "natural" acts of bonding, which *exclude* Black bodies and bodies of color, his daughter is learning, even if pre-linguistically, to mark Black bodies and bodies of color as problematic bodies, untouchable bodies, or, at the very least, unnecessary bodies. I got the sense that he had only one Black friend who did not live close at all and who he sees far too infrequently. He was thankful for and disturbed by the realization that his little girl was already learning how to perform whiteness through her proximity to other/all White bodies, and how *he helped* to perpetuate this. Because of such monochromatically *White* social spaces, he realized how she was already being taught to perceive Black bodies as "Other," "different," "deviant," "dangerous." It was a painful realization, but one that he tarried with, courageously faced, with no appearance of wanting to flee.

What we need are critical spaces where vulnerability can be nurtured in White students who find themselves faced with critical questions about race that mark their bodies as problem bodies. Creating moments of "trauma" (etymologically, to wound) within the context of classrooms, forms of trauma that unsettle various meta-narratives that ground and underwrite White privilege and superiority, is necessary for White students in order to begin to disarticulate various mythopoetic constructions of whiteness that have reinforced their "naturalized" place of dominance in the world. We need a form of *Bildung* or *paideia* that actually cultivates vulnerability in White students, a cultural space where they are wounded, undergo moments of trauma and narrative disorganization in terms of their whiteness. We need to create a culture of crisis where White students get to face their finitude, their emptiness, and all of the lies that they have been told and raised to believe. To tarry within this space is about being reborn, which is always a painful process. Yet, it is about realizing that this rebirth is always a penultimate process. Given that our White students have lived with a multitude of lies about their "natural supremacy" and "entitlement" for such a long time, they will also need to grieve[21]: to grieve the loss of an imperial self, and to grieve in the form of *gravitas/heaviness*, which, on the flip side, may lead to a form of ethical responsibility or maturity, requiring constant ontological renewal. It is here that White people who have come to embrace the importance of White crisis and the value of losing their way, who will be needed to carry the weight of White anger, White frustration, and White resentment that is so often unleashed upon bodies of color within and outside the classroom, will need to create a "container" whereby White students are able to express crisis and uncertainty felt as they strive to struggle with transformation or metanoia and grieve the process of loss.

Notes

1 Sara Ahmed, *Queer Phenomenology: Orientations, Objects, Others* (Durham, NC; London, England: Duke University Press, 2006), 133.
2 Linda Martin Alcoff, "Alien and Alienated," in *Reframing the Practice of Philosophy: Bodies of Color, Bodies of Knowledge*, ed. George Yancy (Albany, NY: State University of New York Press, 2012), 23.
3 Ahmed, *Queer Phenomenology*, 139.
4 Donna-Dale Marcano, "Re-Reading Plato's *Symposium* Through the Lens of a Black Woman," in *Reframing the Practice of Philosophy: Bodies of Color, Bodies of Knowledge*, ed. George Yancy (Albany, NY: State University of New York Press, 2012), 232.
5 Ahmed, *Queer Phenomenology*, 132.
6 The reader should note that the scholars of color within this text are not restricted to challenging racist hegemony alone. I focus on race here as this was the hegemonic site that scholars of color were asked to address within this text.
7 See George Yancy, *Look, a White! Philosophical Essays on Whiteness* (Philadelphia, PA: Temple University Press, 2012), especially the introduction.
8 João Costa Vargas and Joy A. James, "Refusing Blackness-as-Victimization: Trayvon Martin and the Black Cyborgs," in *Pursuing Trayvon Martin: Historical Contexts and Contemporary Manifestations of Racial Dynamics*, eds. George Yancy and Janine Jones (Lanham, MD: Lexington Books, 2012), 198.
9 Joe R. Feagin, *The White Racial Frame: Centuries Racial Framing and Counter-Framing* (New York, NY: Routledge, 2010), 21.
10 Charles W. Mills, *The Racial Contract* (Ithaca, NY; London, England: Cornell University Press, 1997), 18.
11 Barbara Applebaum, *Being White, Being Good: White Complicity, White Moral Responsibility, and Social Justice Pedagogy* (Lanham, MD: Lexington Books, 2010), 14.
12 Applebaum, *Being White, Being Good*, 46.
13 See Yancy, *Look, a White!*, especially chapter six.
14 Judith Butler, *Giving an Account of Oneself* (New York, NY: Fordham University Press), 79.
15 Important to this course was reading Sara Ahmed's "A Phenomenology of Whiteness," in *Feminist Theory*, 8(2), 2007: 149–168. The discourse of "loss" within this introduction is partly influenced by her work.

16 While I have thought about crisis vis-à-vis whiteness prior to this course, I would like to thank Amber Kelsie for this specific phrasing and for the courage with which she staked her claim.

17 Clevis Headley, "Delegitimizing the Normativity of 'Whiteness': A Critical Africana Philosophical Study of the Metaphoricity of Whiteness" in *What White Looks Like: African-American Philosophers on the Whiteness Question*, ed. George Yancy (New York, NY: Routledge, 2004), 103.

18 Applebaum, *Being White, Being Good*, 42.

19 See Erinn Gilson's "Vulnerability, Ignorance, and Oppression," in *Hypatia: A Journal of Feminist Philosophy*, *26*(2), Spring 2011: 308–332—quote on p. 310.

20 While it is not my aim here to explore this issue in any greater detail, it is important to note that many White infants knew the safety of Black arms during American slavery. This, of course, speaks to the reality of Black enslaved women who were forced to nurture and comfort White infants, White children. Within this context, the ethical contradictions abound, especially as these same nurtured White bodies would grow up to inherit as property the Black bodies that nurtured them, Black bodies that were deemed disposable (relative to White bodies) and wretched.

21 I would like to thank my colleague Kathy Glass for sharing this insight.

1

"THE WHITENESS IS THICK"

Predominantly White Classrooms, Student of Color Voice, and Freirian Hopes

Kirsten T. Edwards

Changes, Movements, and Revelations

"Sexy"

I am a critical scholar.[1] I am a womanist, not a feminist.[2] I incorporate critical race theory, postcolonial studies, counter-narrative techniques, and the like in my research. My desire for teaching, research, and service is always emancipatory.[3] And I try to make these intentions clear in my academic and nonacademic spaces. I am a critical scholar of color in a White academy.

As a Black woman with a PhD who writes about issues of equity and access, particularly in reference to race, class, and gender, I surprisingly look great on paper. One of my colleagues tells me my work is "sexy!". He means my work is provocative and racy (race-y). But, the more I think about this adjective—"sexy"—as a descriptor for my life's work, which is primarily situated within a "White capitalist patriarchal hegemon[ic]" academy,[4] the more I recognize its profound truth.

My scholarship is simply sexy in this place—attractive and alluring, inciting arousal and pleasurable recreation—not substantive, significant, or necessary to what is done here; just auxiliary and marginal. Like Fasching-Varner's claims,[5] my scholarly work on "race and racism remain fictionalized, untrue, and quasi-literary in the imagination of readers, particularly White readers. In this sense, whites never take responsibility or action for racist behavior, belief, and treatments of whole groups of people".[6] Instead of a platform for substantive change, I provide the White academy that little bit of "cut-up,"[7] or discursive disruption. My work is provocative and offers the necessary edge to keep the intelligentsia publically relevant.[8] The intelligentsia or White intellectual establishment publicly supports and privately contains/controls counter-hegemonic discourse, while simultaneously perpetuating a common habitus of enslavement. What does this look like in the day-to-day life of a Black female professor? It means I am more than welcome in my university's diversity report. My Black gendered (read "woman") and classed body and my work are interesting and add creditability to their claims of equity. It also means the university does not have to make any substantive strides towards responding to ongoing issues of access, privilege, relevance, and cultural competency.[9] Every day, I realize more and more just how "sexy" I am.

Class in Session

Nowhere is my shallow, non-substantive, sexy academic existence more apparent than in the classroom. While university administrators and White colleagues may be intrigued by my marginal(ized) and intersectional scholarship, or at least begrudgingly find my radical presence a necessary evil for the maintenance of "White supremacist capitalist patriarchy",[10] many of my White students aren't buying it. Instead, they find my rhetorical pursuit of equity and justice on college campuses laborious. This is the ultimate and ugly result of a sexy existence:

> [W]e must be attentive to the seductive absorption of Black women's voices in classrooms of higher education where Black women's texts are still much more welcomed than Black women ourselves. Giving the illusion of change, this strategy of symbolic inclusion masks how the everyday institutional policies and arrangements that suppress and exclude African Americans as a collectivity remain virtually untouched.[11]

Unfortunately, I believed the "illusion of change." As a doctoral student attending scholarly conferences, discussing my work with other critical scholars or *wanna-be* (seen as) critical scholars, or while reading the kinds of literature that strengthen a critical consciousness, I was able to convince myself that my work was valuable and appreciated; that it was important. I found myself surrounded by people who supported my scholarship, valued my contributions, and encouraged my efforts. I was convinced that I was part of the contemporary revolution. Sometimes, I can still convince myself. However, recently I have found it much more difficult to conjure up the illusion, because as soon as I stepped my Black, stiletto-ed feet into the predominantly White classroom as a teacher it was shattered.

When I began teaching courses on race, gender, class, and sexuality in higher education, the ugly truth surfaced immediately. As a new teacher, committed to critical and liberatory dialogue, I cluttered my syllabus with rich, challenging, provocative readings. I intentionally offered questions and case studies that pushed my students to analyze the systemic character of power, privilege, and supremacy and their manifestations in universities as well as the larger society.

I also encouraged them to question the ways they either support or resist these unjust systems. And, as much as I loved the weekly intellectual engagement and the pride I felt in influencing curriculum for social change, I also labored beyond what I ever could have imagined. It was hard! White students, particularly White men, seemed to resent me. Sometimes, they would just sit in their seats scowling, refusing to participate in the class discussion. No matter how much I worked to create an equitable environment, a safe space where we could thoughtfully engage these ideas, some of my students adamantly refused.

It was here in this pedagogical space that I came face to face with the limits of social justice work. It was in the classroom where I finally recognized the implications of surface-level diversity agendas. I received my first real educational lesson as a Black woman teaching in a predominantly White setting. I learned that, despite all of the rhetoric in support of my presence, I definitely don't belong here.[12]

Pedagogical Locations

Place and Space

To be fair, in hindsight, my early college teaching experiences were tolerable. In fact, in the midst of great struggle, there were some real moments of connection and learning. Admittedly, I looked forward to class every week. It was difficult and a reality check, but, for the most part, still enjoyable. This sentiment would drastically change when I moved to another predominantly White university. As a new professor, I knew there would be an adjustment period. As a Black woman who had experience teaching in predominantly White classrooms, I also thought I was prepared for the more common issues that arise from such a subject position. I was wrong.

This new university was my former difficult classroom experiences times one hundred! I found engaging issues of equity and access almost impossible. The antagonism was all too real. What I was also unprepared for was the frequency with which the White male students attempted to undermine my position as professor in the classroom. This was a particular challenge for me because I worked so hard to maintain a commitment to equity and mutual respect.[13] I struggled with balancing my use of positional power (undergirded by White male supremacy) in the classroom with the pedagogical need for hands-on facilitation of learning and engagement for productive dialogue.[14] I also struggled not to tell these White men off! I was angry, frustrated, frightened, and I felt like a failure. None of my teaching and learning techniques worked. I was alone and confused with no direction on how to respond to this difficult place and space. Sadly, I no longer looked forward to class.

One day, after several weeks of emotional, intellectual, and professional turmoil, I confided in a Black colleague who was also a friend. I explained to him my frustrations and feelings of failure. During my escalating rant, I also mentioned my disappointment in my students of color. This was the first time I openly acknowledged the negative feelings I also held towards them. I felt that, at some level, the students of color had abandoned me. I believed they should also be invested in critical conversations in the classroom as the implications were of particular import for them. In my opinion, the students of color had a vested interest in the dismantling of White supremacy and the promotion of equity and socially just practices at the university and beyond. Instead, this less than a handful of students remained largely silent during these discussions, and, sometimes, when they did speak, actually supported their White classmates' racist, sexist, homophobic, classist, and all around unjust commentary.

Nuanced Perspectives

When I finished my rant and released my pent-up frustration, my colleague told me quite matter of factly, "The whiteness is thick here." I had never heard this phrase before. It took me a while to process what he was saying. Within a few moments, it began to make sense to me. I had always considered White supremacy a monolithic, unilateral evil. White supremacy just is. It is global, cultural, and systemic, and it has implications for every aspect of our lives. However, what I had not considered was the varying levels of its pervasiveness in the lives of students of color in different locales. What I also had not considered was the influence a collective Black politic (or any raced politic) had on the degree to which White supremacy manifested.[15] Don't misunderstand me. I realized that an individual's experiences with racism were complicated by location. I understood that I may be afforded the luxury of political correctness in Connecticut that may not be offered in Mississippi. Nevertheless, what I did not expect was a space where the belief in the superiority of a White cultural, sociopolitical identity could exist unchecked, unmitigated, and fundamentally absolute.

I am a Southern woman; a Deep South woman. I am intimately familiar with racism, racial antagonism, colorism, and the like. What I am unfamiliar with is a complete absence of a Black politic. When I use the term "Black politic," this is a personal definition, informed by several scholars,[16] that helps me delineate between multiple White spaces as I understand them now. For me, a Black politic is an adherence to a healthy, positive valuation of an African-descended identity. It is the recognition of the ways White supremacy undermines the richness of Black culture and community, and a commitment to responding to the material circumstances that manifest under White supremacy. In this new, predominantly White space, a Black politic was largely absent.

Alternatively, the institution I had come from had a small, underrepresented yet thriving Black community that possessed a strong Black politic. Black students along with faculty and staff were constantly engaging in programming and activities to raise awareness about issues of concern to Black members of the academic community. There were opportunities for Black students to commune and support one another. Important yearly markers such as Martin Luther King, Jr. Day (MLK Day) and Black History Month were always recognized and celebrated campus-wide, with high publicity and student involvement. In fact, these events were often student-led and organized. Also, there were specific physical spaces on campus that were "Black spaces," spaces where Black students could find solace and reprieve and commune with others of like mind and spirit. Most importantly, when issues of blatant injustice were recognized, there was a solid cohort of Black students to respond in protest. The students at my former institution were vocal, active, supportive, and socio-politically Black.

I did not find that to be the case at my new institution. All the markers of a vibrant Black politic, or any type of raced politic, were largely absent here. At the micro level, Black students did not seem to form any kind of strategic collective to support one another. On a more macro level, there was no evidence of a Black consciousness campus-wide. This institution did not have any type of highly visible activity or volunteer opportunities officially in place to commemorate MLK Day. There is also no program of events in February to celebrate Black History Month. And these are simply the obvious absences and silences. It is not that the recognition of MLK Day or Black History Month makes a campus equitable and accessible. In fact, I would argue that my former institution, as a whole, significantly struggles with issues of justice and equity. In a lot of ways, my former institution is an immensely racist space. But in the midst of that racism (and sexism, and homophobia, and classism) is a space of resistance. I did not find a similar resistant space at my new institution. Now, as a new faculty member, I may concede that I might have overlooked these types of activities actually taking place on campus. Yet, I would argue that, if the efforts were significant, then I would not have to look so hard to find them. Probably more importantly, my students should not have to look so hard to find them.

Black Student Voice, Counter-Narrative, and My Pedagogical Toolbox

As I began to mentally unravel what it meant to teach in thick whiteness, I also began to recognize the beauty of my first predominantly White experience: Black student voice. While both universities are predominantly White institutions, at my former institution, I could depend on the Black students to offer a critical read and a resistant analysis. I knew that the Black students would provide counter-narratives informed by the experiences of a Black subjectivity in a White supremacist culture in response to the master narratives undergirded by injustice proposed by their White counterparts. As part of my pedagogical engagement, I could trust that unsubstantiated ideologies that disenfranchise would not go unchallenged. I could trust that, if I were to assign a reading that discussed the challenges people living in poverty encounter attempting to access higher education, when one of the White men decided to use the example of the "Black welfare queen" to argue for why it is not an issue of access but "personal responsibility," there would be a Black student ready and willing to offer a real-life testimonial attesting to the fact that all of his imagined understandings of Black poverty were flawed and false.

These types of expected classroom relationships altered my practice without me recognizing it. What I had not realized was that I learned to use my Black students' voices (and those of other students of color) as pedagogical resources. Part of my use of their lives as text[17] meant that I developed the practice of limiting my own voice. Integrated in my emerging pedagogical technique was the concept of trust. I trusted that, if I gave my students enough space in the classroom, they would challenge one another in productive ways. As a teacher, I found it more beneficial for my students' learning if they struggled with one another. They interpreted those types of interactions as more equitable and safe. I interjected, primarily, to provide information, clarification, direction, and facilitation. When I did find it necessary to push an idea, I did it with great care, knowing that my students often interpreted the voicing of my ideals and commitments as a reprimand, if not in agreement with theirs.

I came to my most recent institution with this unconscious understanding of classroom practice. I realized fairly quickly that what I had known to be true previously was not true here. My pedagogical truth had changed. I watched students contribute to class discussions with responses that were informed by the rants of their favorite Fox News pundit. I watched them display an almost illogical commitment to not understanding the impact difference could have on one's life experiences. These seemingly bright, intelligent, by all accounts smart White students were trapped in their own worlds and the figments of their imaginations about Other people's worlds.[18] This, however, was not the most disturbing revelation. I had taught racist, misguided White students before. When my students of color did not respond to these illogical and unjust attitudes, that's when I was left unawares. Or, when students of color did respond, it was with comments as shallow and unperceptive as their White colleagues. More disheartening still is the realization of how silenced, discarded, and epistemologically absent my students of color were at this new institution.[19]

Sadly, as the semester carried on, this revelation was confirmed. It was first confirmed when one of my students of color met me after class in tears. She was distraught after hearing the hateful assumptions her White colleagues held about "people like" her. Not knowing her humble beginnings, assuming that all graduate students possessed middle-class sensibilities, the White students had implicitly labeled poor, uneducated communities as incompetent, incapable, and unmotivated. In her words, lacking the ability to "talk White," and knowing that the way she verbally expressed herself would not be validated by her White colleagues, she expressed fear of voicing her truth in class. Moreover, she knew her emotional response would be discredited as irrational and subjective. I, of course, encouraged her to speak up in class, and let her know I would support her. I let her know that her voice was important and necessary. Fortunately, after that meeting, she spoke more. Unfortunately, her newfound freedom was not contagious.

I soon realized my pedagogical toolbox was lacking. While through my previous teaching experiences I had learned to use restraint and patience in the classroom to meet more equitable and emancipatory aims, I had to now learn how to push important ideas without wielding unjust teacher privilege.[20] I had to figure out ways to maintain my commitment to modeling justice and fairness and a safe learning environment, while also strongly encouraging my students to engage in a critical consciousness and self-reflexivity.[21] I have to admit, part of me was quite resistant to the pedagogical push. I had developed all of these personal ideals for the educative space; ideals about how learning could be mutually beneficial and supportive to all involved. Much of this commitment was related to the way I had interpreted my own experiences with formal education as a student. It had been a process that supported racism, patriarchy, and classism, which did not significantly change until I was a graduate student. I was adamant that, as a Black woman teacher, I would be committed to radically changing that space, or at least the space I occupied as teacher. To the extent possible, I would not reenact systems of injustice, even if those systems were now available to me, even if it made my job easier. I was committed to doing something different. And thankfully in my early career, my Black students' voices helped make my vision possible.

Freirian Hopes

While these shifts and movements in my teaching career have been difficult, they have also been the impetus for the development of a scholarly agenda. I am now more interested in the curricular import of student of color voice in predominantly White spaces. One theoretical avenue that has assisted me in considering this idea more thoughtfully is the work of Paulo Freire.[22] In particular, I have found myself drawn to Freire's concepts of mutual humanity and oppression as inhumanity. I am beginning to question what the humanization of oppressors in relation to the oppressed looks like in the classroom.

Love

Freire argues that the very act of hate and oppression dehumanizes the oppressor. The oppressed, because of their more human yet historically dehumanized position, have a responsibility to bring humanity back to both themselves and their oppressors. He writes:

> Concern for humanization leads at once to the recognition of dehumanization, not only as an ontological possibility but as an historical

reality. And as an individual perceives the extent of dehumanization, he or she may ask if humanization is a viable possibility. Within history ... both humanization and dehumanization are possibilities for a person as an uncompleted being conscious of their incompletion ... [However humanization] is thwarted by injustice, exploitation, oppression, and the violence of the oppressors ... which marks not only those whose humanity has been stolen, but also (though in a different way) those who have stolen it, it is a *distortion* of the vocation of becoming more fully human ... This struggle is possible only because dehumanization, although a concrete historical fact, is not a given destiny but the result of an unjust order that engenders violence in the oppressors, which in turn dehumanizes the oppressed ... [I]n seeking to regain their humanity [the oppressed cannot] become in turn oppressors of the oppressors, but rather restorers of the humanity of both. This then, is the great humanistic and historical task of the oppressed: to liberate themselves and their oppressors as well.[23]

How do "student-teachers" and "teacher-students" facilitate this process of humanization?[24] Freire's solution to this (de)humanizing conundrum is love. Through the loving albeit difficult relationship between oppressed and oppressor, humanity can be restored to both. The oppressed must be fearless and strong enough to address the oppressor with their truth in love. Simultaneously, the oppressor must recognize this difficult response as truthful. Freire posits:

[The oppressed] will not gain this liberation by chance but through the praxis of their quest for it, through their recognition of the necessity to fight for it. And this fight, because of the purpose given it by the oppressed, will actually constitute an act of love opposing the lovelessness which lies at the heart of the oppressors' violence.[25]

A Freirian classroom exists in White spaces where students of color are present, not only physically, but also epistemologically, ontologically, and axiologically. For me, the praxis of developing or encouraging the development of a Freirian classroom means creating space for the ways of knowing, being, and valuing connected to a raced identity to manifest, not benignly, but as an act of resistance to White supremacy. Furthermore, this identity must emerge in loving relation to White identity as an act of teaching and learning for emancipation, not oppression. It must exist in a way that offers access and equity for both White students and students of color to be more fully human.

Radicalization

In conjunction with love, the humanizing classroom must also embrace radicalism, or a commitment to a radical response to injustice and oppression. The need for a radical ethic is connected to a fearless engagement with the injustice of the oppressor. Additionally, radicalism fundamentally undermines attempts at assimilation. As mentioned previously, in the second predominantly White setting within which I taught, during the rare moments my students of color did contribute to class dialogue, their comments were often assimilative. In these moments, their voices were present but supportive of racist commentary. Clearly, the presence of their voices is not enough.

Alternatively, the pedagogical import of a raced politic lies in its ability to be obviously contradictory and oppositional.

> Radicalization, nourished by a critical spirit, is always creative. Sectarianism mythicizes and thereby alienates; radicalization criticizes and thereby liberates. Radicalization involves increased commitment to the position one has chosen, and thus ever greater engagement in the effort to transform concrete, objective reality.[26]

What is significant about a radicalized student of color voice is its potential to "transform [the] concrete, objective reality" of White supremacy in the classroom. A radical, oppositional student of color voice prevents White supremacy from existing unchallenged. It gives White supremacy something to deal with. It acknowledges, identifies, and clarifies racial antagonism. Furthermore, it makes the evils of White supremacy real. White supremacy can no longer exist in the classroom as a benign reality. Instead, a radicalized student of color voice reflects White supremacy back to White students. This reflection reveals White supremacy as not simply a personal validated/valuable opinion, but as it is experienced by students of color, as a cultural violence.

Counter-Hegemonic Narration for Lives in Relation

As mentioned previously, the mere physical presence of students of color does not begin the radicalized reflection process. What I have also noticed in the process of comparing my two teaching spaces through a Freirian lens is the importance of storied lives in the classroom. Radicalism and love apart from narrated life stories is impotent. The storied lives of students of color serve as counter-hegemonic text in the classroom.[27] These stories make the violence of White supremacy real, and its master narratives a lie. They also make mutual humanity through lives in relation essential. When White students have to come face to face with the lived experiences of students of color, they are left with one of two options. They can either choose not to recognize through social cognitive resistance; the apathetic refusal to learn through others' lives and experiences. Alternatively, they can acknowledge the cognitive dissonance that results from hearing the counter-hegemonic narratives of their colleagues of color and begin the work of integrating these "new" narratives into the collection of their personal life histories. One choice requires a social, ontological denial that limits authentic humanity by building one's personal reality on an untruth, while the other opens up space for the development of a more fully truthful understanding of oneself in relation to a more expansive community of people.

Freire argues that, "Education is suffering from narration sickness".[28] This "sickness" is the result of teachers and students assuming that the educative process can stand apart from individuals' and communities' storied lives. There is a need for White students to see themselves in relation to Others beyond the text. This can be achieved primarily through classroom dialogue with fellow students who embrace a raced politic. Within these moments of collective and resistant narration, students of color are able to be seen as same and Other simultaneously. The presence of a critical mass of students possessing a raced politic in the classroom provides the necessary critical or counter-hegemonic narration for pedagogical healing through consciousness raising. Instead of more White-stream narration that supports privilege and oppression systems, the voices of students of color make the abstract concrete by naming White supremacy and exposing its consequences on human lives in relation. Recognizing the struggle that the presence of multiple and conflicting narratives can cause, Freire argues that, "Knowledge emerges only ... through the restless, impatient, continuing, hopeful inquiry human beings pursue in the world, with the world, and with each other".[29] Alas, I will also concede that much of that "restless" "inquiry" "with each other" takes place among perceived equals in perceived safe spaces. While the nature of racism and other forms of systemic oppression complicate perceptions of equality, the official markers of equality (shared titles and roles in the classroom) can assist in the process.

Relational Limits

The teacher will never be capable of relationship with students in the same way fellow students are in relation. The nature of Western, Eurocentric educational institutions loads the role of "teacher" in ways that fundamentally impede completely equitable relationships.[30] As long as I am required to submit satisfactory grades to university administration at the conclusion of every semester in order for students to progress towards degree completion, I will not be seen as completely peer and colleague. My relationship with my students is necessarily and involuntarily tiered, stratified. As a teacher, I may be committed to equitable, respectful classroom engagement. I may adhere to womanist tenets as a scholar and teacher. I may actively seek decolonization in my practice.[31] Nevertheless, as I function within systemic "White supremacist capitalist patriarchy" and, as I am employed by one of the primary social institutions (higher education) that undergirds systems of injustice and inequity in this nation and globally, I cannot fool myself into believing the fairytale of complete equality in the classroom. Even when I have attempted to engage my students as equals, they often resisted my attempts and adamantly restored me to my "rightful" place as knower and oppressor.

This pedagogical conundrum makes it impossible for me, as teacher, alone to serve as a storied Other with which my White students engage in "restless," "continuing" inquiry. This type of meaningful learning that challenges those taken-for-granted assumptions or habits of mind can only hope to arise from substantive engagement with peers who actively resist those assumptions and further narrate the flaws and fissures of White supremacy through the lens of their own lived experiences. Classroom colleagues who possess a raced politic and are willing to verbally express those sociopolitical, cultural values "assist [White] students to [un]cover through cultural meanings and lived experience those ideological frameworks ... that encourage uncritical acceptance of exploitation. [Relational] [e]ducation helps students self-construct counter-hegemonic identities and then act as public citizens against individual and collective oppression".[32] This type of relational education can only exist in safe, equitable, learning environments. Students must believe they are struggling with the ideas of people who will not, cannot do violence to them. The absence of potential violence is fundamental to uncovering or discovering more just and equitable ways of being-in-the-world. Conversely, the presence of threat or potential violence, the lack of a safe space to dialogue and disagree, promotes retrenchment to master narratives and ideologies that support injustice and limit access.

I have seen this retrenchment all too often in my recent classrooms. When I am the only voice disagreeing with taken-for-granted assumptions undergirded by White supremacy, my White students often vehemently support their unthought-ful claims. When I continue to push them to think more critically, they fall silent in seeming protest. There is no exchange of ideas, no critical reflection, just an unwillingness to engage the authority in the classroom. Even when I attempt to push critical ideas through readings, assignments, or media, the students dismiss the text as insignificant or refuse to comment so as not to disagree with me. While I frequently encourage respectful disagreement, my role as teacher and authority often trump my intentions.

I also realize much of this resistance and silent (silencing) protest is a response to how my body is "read as text" in the classroom.[33] Not only am I teacher and authority, but I am concurrently read as oppositional and the antithesis to privileged White male supremacy. Before I open my mouth, my White students have determined my politics, my cultural affiliations, and the validity of my position. Like Baszile:

> I was being read as text, not simply as the teacher, but also as one of the few representations of Blackness in the class and perhaps in their life-worlds. To this end, my effort at neutrality had a destructive, if not absurd, dimension

as it allowed students to subsume me, to locate me—as they saw fit—within the master narrative.[34]

In a White space absent of dissentingly collegial voices "students [have] little or no understanding of how they reproduce race as configurations of the self, of how they only assimilate . . . the 'new' information into unquestioned world views, and basically remain . . . steeped in . . . racism".[35] Substantive engagement with a critical mass of students of color who possess a raced politic can help White students move the critical text assigned in class from assimilated abstraction to concrete reality. In addition, it provides students of color the theoretical gateway to assert their position in academic spaces; spaces that have historically been hostile and contemporarily silencing to them.[36] It offers students of color the language to take ownership within the dialogical and pedagogical community. This is a community that exists within White supremacist parameters and has been a source of epistemological and ontological not-belonging.

Praxis Questions, Concerns, and Moving On

What I hope I have made clear throughout this chapter is that paramount to this entire practice we call pedagogy is the need for lives in relation, and the recognition of some of the factors that facilitate and impede the development of those relationships. Llewellyn and Llewellyn note that it is "critical to allow for students and teachers to see and understand the connectedness of people and thus the relations of power that define and mobilize knowledge".[37] While my professional shifts have been difficult, they have also ignited a deeper level of appreciation for the "connectedness of people" in the classroom and how that connectedness directly impacts the systems of power that (de)mobilize knowledge in (un)just ways. I have also begun to understand the profound potential students of color possess in bridging the lacunae of critical reflection for consciousness raising. I now see my students of color as not only key to the development of mutual humanity between White students and students of color, but also as the catalyst for meaningful communication between my White students and myself. Students of color in many ways are my philosophical translators. They make my pedagogical goals real and relevant.

With this in mind, I am now concerned with how I can incite a raced politic in my students of color, particularly when the whiteness is thick. I realize safe, equitable, dialogical classrooms are not enough. If students do not use that space to voice dissenting and critical ideas, then learning for emancipation will not take place. Instead, these ideals for the classroom must work in tandem. While I am admittedly apprehensive about my life as a teacher going forward, I also find myself reinvigorated. The violence of White supremacy in the classroom is still very real. However, the power of student of color voice is promising. And lately I have found it to be a ray of hope for a weary teacher.

Notes

1 Theodor W. Adorno, *The Culture Industry: Selected Essays on Mass Culture* (London, England: Routledge, 1991); Karl Marx and Frederick Engels, *The Communist Manifesto* (Minneapolis, MN: Filiquarian Publishing, 2005); David M. Rasmussen, *Handbook of Critical Theory* (Oxford, England: Blackwell, 1996).

2 Katie G. Cannon, *Katie's Canon: Womanism and the Soul of the Black Community* (New York, NY: Continuum, 1995); Stephanie Y. Mitchem, *Introducing Womanist Theology* (Maryknoll, NY: Orbis Books, 2002); Alice Walker, *In Search of Our Mothers' Gardens: Womanist Prose* (Orlando, FL: Harcourt, 1983).

3 Paulo Freire, *Pedagogy of the Oppressed* (New York, NY: Continuum, 1970).

4 Michael D. Giardina and Cameron McCarthy, "The Popular Racial Order of 'Urban' America: Sport, Identity, and the Politics of Culture," in *Transnational Perspectives on Culture, Policy, and Education: Redirecting Cultural Studies in Neoliberal Times*, eds. Cameron McCarthy and Cathryn Teasley (New York, NY: Peter Lang, 2008).

5 Kenneth J. Fasching-Varner, "No! The Team Ain't Alright! The Institutional and Individual Problematics of Race," *Social Identities*, *15*(6), 2009: 811–829.

6 Fasching-Varner, "No! The Team Ain't Alright!", 816.

7 Regina Austin, "Sapphire Bound!" in *Critical Race Theory: The Key Writings That Formed the Movement*, eds. Kimberlé Crenshaw, Neil Gotanda, Gary Peller, and Kendall Thomas (New York, NY: The New Press, 1995), 434.

8 Jean Franco, "Beyond Ethnocentrism: Gender, Power and the Third-World Intelligentsia," in *Marxism and the Interpretation of Culture*, eds. Cary Nelson and Lawrence Grossberg (Urbana, IL: University of Illinois Press, 1994).

9 Austin, "Sapphire Bound!"; Fasching-Varner, "No! The Team Ain't Alright!".

10 bell hooks, *Remembered Rapture: The Writer at Work* (New York, NY: Henry Holt, 1999), 27.

11 Patricia Hill Collins, "What's in a Name? Womanism, Black Feminism, and Beyond," *The Black Scholar*, *26*(1), 1996: 9.

12 Denise T. Baszile, "In This Place Where I Don't Quite Belong: Claiming the Ontoepistemological In-Between," in *From Oppression to Grace: Women of Color and Their Dilemmas Within the Academy*, eds. Theodorea Regina Berry and Nathalie D. Mizelle (Sterling, VA: Stylus Publishing, 2006).

13 Tamara Beauboeuf-Lafontant, "Womanist Lessons for Reinventing Teaching," *Journal of Teacher Education*, *56*(5), 2005: 436–445; Bruce J. Burke and Michelle Johnstone, "Access to Higher Education: The Hope for Democratic Schooling in America," *Higher Education in Europe*, *29*(1), 2004: 19–31; D. Jean Clandinin, "Lives in School: The Interwoven Lives of Children and Teachers," in *Proceedings of the 2005 National Biennial Conference of the Australian Curriculum Studies Association: Blurring the Boundaries, Sharpening the Focus* (Canberra, Australia: Australian Curriculum Studies Association, 2006).

14 Roland W. Mitchell and Kirsten T. Edwards, "Power, Privilege, and Pedagogy: Collegiate Classrooms as Sites to Learn Racial Equality," in *Managing Diversity: (Re)Visioning Equity on College Campuses*, ed. T. Elon Dancy (New York, NY: Peter Lang, 2010).

15 Lindsay Mack, "Does Every Student Have a Voice? Critical Action Research on Equitable Classroom Participation Practices," *Language Teaching Research*, *16*(3), 2012: 417–434.

16 Na'im Akbar, "Nigrescence and Identity: Some Limitations," *Counseling Psychologist*, *17*(2), 1989: 258–263; Craig C. Brookins, "The Relationship Between Afrocentric Values and Racial Identity Attitudes: Validation of the Belief Systems Analysis Scale on African American College Students," *Journal of Black Psychology*, *20*(2), 1994: 128–142; Kevin O. Cokley, "Racial(ized) Identity, Ethnic Identity, and Afrocentric

Values: Conceptual and Methodological Challenges in Understanding African American Identity," *Journal of Counseling Psychology*, 52(4), 2005: 517–526.

17 Baszile, "In This Place Where I Don't Quite Belong"; Mary Jo Maynes, Jennifer L. Pierce, and Barbara Laslett, *Telling Stories: The Use of Personal Narratives in the Social Sciences and History* (Ithaca, NY: Cornell University Press, 2008).

18 T. Minh-Ha Trinh, *Woman Native Other* (Bloomington, IN: Indiana University Press, 1989).

19 Mack, "Does Every Student Have a Voice?".

20 Mitchell and Edwards, "Power, Privilege, and Pedagogy."

21 Freire, *Pedagogy of the Oppressed*.

22 Ibid.

23 Ibid., 43-44. Emphasis is in the original.

24 Ibid., 7.

25 Ibid., 45.

26 Ibid., 37.

27 Charles Lawrence, "The Word and the River: Pedagogy as Scholarship as Struggle," in *Critical Race Theory: The Key Writings That Formed the Movement*, eds. Kimberlé Crenshaw, Neil Gotanda, Gary Peller and Kendall Thomas (New York, NY: The New Press, 1995).

28 Freire, *Pedagogy of the Oppressed*, 71.

29 Ibid., 72.

30 Mitchell and Edwards, "Power, Privilege, and Pedagogy."

31 Nina Asher, "Decolonizing Curriculum," in *Curriculum Studies Handbook: The Next Moment*, ed. Erik Malewski (New York, NY: Routledge, 2010); bell hooks, *Teaching to Transgress: Education as the Practice of Freedom* (New York, NY: Routledge, 1994).

32 Kristina R. Llewellyn and Jennifer J. Llewellyn, "A Restorative Approach to Learning: Relational Theory as Feminist Pedagogy in Universities" (paper, 13th Annual Curriculum and Pedagogy Conference, New Orleans, LA, November 7–10, 2012), par. 6.

33 Denise Taliaferro Baszile, "Beyond All Reason Indeed: The Pedagogical Promise of Critical Race Testimony," *Race, Ethnicity and Education*, 11(3), 2008: 252.

34 Ibid.

35 Ibid.

36 T. Elon Dancy and M. Christopher Brown, "The Mentoring and Induction of Educators of Color: Addressing the Imposter Syndrome in Academe," *Journal of School Leadership*, 21(4), 2011: 607–634.

37 Llewellyn and Llewellyn, "A Restorative Approach to Learning," par. 2.

2

THIS BRIDGE CALLED MY BODY

Talking Race Through Embodying Difference

Antonia Randolph

First Day

One hundred and fifty students, not the normal two hundred and fifty, a concession to the fact that this is my first semester here, my first time teaching as a tenure-track assistant professor, not an instructor. The difference is that now I have my PhD. Is that a difference that makes a difference to how the students see me? Walking to the front of the class, down the steep stadium-styled steps of this three hundred plus-seat auditorium, I choose the aisle nearest to the doors, not the middle one where I would have to walk between the students that surround me. Back straight, eyes level with the podium, slow, deliberate pace, and shoulders pulled back; all physical sleights of hand to hide the clenched stomach, sweaty palms, and held breath that I hope doesn't show. I reach the front, drape my coat over the chair, retrieve my notes from my bag, skim them, and then finally turn to face the students.

What do they see? Black dreadlocks that are pulled back from my face with a band; they hang to my waist and hide my black leather belt. Dark skin with a broad nose that holds up smoky green glasses. A solid body at 5'6" and about 250 lbs then. A French blue dress shirt with light starch tucked over chocolate brown khakis, both from Ralph Lauren, and polished black Kenneth Cole loafers. Small silver hoops in each ear that get lost in high cheekbones and abundant hair. My clothes, my style say that I am the right class to be here, middle-class, but everything else is wrong. The wrong gender: not only female, but masculine. And the wrong race: Black. And young looking to a bunch of under 21 year olds at 31.

And what do I see on that day? A blur of whiteness closing in from all sides. In the glare of the auditorium light, they are one massive White blob, even with the students of color that are sprinkled throughout the class. They are a single breathing, White entity, waiting for me to teach. And I feel fear, not just the fear of any new teacher, but the specific fear of a Black person in front of a sea of White bodies. When else would I have been standing in front of so many White people with all of their eyes on me? The tight stomach, sweaty palms, and constricted breathing are the residue of racism seeping into my nervous system, sending my body into a heightened state of awareness, preparing me to bolt if the room turns dangerous. The history of what those ratios of Black to White bodies gathered in a public space have meant is in the room with us; it is part of the lesson even if it is not part of the lecture.

Bodies on the Line

This chapter is about what it means to be in this Black body and teach White students about race. It begins from the assumption that teaching is an embodied practice that intersects with how I embody other identities such as race, gender and gender identity, and class. I present a series of vignettes from my classes to argue that my body is unavoidably part of my pedagogy. The vignettes show how I deliberately use the various ways that I embody difference to open up a space to talk about race. By playing up my class sameness, but amplifying my gender otherness, I destabilize students' expectations of what Blackness means. Through this process, students sometimes become aware of their investment in the idea of Blackness as inferior, inhuman, and strange.

However, as my account of the first day shows, I cannot completely control how my body is read or how it matters to those I teach. Thus, drawing from sociology, I pay attention to signs given, or information that I intend to convey, and signs given off, or information that students inadvertently ascribe to me.[1] For instance, the students give off a sense of ease and belonging at a university, due to their racial and class privilege, which renders me an outsider even with my middle-class background. Each first day, I have to prove my right to be there in a way that feels demoralizing and specific to my status as a Black teacher at a predominately White university. As the concept of stereotype threat suggests,[2] my fear of confirming negative stereotypes about Black incompetency can hinder my performance without any student actively creating a hostile racial environment.

Fear of confirming negative stereotypes, anxiety about feeling out of place in the classroom … these are all indications that my body is on the line when I teach. Race is a bodily discourse that attaches social meaning to physiological differences, and we feel its affect in and through our bodies.[3] Of course, teaching is a performance, and thus a bodily practice, for all professors, not just racial minorities.[4] However, this chapter catalogs some of the bodily manifestations of the costs of teaching while Black. It also shows that, when I deliberately incorporate my body into my teaching, including the strategic use of storytelling, humor, and irreverence, I can interrupt the blithe functioning of everyday racism and help students become aware of how race structures their understanding of social reality.

This chapter contributes to the growing body of literature that analyzes how the racial, gender, and sexual embodiment of professors of color informs their pedagogy.[5] Additionally, I am indebted to feminists of color from earlier generations who wrote about how to bring their whole selves to their work with White allies against social injustice.[6] In that spirit, the title of the chapter pays homage to the seminal book *This Bridge Called My Back*, which collected the stories of many different persons of color who worked in community with Whites. The dilemma then, as now, was how to take advantage of women of color's liminal status, as the bridge between multiple communities, without exploiting our bodies, stories, and talents. I offer these preliminary reflections about my own teaching practice in hope of advancing that conversation.

"It's Not That Kind of Story"

The first day of Introduction to Sociology begins with a story. Actually, it begins with a necessary, but tedious, recitation of highlights from the syllabus about which students lose interest half way through. To recapture their attention and set the tone for the class, I tell them the story of why I became a sociologist. I usually lean against the desk at the front of the class to signal a shift to a more casual mode and talk about growing up middle-class in Philly with my older brother. I litter symbols of cultural capital throughout the story, from getting a PhD at Northwestern to attending one of the top public high schools in Philadelphia, in order to establish common ground on the basis of class. My clothes also vouch for my class status, as does my fluency in normative American English. After putting students at ease, I launch into the real lesson of the story.

There are actually two lessons in the story. Officially, I tell students about how my brother and I started off in similarly accelerated classes, but wound up on divergent paths, to get them thinking about how social forces affect the life chances of individuals. The punch line of the story is that my brother became a paramedic and I became a professor, even though we both grew up in the same family and were in intellectually gifted classes as kids. I invite students to think of social factors, like peers and gender, which might explain why our educational attainment and professions were so different.

However, when telling the story the first time, I noticed a moment in class when the students assumed something horrible happened to my brother. I had not consciously built that expectation into the story, though I did build in a dramatic fork in the road where I choose to go to the magnet school downtown and he decides to go to the neighborhood junior high school. From there, I say that I went to the prominent high school and he went to a vocational technical school to show that these "innocuous" choices set our lives on different trajectories. Then comes the part the students already know: I became a professor and he became . . .

This might be when I became aware that teaching was an embodied performance. I had been telling the story in a naturalistic way, as it occurred to me from my memory with little embellishment. In fact, I was so lost in memory that I had barely noticed that the students were figuratively holding their breath. What happened to my brother? When I checked back into the classroom, I saw concern combined with anticipation on many of the students' faces. They thought they knew the ending to the story; they had heard it so many times on the news. A young Black man gets a raw deal in the school system and gets killed/hooked on drugs/becomes a criminal. Talk about signs given and signs given off. I meant to be talking about social forces and the students were expecting a story of "Black pathology." The widely circulating racial narratives about Black men as violent supplied the rest of the story for them.

At that moment, I switched from a naturalistic mode of storytelling to self-consciously performing my racial identity. I paused, and said something like, "It's not that kind of story. He became a successful paramedic and probably makes as much money as I do." By acknowledging the students' racialized and gendered expectations of what happened—"It's not that kind of story"—I created a meta-conversation about the content of the lecture. The official lesson was still there, but I interrupted another lesson about Blackness that would have been taught if I had not taken control of the story that the students were telling themselves about my brother.

These days, I am even more deliberate about playing with my students' racialized expectations of what happened to my brother. I ham it up; I pause more dramatically each time. I add more details about how long the trip was on public transportation to the magnet school. I ask them how many of them had attended vocational school or know someone who attended. I intentionally play with the racial (and class) dynamics that the students have already infused into the story to achieve a different effect than the one they expect. Through doing so, I hope students notice their expectation that tragedy befell my brother due to his racial/gender status. On that first day, as now, students laugh when I say, "It's not that kind of story." I read the laugh as relief, but also, hopefully, a budding awareness of how race played a role in the ending they were building in their minds.

Hair Piece

I have found it easier to talk about race in classes where race is considered with other identities, such as gender, class, and sexuality. I teach several courses in the gender rotation at my university from an intersectional perspective. In these classes, I draw on the disjunction between my gender (female) and gender identity (masculine) to denaturalize students' assumptions about gender. However, my gender embodiment can also be a resource for talking about race.

Like race, gender is a bodily discourse in which we ascribe physical differences with meaning that supports the idea of a gender binary, or the belief, among other things, that there is an unbridgeable gulf between men and women.[7] However, as my description suggests, my style of dress is legibly masculine as are my mannerisms. When students are surprised to see that I am their teacher, they are likely responding as much to my gender difference as my racial difference. I expected that it would be hard to connect with my students at a predominately White university because of the multiple ways I am non-normative.

I now see my excess of visible differences to be more of a help than a hindrance, particularly in gender classes. I denaturalize the relationship between being female and having a feminine embodiment. I rarely claim a gendered subjectivity in class, such as by making statements about what "we" women are like or "we" men are like. Instead, I hold my knowledge of what is expected of men and of women at arm's length, making that knowledge visible as produced and socially required.[8] "Why don't women's pants have pockets?" I ask this question with a feigned ignorance that shows my familiarity with feminine expectations, but also draws attention to my pocketed (and, thus, "made-for-men") pants. I walk leading from my shoulders then walk leading with my hips to show the differences in how we expect men and women to inhabit their bodies. However, my visible stiffness in walking from the hips (the stereotypically feminine way) and ease with walking chest forward (the stereotypically masculine way) is meant to disrupt the connection between gender and gender identity. In this way, my gender embodiment is a text that supplements the actual text of the class.

My embodiment of multiple types of difference is useful in a lecture that I present about racialized and gendered beauty standards. The reading is about the way Black women have felt estranged from standards that say that long, flowing hair is the measure of feminine beauty. During the lecture, I fling my waist-length dreadlocks and note that I have long hair. In that moment, I offer my body as a text to read alongside the textbook. My long hair is not the same as the type that is portrayed in fashion magazines, as the reading itself notes when it says that long *straight* hair is the mark of beauty.[9]

Yet, I believe my masculine gender performance also makes the artificiality of long hair as a feminine marker more visible. Flinging my hair invites the students to consider what, if any, meaning they attached to it before I made it part of the lecture. If my hair does not read as beautiful, it is because both my masculinity and my race work against reading it as such. Until that point, I suspect my students registered my hair as communicating racial identity, because of its dreadlock style. By flinging my hair, I actively ask students to consider its gendered meaning, too.

Fighting Bad Taste With Bad Taste: Talking Openly About Racism

So far, I have recounted incidents when I talked about race indirectly or in the context of other identities. What happens when race—specifically, racism—is the topic of the lecture? I often feel like I am acting in bad taste when I deal with racism directly in class. I feel rude piercing the colorblind illusion that is common among my White students.[10] To name racism is to break my tacit bargain not to make them uncomfortable. If race does matter, it does not matter very much, and it only matters to individuals, not whole groups of people. Colorblind discourse says that the person that brings up racism is impolite, not that racism itself is in bad taste.[11]

I have found that irreverence and humor helps me productively talk about race when it is at the heart of a lecture. I create absurd scenarios, strategically use coarse language or slang, and ask students mocking questions to antagonize them into thinking critically about racism. Drawing from Dwight McBride's book, I present a lecture on the "banality of evil" in Sociology of Popular Culture in which I compare the images from Abercrombie & Fitch clothing ads to images from Nazi German propaganda.[12] It can be hard for students to swallow that comparison, though, so I say things that catch them off guard in the hope of opening up their minds to new ideas. For instance, I ridicule the cheesiness of the shirtless, hairless, muscled men in the Abercrombie & Fitch ads and tease the students about still wearing the brand, which they then vocally dismiss as passé. This teasing humor eases the tension in the room, sometimes enough to soften their defenses against thinking of the ads as contributing to White supremacy.

However, I reach for bad taste to drive the point home. I riff on the idea of "as American as apple pie" by offering another set of possible endings to the saying that underline the racial assumptions that undergird it. What if we changed it to as American as "gun violence," or "eating disorders," or "segregation"? I list alternate endings to the saying that are deliberately absurd, shocking, and possibly in bad taste. But they have just enough resonance for students to notice their assumptions about what it means to be American.

When Embodiment Fails

As much as I try to consciously use my body as a tool to teach about race, racism can act back against me. My embodiment cannot overturn the enormous weight of negative meanings that the dominant culture attaches to my multiple identities. The powerlessness I felt on my first day of class can come back any time. Racism still structures my White students' imagination about what Blackness means. For instance, racism is at play when students only question the facts in the textbook when they show the persistence of racial inequality.[13] Likewise, no amount of humor, irreverence, or embodied performance can engage those students in every class who sigh heavily, roll their eyes, or talk more loudly with their neighbors whenever I mention racism.[14]

My embodiment is particularly ineffective for challenging beliefs that construct Blacks as poor and that treat Black poverty as pathological. My class embodiment is the Achilles' heel of my strategy to push past students' racist assumptions, since so much of their racial animosity is tied in with class animosity. The idea of the superiority of the middle-class, due to their normalcy, justifies White supremacy.[15] To the extent that I appeal to students' sense that being middle-class is normal and desirable, I help perpetuate racism.

Recently, my embodiment failed as a supplementary text when I was using Byron Hurt's documentary *Hip-Hop: Beyond Beats and Rhymes* (2006) to teach about the social context of the misogyny and homophobia in rap music. The movie features interviews with famous rappers, music industry personnel, and cultural critics, but also shows the filmmaker talking with Black fans at hip-hop events around the country. In a disturbing scene, the filmmaker shows a small group of Black women trying to walk through a large crowd of Black men at a Black Spring Break event. The women's body language shows fear and discomfort, as they huddle together and link arms to move between the men, some of whom are grabbing at them and filming them without their permission.

My alternative Black masculine embodiment is no match for the power of those images to reinforce the myth of the violent Black male. Indeed, the film-maker's own desire to use the scene as part of his broader project of showing that the misogyny in hip-hop is socially produced, not inherent, is frustrated by the "truth" of what those bodies signify to my predominately White and female class. To be clear, the Black men in that scene are acting in aggressive and violent ways, but that is not proof of an inherently violent Black male sexuality. The filmmaker could have shot the same scene of White male college students grabbing at a group of White women at Spring Break, but it would not have the same meaning. It would not echo with the history of racist images and racial fears that have been used to justify White supremacy.[16] The image of hip-hop-attired Black men behaving in misogynistic ways towards women (across "racial" differences) has been immortalized in so many rap videos, which themselves rehearse the myth of the Black male rapist, that any attempt to read it another way seems doomed.[17]

Indeed, the documentary and I may have the same shortcoming of securing the trust of a White audience by appealing to a sense of middle-class commonality. The Black men in the movie who interpret the social context of hip-hop—that is, the "talking heads," not the rappers and industry personnel—all read as middle-class. When Black antisexism activist Kevin Powell critiques the misogyny of hip-hop in his tan suit on his cream sofa, his embodiment of middle-class respectability might add another text that undermines his critique.[18] He indicts the White-dominated music industry as the ultimate engine of the misogyny in rap, suggesting that Black (and Latino) male rappers are part of a broader structure that profits off of images of male dominance. However, Powell's personification of a "decent Black man" may help the Black male rappers who are the subject of the movie remain "Other" in the viewers' mind. I fear my performance of "middle-class respectability" has the same effect in my classes.

Bodies As the Line

Teaching is unavoidably embodied, but I intentionally put my body on the line to teach about racism in my classes. Whether I am playing off of my gender identity or signaling class cues by my style of dress, I try to make my body a part of the text of the class. Students are reading my body anyway, so I want to be the author (as much as this is possible) rather than the object of the narrative. I have argued that by strategically calling attention to my multiple forms of difference and by using humor, storytelling, and irreverence, I open up a space for students to notice their racist assumptions. In this way, my body can be a bridge to a different understanding of race in the classroom.

I have also pointed to the limits of this strategy for talking about race on predominately White campuses. In particular, I have struggled with finding a way to challenge the alienation, fear, and contempt that students seem to have for poor Blacks. My reliance on performing middle-class cues as a way of bonding with my students will always have limited utility as an antiracist strategy as long as racism is so tied to classism. While I cannot embody a working-class Black identity, I need to think of ways to interrogate my own class privilege and biases to effectively teach and talk about race.

I want to conclude this chapter by returning to the notion of the "residue of racism" that settled on my body during the first day of class. It costs Black professors (and other teachers of color) something to teach on predominately White campuses. I know that I often come back from class exhausted, even when the teaching went well, because of the effort it takes to engage in all of these performances. Fending off racist assumptions about what happened to my brother with humor, rather than anger, takes work. Using anger productively in class by channeling it into irreverence that opens up a space for questioning takes work. Drawing attention to my non-normative gender embodiment is risky. While I am arguing that teachers of color might consciously use their bodies in their teaching, I want to acknowledge that it is costly. However, we already pay the price of putting our bodies on the line. We might as well reap the benefits that can come from using our bodies *as* the line that connects us with students.

Notes

1 Erving Goffman, *The Presentation of Self in Everyday Life*, 1st ed. (New York, NY: Doubleday Anchor, 1959).
2 Claude M. Steele, "A Threat in the Air: How Stereotypes Shape Intellectual Identity and Performance," *American Psychologist*, 52(6), 1997: 613–629, doi:10.1037/0003-066X.52.6.613.
3 Michael Omi and Howard Winant, *Racial Formation in the United States: From the 1960s to the 1990s*, 2nd ed. (New York, NY: Routledge, 1994).
4 John Evans, Brian Davies, and Emma Rich, "The Body Made Flesh: Embodied Learning and the Corporeal Device," *British Journal of Sociology of Education*, 30(4), 2009: 391–406, doi:10.1080/01425690902954588.

5 Mae G. Henderson, "What It Means to Teach the Other When the Other Is the Self," *Callaloo*, *17*(2), April 1, 1994: 432–438, doi:10.2307/2931741; Mel Michelle Lewis, "Body of Knowledge: Black Queer Feminist Pedagogy, Praxis, and Embodied Text," *Journal of Lesbian Studies*, *15*(1), 2011: 49–57, doi:10.1080/10894160.2010.508411.
6 Cherríe Moraga and Gloria Anzaldúa, eds., *This Bridge Called My Back: Writings by Radical Women of Color*, 3rd rev. ed. (Berkeley, CA: Third Woman Press, 2002); Gloria T. Hull, Patricia Bell Scott, and Barbara Smith, eds., *All the Women Are White, All the Blacks Are Men, but Some of Us Are Brave: Black Women's Studies* (New York, NY: Feminist Press, 1992).
7 Judith Butler, *Gender Trouble: Feminism and the Subversion of Identity*, 2nd ed. (New York, NY: Routledge, 2006).
8 Candace West and Don H. Zimmerman, "Doing Gender," *Gender & Society*, *1*(2), June 1, 1987: 125–151, doi:10.1177/0891243287001002002.
9 Ingrid Banks, "Hair Still Matters," in *Feminist Frontiers*, 9th ed., eds. Verta A. Taylor, Leila J. Rupp, and Nancy Whittier (New York, NY: McGraw-Hill, 2012), 142–150.
10 Antonia Randolph, *The Wrong Kind of Different: Challenging the Meaning of Diversity in American Classrooms* (New York, NY: Teachers College Press, 2013).
11 Eduardo Bonilla-Silva and Tyrone A. Forman, "'I Am Not a Racist but . . .': Mapping White College Students' Racial Ideology in the USA," *Discourse & Society*, *11*(1), 2000: 50–85.
12 Dwight A. McBride, *Why I Hate Abercrombie & Fitch: Essays on Race and Sexuality* (New York, NY: New York University Press, 2005).
13 C. T. Pittman, "Race and Gender Oppression in the Classroom: The Experiences of Women Faculty of Color with White Male Students," *Teaching Sociology*, *38*(3), July 20, 2010: 183–196, doi:10.1177/0092055X10370120.
14 Ibid.
15 Leslie Margolin, "Goodness Personified: The Emergence of Gifted Children," *Social Problems*, *40*(4), November 1, 1993: 510–532.
16 Patricia Hill Collins, *Black Sexual Politics: African Americans, Gender, and the New Racism* (New York, NY: Routledge, 2005).
17 Ibid.
18 Cathy J. Cohen, *The Boundaries of Blackness: AIDS and the Breakdown of Black Politics*, 1st ed. (Chicago, IL: University of Chicago Press, 1999).

3

STAYING IN THE CONVERSATION

Having Difficult Conversations about Race in Teacher Education

Dyan Watson

"Urban kids don't want to learn as much as the other students in class," Josh stated in a frustrated voice.

"I don't understand," I said. "You teach in a school that only accepts the neighborhood kids. Who ... who are the 'urban kids'?"

Josh was a White teacher candidate at my university who did his student teaching in a school where all of the students were neighborhood kids in the middle of a small city. Racially, the students are diverse—nearly half are White, about 40% are Latino, with the rest of the student population being Asian American, African American, and Native American.

Just who are the "urban kids" in his class that don't want to learn as much as "the other" students? It took some probing, but finally Josh admitted that the urban kids in his classroom were the kids of color; specifically, the Black and Latino children. Josh is not alone in characterizing his classroom as a mix of children, both urban and suburban. I hear teachers use this type of language all the time. Impossible, right? If a student is suburban, doesn't that mean he or she resides in or is schooled in a small, residential town on the periphery of a large one? Isn't that the definition of "suburban"? Not anymore. We have come to a place where these terms, "urban" and "suburban," are cultural constructs where both are defined primarily by race—and, to a lesser extent, class—and the perceived behaviors, beliefs, and values associated with each.[1]

By using "urban," Josh was allowed to freely talk about race without using race words, thus enabling him to say things he might not say if he used "White" or "Black," for example. This is a linguistic move employed by educators all over the nation. However, I've especially seen it in my own practice and classroom. But why? Why use code words for race? It is because we often have stereotyped views of children and their families, and how these play out in schools. In other words, we tend to think that Black and Latino students and families don't value education as much as middle-class White students and families. "Oh, it's not their fault," some of my White students say. "They live in crime-ridden neighborhoods," "They don't have familial role models," "They are poor" . . . the list goes on. The problem with this—aside from it not being true—is that the thoughts we have about African, Latino, Asian, Native, and European American children and their families influence how we think of teaching them. And, in my field, that is especially problematic.

I teach a variety of education courses; most are geared toward Master's-level students who are becoming secondary teachers. The vast majority of my students are White. In fact, I have never had more than two students of color in a cohort; some years, I've had none. My aim is to send into schools teachers who are adept at designing curricula that respond to the diversity of the community and prepare their students to be kind, socially just participants in our democracy. I want my students to understand how race influences how they teach and interact with students. I want them to constantly think about how race intersects with both teaching and learning. The majority of my students of color seem to understand this in some fashion, even if only experientially. I think they are aware of the interplay, even if they don't understand the intricacies of this intersection. My experience is that my White students tend to be less cognizant of how race mediates teaching and learning. Even those who can articulate that an intersection exists often struggle with the reality and subconsciously resist learning about it.

Because of these goals, my objective for all difficult conversations, but especially those that involve race in some explicit way, is for my students and me to stay in the conversation. What this means is, no matter how hard it gets, keep talking and listening. It means each participant needs to seek to understand what other folks are saying and not to assume that they know in advance what someone means. Staying in the conversation involves giving of self; it involves listening with the heart and being fully present. White students often find this difficult since they tend to characterize courses and conversations that center on race as acts of violence.[2] By giving wholly, they feel they will experience a loss of self and/or authority; thus, they resist it.

Practically, staying in the conversation means asking a host of questions in a tone that suggests genuine interest and invites people in, in lieu of sarcasm or in ways that threaten the respondent. In the example above, asking Josh to explain who were the urban kids took effort to ask it in a way that invited his honest response instead of a canned, intellectual one that any of my students can proffer any day of the week.

It is difficult to keep students in the conversation if I don't establish an environment that welcomes honesty, disagreement, respect, openness, and regularly questioning of normativity. It helps to tell and show my students that I care about them, and to share my own shortcomings with them as much as I can without supporting a sense of incompetence. This is a difficult task at best, but I've learned a few ways of encouraging this work.

The first is to start my classes with an educational autobiography. This is something that a group of friends of mine used in their course at the Harvard Graduate School of Education years ago. On a half sheet of paper, I write:

> Who we are influences how we form relationships and understand others. Thus, we begin this experience with an educational autobiography. In this assignment, I hope you will learn more about your beliefs and assumptions about students and learning, where these assumptions come from, and how these assumptions may influence your relationships with students and your interpretations of student behavior. In no more than four, double-spaced, typed pages, write the story of your schooling career. Include formal and informal learning experiences that led to your decision to enter the Master of Arts in Teaching program. Please provide contextual information (e.g., race, social class, family structure, environment growing up, etc.) that informs your experiences.

The first year that I did this, the responses were disappointing. Students wrote about having ADHD, being poor(er), the only Christian, one of many Christians, chubby, shy. But hardly any student wrote about race. So, the next year, I penned one and read it to them. I wrote, in part:

> The journey to my decision to teach and since then has been full of experiences that have cultivated my resolve to teach. Since the age of nine, I was raised in a single parent home in NE Portland (12th and Killingsworth). In middle school, gangs moved up from California and into my neighborhood, making walking around certain streets very dangerous. Simultaneously, I was bused into a White school across town. We were very poor and on free lunch and had to stand in a separate line to receive our lunch tickets. I matured a lot at that school. And, by the time it was over, I had had enough of being the minority and decided I wanted back in to my neighborhood. So, for high school, I went to Jeff, where the Black population was around 65%. It wasn't easy. I had been mostly with White people for three years and, before middle school, had spent most of my elementary years with White students and families in Paterson, New Jersey. So now I had to code switch in a number of ways, and learn to be just black enough to fit in, but not too black, so that my teachers would like me and think I was smart.

Then I invited them to write theirs. The difference was night and day. Students wrote about not seeing any people of color until high school or never having a teacher of color until now. And, as the years have worn on, I have done a better job of prepping them for responses that really interrogate their perceptions of race. This past year, one student wrote:

> After high school graduation, I moved to Florida for six months. That was the first time I had ever seen (much less lived in) a place with a high percentage of African Americans. From then on, whenever anyone asked about Idaho, it wouldn't take long before I mentioned the whiteness of Idaho. To support this claim I often mentioned how, in my high school of about 600 students, fewer than 10 were black. It was several years after graduation, while skimming through my old yearbooks, that it dawned on me that my spiel about the complete whiteness of my high school wasn't true at all. Looking through the photos, I noticed many Hispanic students, mostly unfamiliar faces. I didn't share the same classes with these students, or see them at lunch or at school dances. In elementary school, there [are] usually a couple of Hispanic students in my class, but, at that time, I felt oblivious to race. By junior high and high school, they had all but disappeared from my line of vision. I am embarrassed to say that I simply didn't see them. I didn't see them even though my best friend was Mexican American. My first fleeting inkling that race matters was when she got upset after a mutual friend of ours said, "But you're not really Mexican." I recognize now that the most offensive part of that statement was that it was meant as a compliment.
>
> *Sara*

Some of my students had simply not thought about their interactions and experiences around race. Others often don't know what to make of them, but describe these incidents and moments anyway. I then respond to each student, sometimes asking them questions, but often just reassuring them that their experience is real, that I'm glad to have them as my student, and that I look forward to being a part of their journey to teach. I find that this exercise sets up the classroom as a safe space to talk about race.

And by "safe," I don't mean a place where folks won't get offended, or angry, or feel pain. I mean safe enough to feel all of these emotions and more, but still want to come back because the learning is that good and productive. The more I make race visible to my students, the more they talk about it and become comfortable with the uneasiness of talking about race with people of color.

What I like about Sara's autobiography is that there is no talk of guilt—yes, she's embarrassed, but not guilty. I think White guilt can detract from the real issues at hand and provide an unsafe space that promulgates White progressivism— a notion of feeling badly because "my ancestors did bad things" and now "please take care of me and my feelings." So, I'm sure to address this, too. In fact, this past Fall, a White student offered: "I feel so guilty and horrible about being White." My response: "You should feel guilty if you go into schools and continue to perpetuate the systematic oppression of people of color." I try to make it clear that I'm not here to absolve them of guilt or make them feel badly for the past. My concern is kids and what kind of teacher my students are going to be. If, after taking my class, any one of my students does not recognize how race mediates learning and teaching, and aren't proactively using this knowledge to make a positive difference, they should feel horribly guilty. And I hope they don't stay in teaching. Instead of guilt, I ask students to think about privilege and the consequences of injustice.

One of the ups in my years of exploring race and teaching with students is to allow them to ask any question that they want. I tell them that, if I'm offended, I'll tell them that I am and I'll tell them why, and that I promise to keep the dialogue open, no matter what. This has usually worked. In the case of Josh who insisted on saying "urban" instead of Black and Latino, this worked out well. He realized what he was saying and what it was hiding, and began to think about his assumptions of the Latino and Black children in his care.

However, in the case of Pete, it turned out badly, at least temporarily. During orientation, all of the professors introduce themselves—name and what you teach. Nothing personal; no interesting tidbits. I announced: "My name is Dyan Watson and I primarily teach the Social Studies folk, but this year I'll also be your Multicultural Education instructor." After we finished our introductions and there was a break, a young, White student named Pete came over to me and said, "Why are all of the Social Studies teachers always so cool?" I just stared at him because there were too many competing thoughts in my mind, and I was trying to figure out how he surmised that I was "cool" based on 23 words of introduction with no personal stories. A few months later, Pete was a student in my Multicultural Education course. I noticed that, when he spoke to me, he put on a "Black" accent. After a few weeks of this, I called him on it: "So, I just want to stop you right there and point out the words and tone you are using, and I'm trying to figure out why you are talking like this." He stammered through a response about hanging out with Black kids growing up and that it had nothing to do with my being Black. It didn't go well. He didn't speak for the rest of the session. The following week, he asked to meet with me. I told him I was glad he wanted to talk because I knew I'd hurt him and wanted to rectify that. We worked it out, but I clearly didn't play that one well. And, because I didn't play that one well, I addressed it with the entire class in a different session. I told them that one of the most important aspects of moving forward in conversations about race is to stay in conversation. So, even though Pete was angry, he came to me and we talked it out. And even though I had been offended, I listened and, this time, asked clarifying questions and truly sought to see where he was coming from.

In addition to self-exploration, I want students to examine and critique societal institutions that perpetuate inequality, such as schools—both in K–12 and in higher education. So, I send them on a mission to answer the following questions:

> Who does your university serve? What is your evidence? Over the next week, collect data to answer this question. Look at the art on the walls, names of professors, accessibility, etc. Record this data and be prepared to discuss it next class.

We follow up this activity with a "climate case study" that asks students to explore the secondary school in which they are placed. Students are asked to gather demographic data on the school community and specifically think about the following:

1. What are the most obvious manifestations of culture that you observe when you first walk into the school? (Name of school, language(s) of signs, language/appearance of people in the office, bulletin boards, pictures, decorations, etc.)
2. How do you think you would feel entering the school if you were a parent? A child of color? Of a poor family? Non-English speaking? Special needs? Talented and Gifted?
3. Observe student and teacher behavior before and after school, at break/ recess, and lunch.
4. Observe the attire and nonverbal behavior/communication of students and teachers.
5. Identify other evidence of a school culture.

Students are then asked to compare the culture of their practicum site and the culture of their own high school or middle school. Students produce rich narratives of differences and similarities, and how these aspects either welcome or alienate students, faculty, and parents of color. Sam, a White student, wrote:

> Reynolds High has a dim interior. Labyrinthine halls branch out from the main cafeteria area, and each section is walled off from the next. To pass from one hall to the next, students must push through doors, giving the building the feeling of a well-contained institution that can be locked down and sealed off at a moment's notice. Sunset High, on the other hand, is well lit with an open, free-flowing feel. Things are mostly new and functional at Sunset; not so at Reynolds, where many things in my mentor's room are old and half-functional. Sunset is equally mazelike and institutional, but, whereas Reynolds has the feel of a prison or mental ward, Sunset feels more like a nursing home or hospital.

Sam goes on to discuss the racial demographics of the two schools. He mentions the prison-like one having a large Latino population, and the nursing home-like school having a largely White, middle- and upper-class student population. As a class, we talk about how schools are microcosms of our stratified society and the implications of this in our teaching. By looking outside of personal stories (i.e., autobiography), the conversation gets moved to systems of oppression so that students see how both micro and macro hegemony is at play.

Staying in the conversation takes a lot of emotional and intellectual effort. I don't always want to use nice words and soften my voice. I am constantly aware of coming across as the angry Black female. It doesn't matter that I don't do a lot of eye rolling and head moving. It's scary for many Whites to have a Black woman check them on a statement that might be racist, or to point out the structures that maintain the racial status quo. Students want to know that their teacher cares for them, and I do. But caring for them in this circumstance can prick the heart, and, well, that's not what the typical teacher–student relationship looks like in our White, female-dominated institutions. I know that I'll see whatever I may have missed during the semester on my course evaluations at the end of the semester. So, I'm constantly second guessing myself, replaying what I've said, and rehearsing how I might fix it the next day. The work this takes is taxing and can take a heavy toll on my well-being if I don't take measures to adequately deal with having to pay this tax.

It is crucial to my survival that I assemble a White team of support. These allies are folks who are steeped in the literature and research on whiteness and antiracist pedagogy. These are teachers who practice what they preach, and, when they miss the mark, admit it and seek to rectify their shortcomings. Further, these are the ones that go to bat for me in meetings with other faculty who don't understand these phenomena, and bring up issues of race without my prompting and often before I get the chance to.

Unfortunately, I have also taught in universities where I did not have this team. I had "allies" who did back me up, but only once I had spoken, because they did not live and breathe the literature; they simply agreed with what I stated because it made sense. I maintained my sanity primarily by doing two things. The first was to allow myself to cry when it got to be too much. The release of this emotion functioned much like the vents on a well-built house. As the warm air of racialized tension filled my working self, I emoted, allowing the "house" to breathe and not suffer structural damage. The second strategy is one I continue to employ, and that is to write these instances down. Sometimes, these musings and recountings serve as sources for future publications. Other times, they serve as a catharsis; cleansing me from the microaggressions and the tax owed of being one of the only faculty of color serving a predominantly White population.

The two most helpful ways I've dealt with this burden in the classroom are to do a lesson on African American Vernacular English (AAVE), and on my fears as a parent of raising Black boys.

The lesson about AAVE usually comes within a unit on language and power. I begin with an exercise I got from author and social justice educator, Linda Christensen. I ask the class of Master's degree-seeking candidates to do the following:

> Write a response to the following prompt: "Why do you want to be a teacher?" Use the following rules as you write:
>
> 1.   No "s" on plural;
> 2.   No "s" on possessive;
> 3.   No "s" on third-person verb: I swim. He swim. We swim. They swim.

After a few minutes, I ask the students to draw a line beneath the last thing they wrote and write a reflection about the process—the strategies they used and how it felt. Here is a sample of how students have responded:

> "I took a step back in the complexity of what I was writing because it was too hard."
> "It's hard to think about grammar and answer the prompt."
> "I thought about the rules too much. I decided to write and then go back and cross out things."
> "I had all these ideas, but, then, when I saw the rules, I abandoned them."

I point out that when students have to focus on rules instead of ideas, the ideas suffer, and that when teachers prioritize speaking in a language or manner that isn't natural or native, it diminishes self-worth. We spend some time going over a few of the rules of AAVE, so that they can see there is structure to the dialect, and that it is not just "lazy English" or "slang." And then I get personal and tell them about my own experiences with speaking AAVE.

In doing so, I share with them a very short passage from *Wild Meat and the Bully Burgers* by Lois-Ann Yamanaka.[3] In this story, the teacher asks his students—all of whom are Hawaiian and speak pidgin English—to "stand up and tell me your name, and what you would like to be when you grow up."[4] The command is simple enough. Many teachers across the country, if not the world, have asked their students to talk about what they aspire to be. The hitch is he has mandated that they use Standard English (SE), both without providing them the tools with which to be successful and the caring encouragement that is needed when SE isn't your first language. The first student responds:

> "Ma name is Mal-vin Spenca." . . . Before he begins his next sentence, he does nervous things like move his ankles side to side so that his heels slide out of his slippers. He looks at the ceiling and rolls his eyes. "I am, I mean, I wanna. I like. No, try wait. I going be. No, try wait. I will work on my

Gramma Spenca's pig farm when I grow up cuz she said I can drive the slop truck. Tank you."

I tell my students that, every August, when the faculty return from summer vacation, we go around the table and share what we did during the summer. Every summer, I am Melvin. My hands sweat and I twitch in my seat. I stutter, and then I mumble. I am a college-educated woman. I have a Bachelor's, Master's, and doctorate. But, ask me what I did for summer and I become inarticulate. It isn't that I can't express myself in either AAVE or SE. It's that I want to use them both, simultaneously. But only one of these languages will be validated. Only one of these languages matches the fact that I have a doctorate. Only one of these languages makes me look smart. Only one of these languages makes me feel like I got into an Ivy League school because I was qualified and not because I am an affirmative action case. However, it is only through both languages that I can express what I did this summer. It is only through them both that I can share the joy I had riding my bike with my 11-year-old niece or the birth of my sons. It is only through them both that I talk about the disappointment of not getting my latest article published or the lesson that did not go so well.

Students are often shocked to hear that I speak in AAVE and that I feel ostracized when I do. We then have a rich, honest discussion about language, discrimination, and race. I tell them they can ask me any question they want. At the end of the semester, I read to them, *A Letter From a Black Mom to Her Son*.[5] This, by far, is one of the most powerful lessons I do with them. It humanizes White hegemony, yet is hopeful. It is a letter written to my oldest son, Caleb, when he was almost 2 years old, about the education that I received and how it influences the hopes and dreams I now have for him. In it, I write: "I hope you will have teachers who realize they are gatekeepers. I hope they understand the power they hold and work to discover your talents, seek out your dreams and fan them, rather than smother them."[6] Taking a cue from another social justice educator and colleague, Amy Dee, I then ask them to write back to me as the teacher they hope to be. How will they, with their new understanding of how race mediates teaching and learning, work to discover my son's talents, seek out his dreams and fan them, rather than smother them?

The best part of this experience is that usually by the end of the semester, my students—who are going to have their own students in just a few months—are asking different questions than the ones that they asked at beginning of the semester. "Dr. DW, how do we empower students to use their home language AND provide them the tools to be successful in a racist world?" they ask. "What's the best way to teach a book that has the N-word in it that validates differing opinions, but creates a safe learning community?" "Do you have the lesson plan for the autobiography assignment we did at the beginning of the year? I want to do it with my tenth graders." When we get to these type of questions, I know I've stayed in the conversation—and I am proud of them for doing so as well.

Notes

1 See Dyan Watson, "'Urban, But Not Too Urban': Unpacking Teachers' Desires to Teach Urban Students," *Journal of Teacher Education, 62*(1), 2011: 23–34; and Dyan Watson, "Norming Suburban: How Teachers Talk About Race Without Using Race Words," *Urban Education, 47*(5), 2012: 983–1004.
2 Robin DiAngelo and Özlem Sensoy, "Getting Slammed: White Depictions of Race Discussions as Arenas of Violence," *Race Ethnicity and Education, 2*(20120518), 2012: 1–26, doi:10.1080/13613324.2012.674023.
3 Lois-Ann Yamanaka, *Wild Meat and the Bully Burgers* (New York, NY: Farrar Straus Giroux, 1996).
4 Ibid., 11.
5 Dyan Watson, "A Letter From a Black Mom to Her Son," *Rethinking Schools, 26*(3), Spring 2012: 16–18.
6 Ibid., 18.

4

RACE-ING THE CURRICULUM

Reflections on a Pedagogy of Social Change

Kathy Glass

Is it *racist* to discuss race? Does racial analysis *perpetuate* insidious racial notions? Heartfelt White students often pose these questions in predominantly White college classrooms. Such questions recur in academic settings when students engage literature produced by and about nonwhites. As a Black woman teaching African American literature, I get these questions frequently, and, in the following chapter, I'd like to explore the embedded optics and cultural assumptions in these inquiries. White students often feel discomfort, denial, detachment, defensiveness, and guilt when reading texts that remove the veil and dare to gaze boldly at whiteness and its socio-structural effects.[1] But these responses may give way to curiosity, openness, awareness, and a critical sensibility that leads to political engagement.

In engaging students in frank discussions about race, faculty of color may encounter unique scenarios not shared by their White colleagues. Some students take refuge in silence so as to avoid making racially insensitive remarks, others make offensive comments without realizing the impact of their words, and yet others question the value of discussing race in (what they believe to be) a post-racial period. How might faculty of color navigate these encounters? How do we transform these challenges into teachable moments? I hope to offer here some lessons learned from these experiences, and propose some teaching strategies that can create classroom spaces conducive to dialogue, agency, and change. I structure this chapter around students' frequently asked questions, and my pedagogical responses to their inquiries.

I'm a Black female committed to teaching literature, promoting cross-cultural dialogue, endorsing democratic ethics, and foregrounding social justice. My teaching method derives from the educational philosophies of Paulo Freire and bell hooks, who theorize the classroom as a potential site of social and intellectual transformation. hooks writes that her "pedagogical practices have emerged from the mutually illuminating interplay of anticolonial, critical, and feminist pedagogies."[2] Similarly, the same antiracist, feminist, and critical frameworks also shape my scholarship. Like Freire and hooks, I reject the "banking" model of education that renders students passive vessels that consume knowledge dispensed by their instructors.[3] Instead, I invite students to actively engage texts and one another in the classroom. This interaction creates contexts in which students can exercise their critical thinking skills, and challenge received truths about literature, culture, race, and society.

"White supremacy" is the term that hooks uses "to describe the system of race-based biases we live within" because, she notes, it is "inclusive of everyone."[4] She refers here to Whites, as well as Black people/people of color who harbor racist views, even though they may "organize their thinking and act differently from racist whites."[5] hooks correctly notes that racist ideology can operate through persons of all colors and classes. Active confrontation and interrogation of internalized racism are essential stages of the liberation process for minoritized groups. Though I focus exclusively on teaching in predominantly White spaces in this chapter, I am aware that ideologies of whiteness can affect not only White students, but also students belonging to racial/ethnic and minority groups.

"Is it Racist to Discuss Race?"

In February 1998, the U.S. sitcom *Seinfeld* broached the subject of race in an episode entitled "The Wizard." As the episode opens, the camera captures Jerry, and George (soon joined by Elaine), at the local diner. When the conversation turns to Elaine's new, fair-skinned boyfriend, confusion ensues. Perplexed and preoccupied with his racial identity, the three White friends guess at what it might be. Is he Black or is he White? After a brief debate, George ventures: "Should we be talking about this?" Minutes later, when a Black waitress approaches their table to bring their check, Jerry, George, and Elaine guiltily shower her with tips. Though fictional, this revealing scene reflects a broader trend of anxiety among White adults in America who are conscious of race, and yet are uncomfortable discussing it.

Though they are younger and often more progressive than their parents, many of the students I encounter in the classroom have inherited from them—or developed on their own—a degree of discomfort about race. Sadly, this is not an isolated phenomenon. Research suggests that a significant percentage of White students across America feel uncomfortable engaging issues of race in academic settings. In *Being White: Stories of Race and Racism*, Karyn D. McKinney shares the results of her extensive study on the subject. After gathering and reviewing the "racial autobiographies from nearly 200 students in northern and southern universities," she reports that, "for whites who do not want to appear racist, noticing difference at all has been taboo. In other words, whites most often attempt to appear 'colorblind.'"[6] The operative phrase here is that Whites often "*attempt* to appear colorblind" (my emphasis). Arguably, *Seinfeld's* George believes that noticing and commenting on perceived difference is inherently wrong. Though Whites do indeed see the human diversity manifested in shades of skin color, cultural practice, and historical tradition, some are convinced that acknowledging and discussing these differences is racist—in the presence of a person of color (which could pose a significant problem for professors in this category) *and* outside the presence of persons of color. For this reason, Elaine, George, and Jerry feel the need to "redeem" themselves for having discussed race in the absence of Elaine's possibly Black boyfriend. They eventually shower their Black waitress with tips to assuage their guilt over their "race talk."

McKinney's study has explanatory value here, for she encountered in her research groups of White students who believe that "the only way to a truly egalitarian society is through colorblindness."[7] If they ignore race, they imagine it will go away. This avoidance strategy not only denies the reality of diversity—and its attendant sociocultural dimensions—but it also undermines efforts to critically analyze literary works produced by minority communities. And, as McKinney's studies show, students themselves are *consciously* aware of what we have come to understand as "race."[8] This comes as no surprise as in the United States human bodies "are inserted in a comprehensively racialized social structure," such that:

> [o]ne of the first things we notice about people when we meet them (along with their sex) is their race. We utilize race to provide clues about who a person is. This fact is made painfully obvious when we encounter someone whom we cannot conveniently racially categorize ... Such an encounter becomes a source of discomfort and momentarily a crisis of racial meaning.[9]

Seinfeld's "The Wizard" is again illustrative, as the characters in the episode explored above endeavor to fix Elaine's boyfriend on the terrain of racial identity. They "notice" his racially indeterminate body and attempt to render it intelligible. But more fascinating (for this author) than the *racial identity* of Elaine's boyfriend (who laments, at the end of the show, that he and Elaine are "just a couple of White people"—an observation which invites, by contrast, speculations about the "exotic" lives led by people of color) is the other characters' desire to categorize him in the first place. Once Elaine's curiosity is stoked, she spends the rest of the episode looking for "clues" that will render his race legible.[10] Elaine is no aberration, for we all learn some combination of racial stereotypes that shape racial experience and condition "meaning."[11] Unfortunately, colorblind approaches to race result in a denial of these experiences and meanings, and prevent us from addressing the social, cultural, and historical implications of race. In my lower-division courses, I have had students share with me in class and during office hours that they do not see color—only human beings. Others acknowledge that they do *see* color, but that they attach no particular significance to it.

Pedagogical Response and Suggested Reading

Aware that well-meaning students bring to the classroom the assumption that they must appear colorblind—perhaps especially in my presence—I engage them early in the term in a simple yet productive free association exercise. In a course on representations of race in literature, for example, I have asked students to prepare for the semester's readings by considering what and how "Black" signifies in our culture. I invite them to call out whatever connotations come to mind, and I list their responses on the chalkboard. Since "Black" functions in Western culture as the binary opposite of "White," I also ask my students to consider the connotations of whiteness. Invariably and inevitably, these lists reflect racialized, dominant cultural assumptions that have been linked to Black and White bodies in the United States since the nineteenth century. Such questions as "How do you make these associations?" and "How are these notions transmitted in our culture?" serve as the starting point for discussions about the racially coded nature of language, the circulation of racial ideology, and the power of racial discourses to shape our culture, actions, and experience.

Free association exercises combined with a study of generative literary works can further help students to acknowledge and actively interrogate the cultural implications of racial ideology. I frequently use for this purpose Toni Morrison's "Recitatif" —a text that refuses to attach racial clues to racially ambiguous bodies in the story.[12] In the absence of such details, students—as would any other reader—seek to identify, based on authorial description and character dialogue, the "racial identity" of the main characters. Students then reflect on *why* they feel compelled to do so. What is it about the human psyche that needs to make "racial sense" of embodied subjects? These questions often spark discussions about interpretive reading practices, situated readerships, and insidious "common sense" notions about race. Once these racial assumptions have been articulated, acknowledged, and understood to be part of the culture in which we all live, many students feel more liberated to discuss the cultural significance of race as textual and experiential realities. Aware that they are to some extent "swimming" in these racial ideas empowers them to confront—and even challenge—them. Jettisoning the politically correct strategy of "avoid[ing] recognition of difference altogether" makes it possible to identify, describe, and appreciate our differences, even as we analyze how hegemonic forces have historically used these differences to justify unequal sociopolitical conditions, and to divide humanity along racial lines.[13] While illuminating and constructive, the act of rendering visible the effects of whiteness through literary encounters can yield unpredictable results in the classroom.

"How Does This Apply to Me?"—*or*, the Denial of White Privilege

Several years ago, I assigned Ralph Ellison's *Invisible Man* to my sophomore-level literature students. After discussing the content of the battle royal scene with my students—all of whom were White—I asked how they felt about this section of the novel.[14] How did they experience Ellison's rendering of the aggressive, "leading White citizens" who urged the unsuspecting Black men to pummel each other in the boxing ring?[15] How did they feel when violent, White, middle-aged men reduced young Black men to mere figures of entertainment? Silence blanketed the classroom as some of my students looked down at their books, and others looked past me to the chalkboard where I had listed the key themes of *Invisible Man*. So I waited as one minute passed, and then another, wondering all the while if I should move on to the next question.

I was preparing to do just that when one student raised his hand, and said that the battle royal scene made him "uncomfortable." Other students nodded in silent agreement. He went on to say that he felt embarrassed by the Whites' behavior toward the Blacks, and, well, guilty too. He proceeded to make a connection between the power dynamics in the novel and race relations in the twenty-first century. In essence, his encounter with Ellison's novel had made him keenly aware of his own privilege in the *present moment*. While this student's thoughtful reading of the battle royal gave way to a timely discussion about the systemic nature of racism, I have also taught students who emphatically denied the existence of systemic racial inequality in the modern world.

In a freshman course on literature and diversity, one of my students actively rejected the idea that racism operates as a *system* of oppression that advantages some while disadvantaging others. At one point in the semester, she reflected that our discussion of White privilege felt like a tirade against White people. But "opposing whiteness is *not* the same as opposing White people."[16] This student's refusal to "tarry," to borrow George Yancy's term, with the idea that whiteness is a system of domination allowed her to take refuge in the merit-based narrative that outcomes depend wholly on individual effort.[17]

In *Teaching Community*, hooks argues that "it is a positive aspect of our culture that folks want to see racism end; paradoxically, it is this heartfelt longing that underlies the persistence of the false assumption that racism has ended."[18] Whether motivated by positive or insidious intentions, some eagerly assert that racism is dead and that race is irrelevant in the twenty-first century. In her studies, McKinney reports "how infrequently whites think directly and consciously about whiteness and what it entails."[19] Being White, they simply consider whiteness to be the neutral cultural norm—an assumption that works alongside the finding that "racial identity is, almost by definition, invisible when a person occupies the top rung of the racial hierarchy."[20] Student respondents in this category therefore view themselves as raceless, average individuals, unlike the Others who "have" a race. This attitude can manifest itself not only in the classroom, but also at every level of academia.

Black literary scholar Ann duCille observes this phenomenon in the field of mainstream American feminism. To illustrate her point, she quotes White feminist Jane Gallop, for whom "race only posed itself as an urgent issue to [her] in the last couple of years."[21] DuCille laments that "[b]y and large, it is only those who enjoy the privileges of White skin who can hold matters of race at arm's length."[22] But this perception that "racial identity is a property only of the non-white" prevents serious analyses of whiteness *as an invented structure* that ensures benefits for some while channeling them away from the most disadvantaged among us.[23] An unmarked category,[24] whiteness must be rendered visible so that it can be recognized as a structure that shapes lived experience. To this end, I discuss with my students how whiteness emerged in U.S. law, and how it has evolved from the slavery era to the present.[25]

Pedagogical Response and Suggested Reading

Learning about the structural dimensions of whiteness can produce a wide range of effects on students. Some attempt to deny their relation to whiteness as site of privilege, citing their working-class background. Others point to the hard work that has allowed them and their families to advance in life without government assistance or social preference of any kind. Some may resent the implication that they have done otherwise, and believe they are being exposed to far-left dogma in the classroom.

During conversations about White privilege, students frequently (and correctly) observe that things have changed since the 1960s: we have a Black president now, and Oprah Winfrey is one of the richest women—Black or White—in America. These are the facts. And the recitation of these facts provides an opportune time to discuss the workings of structural racism, and its uneven results.

While whiteness constitutes a form of privilege, not all Whites are equally privileged within its system,[26] and certain people of color do enjoy a privileged social and economic status relative to some Whites. In a recent interview with Henry Louis Gates, Jr., historian Nell Painter indicates that whiteness is both "expanding" and "shrinking." It is expanding, she argues, "by letting in people by opening the privileges that used to be preserved for whiteness to people who are brown as long as they are rich, or beautiful or cute."[27] But, as Painter makes clear, "that does not touch the Black poor who … will always be racialized." While it is true that one "no longer has to be White to move with power and assurance," African Americans are "six times more likely than whites to be incarcerated."[28] Moreover, Blacks have less access than Whites to life chances and resources, including health care, housing, education, and employment.

Although Barack Obama dwells in the White House, Black men in America still find themselves routinely stopped and frisked for "driving while Black" in

America; and the Blackness of young men like Trayvon Martin makes them figures of suspicion and potential targets of violence on our city streets. These are not isolated incidents of injustice, but, rather, symptoms of a discriminatory system structured by privilege. These are the facts that I share with my students, and the realities shaping the contexts in which many Black authors write.

One text that makes palpable the effects of whiteness is George Yancy's *Black Bodies, White Gazes*. Chapter 1 of *Black Bodies*, entitled "The Elevator Effect," explores how the "space within the elevator is only a pale reminder of how the Black body has been historically marked and inscribed in derogatory terms, how it has been subjected to inhuman brutality and pernicious acts of violence, and how it has been marginalized and derailed within the space of the White body politic."[29] Yancy's smart, incisive, and compelling text highlights what his Black body signifies for a White female in the social space of an elevator. Although she "'sees'" his "Black body," writes Yancy, what she sees is "not the same one [he] has seen reflected from the mirror on any number of occasions."[30] Instead, she sees the Blackness that has historically been produced and colored by negative association and characterization in the media, public policy, and other "'agents of representation.'"[31] Consequently, the woman in the elevator responds accordingly: "Her body language signifies, 'Look, *the* Black!'"[32]

In the classroom, this chapter prompted one of my students to defend the woman in the elevator, and to question the fairness of the speaker. As Frances Foster notes, from the appearance of "the earliest extant volume by an African American, to the present time, the mimetic details ... and political implications of their texts have been particularly challenged."[33] Another of my students reflected that she did not "see" the Black body through a negative lens and that, moreover, she did not view her own body as socially privileged. Another student acknowledged that White privilege exists as a system that determines life chances and opportunities in general, but he denied the system's power to shape daily social encounters. Although a few of the students in the class took issue with some of the chapter's conclusions, *many more* indicated that Yancy's text helped them to understand how their socially constructed "positive" whiteness helps to construct "negative" Blackness in social contexts,[34] as these signifiers are interdependent. For them, "the Elevator Effect" lays bare the ways in which history affects institutions and individuals in seemingly mundane spaces.

"Why Is She/He So Angry?": Tone Matters in Literary Texts

David Walker and Malcolm X were angry—and for good reason. The injustices of slavery, segregation, antiblack violence, and racism generally inspired a righteous indignation made palpable in their writings. Some students find "angry texts" off-putting because they feel accused, and made to feel aware of their "race."

Perhaps for the first time, they have access to the "Others'" voices, and are shocked by what they hear. David Walker's *Appeal* argues: "The whites have always been an unjust, jealous, unmerciful, avaricious and blood-thirsty set of beings, always seeking after power and authority."[35] In his *Autobiography*, Malcolm X quips, "He [the White man] may stand with you through thin, but not thick; when the chips are down, you'll find that as fixed in him as his bone structure is his sometime subconscious conviction that he's better than anybody Black."[36] In *Killing Rage*, bell hooks writes of her "killing rage" resulting from experiences and observations of antiblack discrimination.[37] The outrage animating these sentiments signifies the extra-textual factors that necessarily draw readers of these and—by extension—other texts by other African American authors beyond formalist readings.

Many students have not been exposed to what Cornel West calls the "night-side" of Western modernity;[38] they have learned about the nation's founding documents, but have not studied how slavery made possible the freedom outlined therein. They have learned about the nature of democracy, but have not studied the antidemocratic practices and policies that have historically structured unequal social and economic realities. Some students feel angry and betrayed when exposed to the "unsanitized" version of our nation's history. Others feel sad. For the first time in their lives, perhaps, they confront in the college classroom the fact that the nation's promises have not been historically accessible to all—and still remain inaccessible to many. Once armed with this knowledge, however, students can become more socially conscious, culturally sensitive, and more effective readers of texts.

Pedagogical Response and Suggested Reading

Literary texts are social documents that reflect and seek to transform the culture in which they emerge. Considerations of authorial tone can enhance students' understanding of historical conditions, and of the sociopolitical change that texts have attempted to enact throughout history. For these reasons, I have come to appreciate the oft-asked question ("Why are these authors so angry?"), but, in the classroom, we go beyond it to consider the sociocultural contexts in which authors write, the assumptions undergirding their texts, and the cultural work that literary texts seek to perform. These discussions connect cultural production to overarching sociopolitical issues that may not appear in elementary and middle school history and political science books. Simple awareness can be the first step toward deeper understanding.

James Baldwin wrote *The Fire Next Time* to increase readers' awareness of the urgent state of race relations in the 1960s.[39] In the book, his tone ranges from sadness to despair and outrage. It positions readers to imaginatively experience with Baldwin the indignities of discrimination, and the "crime" of being passive in its presence. In section 2 of the book, Baldwin recounts an incident that took place when he and two Black friends arrived at the Chicago O'Hare airport in advance of their flight to enjoy a drink at the bar. The White bartender did not serve these men, however, who were all "well past thirty and looking it."[40] A confrontation ensued. After Baldwin and his friends repeatedly asked to see the manager, the latter appeared and defended the bartender, who was apparently "new," and as yet unable to tell a "Negro boy of twenty and a Negro 'boy' of thirty-seven."[41] Although Baldwin and his friends eventually got their drinks, they were conscious of the fact that not one of the White onlookers at the bar had interceded on their behalf. When a "young White man" belatedly approached to ask if they were students, assuming that only students would bother "putting up a fight," Baldwin's friend responded: "[T]he fight that we had been having in the bar was [your] fight too." The young White man could only answer that he "had lost his conscience a long time ago," before turning to exit the bar.[42] This disturbing display of indifference *understandably* angers Baldwin, who argues that civilization is destroyed not only by "wicked" but also by "spineless" people who refuse to protest discriminatory attitudes and systems.[43] This disturbing indifference is designed to anger readers, too, and to move them toward productive social action.

I recently spoke with a former student who said that he had been disturbed two years ago by our readings on race theory, which had "opened his eyes" to the construction of whiteness. He was somewhat dismayed after the course, but he said he wanted to learn more so that he could "do something" about its structural effects. He felt inherently that unearned privilege was just "wrong." Being exposed to Black intellectuals like hooks, Baldwin, and Yancy had created in him a hunger to learn *more*. But what about those students who refuse textual encounters?

"No comment"

Some students are highly resistant to speaking about race in the classroom. Given my embodiment as a woman of color, I realize that a portion of these students may withhold their interpretations of Black literary texts because they fear offending me, or their classmates. Perhaps they are uncertain as to which language to use, and how to discuss race in an academic setting. Some detach emotionally from the conversation, and refuse to participate.

Earlier in my career as a college professor, I ignored these silences and lectured doggedly on to cover up the awkwardness of the quiet classroom. But, over the years, I've undertaken what I believe to be a more effective strategy: I acknowledge and confront the silence. What lies beneath that silence can often enrich classroom discussion. But drawing it out is not always easy. As McKinney notes, "[A]t least for young whites, the question is under what circumstances one should notice or speak about race."[44]

Pedagogical Response and Concluding Thoughts

Given the sensitive nature of the issues discussed and the slipperiness of language, the meaning of which cannot be guaranteed, I establish my classroom as a space of respectful listening and learning. While the catchphrase "safe space" could be invoked to describe my classroom, I prefer to use what I call a "dialogic space" to make clear to students that they are free to ask questions and to exchange ideas with me and their peers. They might not always feel emotionally comfortable or "safe" during these encounters, as honest participation requires some degree of vulnerability.

Designating the classroom as a non-punitive space where any one of us might in fact misspeak while grappling with such sensitive issues as race, racism, and other systems of oppression helps to create a more relaxed environment. In such a context, misunderstanding and even disagreement can create opportunities for learning and growth.

Far from being a show about "nothing" (which is how two of *Seinfeld's* characters describe a sitcom pilot that reflects the ordinariness of Jerry Seinfeld's life), *Seinfeld* often got its viewers' attention by focusing on issues germane to contemporary culture. "The Wizard" foregrounds racial issues, reflecting back to viewers their racialized habits and ways of being-in-the-world. It mirrors our blindness and our ignorance, as well as our capacity to change. Years ago, I showed clips from "The Wizard" to the students in my composition class, who found the show highly entertaining. Describing the program's "argument," one student said it was an obvious one: our society is obsessed with race. Her assessment served as a springboard in to a discussion about identity, literature, and the absolute necessity of linking the act of reading to the broader cultural contexts in which we live.

Notes

I would like to thank George Yancy and Greg Barnhisel for their valuable feedback on a draft of this chapter.

1 I use the term "whiteness" to refer to a dominant category of social and political authority. Though whiteness is a social construction, it has measureable structural effects.
2 bell hooks, *Teaching to Transgress: Education as the Practice of Freedom* (New York, NY: Routledge, 1994), 10.
3 hooks, *Teaching to Transgress*, 51, 52.
4 bell hooks, *Teaching Community: A Pedagogy of Hope* (New York, NY: Routledge, 2003), 28.
5 Ibid.
6 Karyn D. McKinney, *Being White: Stories of Race and Racism* (New York, NY: Routledge, 2005), 179.
7 McKinney, *Being White*, 21.
8 "Race" is a social construction, though I use it here in its most casual sense.

9 Michael Omi and Howard Winant, *Racial Formation in the United States: From the 1960s to the 1990s* (New York, NY: Routledge, 1994), 59.

10 During a visit to her boyfriend's apartment, for example, Elaine hears loud rap when she approaches his door. She nods and smiles, and is satisfied—for the moment—as the music "Blackens" her boyfriend in her mind.

11 Omi and Winant, *Racial Formation*, 59.

12 Toni Morrison, "Recitatif," in *The Heath Anthology of American Literature, Volume E: Contemporary Period: 1945 to the Present*, ed. Paul Lauter (Boston, MA: Wadsworth, Cengage Learning, 2010), 2819–2832.

13 McKinney, *Being White*, 179.

14 Early in the novel, the narrator recalls a humiliating experience that occurred during his youth. Although he had been invited to give his graduation speech before a group of prominent White citizens, the narrator was first forced to participate in a boxing match with his Black peers while blindfolded, to watch a naked White woman dance, and to scramble for coins on an electrified rug.

15 Ralph Ellison, *Invisible Man* (New York, NY: Vintage, 1995), 17.

16 George Lipsitz, *The Possessive Investment in Whiteness: How White People Profit from Identity Politics* (Philadelphia, PA: Temple University Press, 1988), viii; emphasis mine.

17 George Yancy, "Looking at Whiteness: Finding Myself Much like a Mugger at a Boardwalk's End" in *Look, a White!: Philosophical Essays on Whiteness*, ed. George Yancy (Philadelphia, PA: Temple University Press, 2012), 39.

18 hooks, *Teaching Community*, 29.

19 McKinney, *Being White*, xii.

20 McKinney, *Being White*, xii.

21 Quoted in Ann duCille, *Skin Trade* (Cambridge, MA: Harvard University Press, 1996), 99.

22 duCille, *Skin Trade*, 99.

23 For more on this point, see Lipsitz, *The Possessive Investment*.

24 See Richard Dyer, "White," *Screen*, *29*(4), Fall 1988: 44–65.

25 Some of the excellent books on this subject include Lipsitz's *Possessive Investment*; George Yancy's *Black Bodies, White Gazes: The Continuing Significance of Race* (Lanham, MD: Rowman & Littlefield, 2008); and Omi and Winant's *Racial Formation*. These works discuss whiteness in its historical, social, and cultural contexts.

26 See Yancy, *Black Bodies*, and Lipsitz, *Possessive Investment*.

27 This interview is available online at http://dubois.fas.harvard.edu/video/professor-nell-painter-interviewed-henry-louis-gates-jr-du-bois-review-nell-irvin-painter.

28 Yancy, *Black Bodies*, 58–69.

29 Yancy, *Black Bodies*, 25.

30 Yancy, *Black Bodies*, 4.

31 Ibid.

32 Ibid.

33 Frances Foster, "Resisting Incidents" in *Harriet Jacobs and Incidents in the Life of a Slave Girl: New Critical Essays*, eds. Deborah M. Garfield and Rafia Zafar (New York, NY: Cambridge University Press, 1996), 58.

34 Yancy, *Black Bodies*, 21.

35 David Walker, "From 'David Walker's Appeal, in Four Articles, Together with a Preamble, to the Coloured Citizens of the World, but in Particular, and Very Expressly, to Those of the United States of America'" in *The Norton Anthology of African American Literature*, 2nd ed., eds. Henry Louis Gates Jr., and Nellie Y. McKay (New York, NY: W.W. Norton, 2004), 237.

36 Malcolm X with Alex Haley, *The Autobiography of Malcolm X*, 2nd ed. (New York, NY: Ballantine Books, 1999), 28.

37 bell hooks, *Killing Rage: Ending Racism* (New York, NY: Henry Holt, 1995), 11.

38 Cornel West, "On My Intellectual Vocation" in *The Cornel West Reader* (New York, NY: Basic Civitas Books, 1999), 25.
39 James Baldwin, *The Fire Next Time* (New York, NY: Vintage International, 1993).
40 Baldwin, *The Fire*, 55.
41 Baldwin, *The Fire*, 56.
42 Ibid.
43 Baldwin, *The Fire*, 55.
44 McKinney, *Being White*, 179.

5

TEACHING WHITE SETTLER SUBJECTS ANTIRACIST FEMINISMS

Jo-Anne Lee

Introduction

I teach courses in racialization and antiracist feminisms in a women's studies department in a predominantly White and proudly British colonial city and university. In this outpost of Empire, whiteness—understood as a historically emergent cultural formation that has become naturalized as ordinary and normal—must be explicitly and mindfully named and outed from the shadows. In an environment of overwhelming White hegemony, teaching about racism and racialization cannot proceed unless whiteness is outed. The irony of whiteness is that it is everywhere and nowhere, present and absent, inescapable but denied.[1] Teaching antiracist feminisms in such a context requires a conscious critical pedagogy of whiteness.[2]

Recent studies of antiracist whiteness have focused on its invisibility,[3] its unearned entitlements,[4] its social construction within specific contexts and social relations,[5] and the dangers of its reification in scholarly and popular discourse.[6] Deliberately engaging in critical whiteness pedagogy is called for, but is not without risk. White students who are not accustomed to being perceived as having a racialized identity, to being named as White, and to being asked to reflect on the meaning of whiteness in terms of racism and racializing processes tend to find the experience unsettling. The same is true for racialized minority students. And, although there is a long tradition of minority women faculty writing critically about racism in Canadian postsecondary institutions, literature on classroom pedagogy about teaching antiracist feminisms from a marginalized perspective remains scarce.[7] This chapter contributes to a needed conversation about teaching antiracisms to White subjects in predominantly White classrooms from the perspective of racialized Others.

One reason for the limited literature by minority women faculty on teaching antiracism to White subjects might lie in psychic and emotional tensions that minority faculty such as myself experience when teaching in White-dominant postsecondary institutions where racism and sexism are facts of everyday life.[8] Given a culture of silence and the reticence of institutional officers to openly discuss racism and sexism, it is not surprising that minority women faculty might be reluctant to voice their concerns. Systemic and persistent racism and sexism in postsecondary institutions shape the context of our work.[9] In multiple ways, minority women faculty are encouraged and disciplined to stay quiet, to not name the sexism and racism they encounter, and to avoid openly addressing the realities that they and students of color face. Every postsecondary institution in North America issues aspirational statements about valuing equity and diversity, but, in the majority of institutions, few specific policies, administrative procedures, designated staff, or programs exist to operationalize policy goals and mission statements.

This context was my starting point for writing this chapter. While writing, I became aware of how conflicted I felt about revealing my personal experiences. Each time I sat down to write, questions and anxieties surfaced. *How do I contribute to this necessary conversation without, once again, being positioned as "the race lady who whines about racism"? How do I write my experience into words in other than an abstract, academic, objective voice? How do I bring the unspoken flesh and bones of me into my writing? What is it exactly that I want to share? Why do I feel the need to be cautious, sensitive, and careful about how I might be read? After all, hasn't this already been said?* Given these trepidations, I wondered what moral regulations I have been party to. *Have I willingly participated in regulatory practices? How deeply have I imbibed and integrated these modes of conduct, these dominant values of institutionalized whiteness into my conscious and unconscious values, beliefs, and practices?*

With these doubts and uncertainties, this chapter reflects my struggle to speak coherently about what still feels very tentative and incoherent. As the interlocutor, I move constantly in and out of positions and emotions: victim, agent, cynical, angry, hopeful, resigned, and amused. I am simultaneously a novice and a seasoned instructor traveling tricky terrain. My hope is that some readers will recognize themselves in what I share, and that my writing will validate what has been for them, as for me, for whatever reasons, unspoken and submerged for too long.

Silence and Possessive Investments in Whiteness in the Classroom

In my classrooms, about 80% of the students are White identified, and it is their voices, experiences, attitudes, and responses that are centered. If White normalization in the classroom is to be challenged so that students can become conscious of White cultural identity and White culture and knowledgeable about their personal investments and implications in and with hegemonic whiteness, then the classroom space and students' assumptions about how and what is discussed in this space and how to be present in it need to be decentered and deconstructed.[10] In the context of teaching race, racialization, and antiracism where White female students dominate and racialized minority students are numerically and culturally marginalized, I strive to ensure that all students, White and nonwhite, locate themselves subjectively and experientially within the course content. To do otherwise is to allow majority White students to have the privilege of staying emotionally disengaged from the material, learning abstractly and objectively, while minority students struggle with the emotional impact of learning subjectively and viscerally through their actual lived experiences. The invisible inequality in hegemonic White classrooms serves the learning needs and outcomes of majority White-identified students at the expense of those on the margins. My ethical responsibility as an antiracist feminist teacher is to confront and change these dynamics. For White students, this means I must teach them to see themselves through the lens of critical whiteness. I must show how they, individually and as members of historic communities, have created, reproduced, and benefit from ongoing institutionalized discourses and practices of racialization in the interests of colonization and nation-state formation. In the women's studies classroom, I must show how gender and sexuality are insufficient on their own to account for social injustice by insisting on intersectional analytical frameworks that expose how links among race, class, gender, sexuality, religion, ethnicity, citizenship, and other systems of inequality work together to maintain whiteness and heterosexual maleness as sites of the taken for granted, as normal, routine, and superior.

Awkward silences are commonplace at the start of most of my classes; a topic of much concern to many who write about the challenges of teaching critical whiteness in the context of antiracism.[11] I view these silences as a manifestation of an unwritten code of hegemonic whiteness that permeates the antiracist classroom. Most students conform, consciously and unconsciously, to these unwritten rules. A recent incident helps to explicate some of the challenges of encouraging students to break the code of silence over White dominance in the classroom.

In a discussion on "the oppositional gaze" in film,[12] I asked students to break into discussion groups. Students were to form groups on the basis of self-identification as racialized, White, or neutral. To ensure that everyone would have an opportunity to speak, I instructed students to form groups of no more than eight students. Given the small numbers, there was only one group for racial minority students and several for White-identified students and students who wanted to take the neutral option. My intention in this exercise was to offer space for minority students to have a conversation about the oppositional gaze that was not overly determined by White students' concerns. This exercise decenters and disrupts classroom norms, and it elicits highly charged and unpredictable responses on the part of students. What I find most challenging in facilitating the exercise is staying in tune with everyone's different starting places. Some racialized minority students who identify with whiteness may need to be brought to critical awareness of how commonsense, normalized whiteness unconsciously influences their responses. For others who already have a fledgling oppositional consciousness, I might need only to offer positive encouragement. Many White majority students tend to bristle at the idea of being named as White and at being asked to take action on the basis of their White identity. The exercise can go off the rails at any point because it explicitly and visibly challenges unwritten codes of silence. Nonetheless, when it works, it opens up possibilities for transformation.

On this occasion, I immediately felt a chill after giving instructions on forming the groups. The classroom buzz stopped. Students seemed stunned. The long silence was broken when one student asked for clarification on the instructions, after which several other students reposed the question in different ways. After I repeated my instructions several times, insisting that students follow my instructions, most students moved into small groups to begin the discussion. Some students did not, including a few international students who did not understand the question and who asked again for directions on where they should go. I told them that they should decide on the basis of whether they saw themselves reflected in popular Hollywood films.

A few minutes later, three or four students had yet to join a group. One of them stood up abruptly and walked out, firmly closing the door as she left. This was uncustomary behavior for my classroom, but it was hard to attribute meaning because I did not follow the student into the hall to ask why she was leaving. The class carried on discussing the theme. After 15 or 20 minutes of discussion, I asked the students to reconvene as a large group to report on their discussions. The group with minority students said how refreshing and different it felt to discuss this topic without having to explain or justify their feelings to White students. They felt liberated from the burden of having to care for their fellow students' sense of guilt, shame, defensiveness, or denial. They reported on the lightness of their conversation, how they laughed and shared insider jokes and oppositional readings. In contrast, when White-identified students reported on their discussions, they commented objectively on hooks's text and the concept of the oppositional gaze.

I then asked students to reflect on how they felt when I asked them to divide into groups. I also asked them to explain to me what had happened in the class when I first introduced the exercise. I asked, "Why the silence? Why did you seem so reluctant to form discussion groups, something that we do every class?"

I waited for several long minutes before one student raised her hand. She said that she had felt surprised and offended by the request. It felt exclusionary and racist to her. She felt that race shouldn't matter, that everyone should be treated the same. She felt that I was excluding her from benefiting from the minority students' insights about the oppositional gaze. Another student felt offended that

I had called her White. No one had ever identified her this way, and she felt that I had prejudged her by asking her to form a group on the basis of a racial identity.

This refreshingly honest response prompted a retort from a member of the racialized group:

> "You are getting a taste of what we have to put up with in every class. We never get a chance to talk on our own terms. And, when we do, everyone just assumes we are speaking for all members of our group. You use racial categories all the time to talk about us and it doesn't bother you, but it bothered you this time because it was about you."

In this exchange, the normal expectations of classroom behavior were exposed and named by students themselves. Warren concludes, from observing similar behaviors, that such students "are subjects embedded and constituted in a racialized system that continues to constitute their identities in ways that protect whiteness' normative power."[13]

Furthermore, the exercise revealed the everyday racisms that White students enact and that racial minority students endure. It was one of the rare times when the customary silence about White hegemony in the university classroom was broken. The ways that students, White and nonwhite, collectively enforce informal cultural codes of White solidarity in university classrooms came into visibility. Usually, students conform to silence about not naming whiteness, talking about racism, or asserting entitlement. The exercise opened a fragile space that allowed students to address and name the performance of whiteness as it was taking place.

Each time I have reconstituted the classroom by making race an explicit rather than an implicit criterion for interaction, I have encountered a similar reaction and justificatory discourse. To most White students, students of color exist as a resource for them to learn about "difference" and "oppression." To recapitulate, the White cultural logic that determines the classroom climate is, "How can I/we learn about racialization and racism or oppression, if I/we are denied access to minority students' experiences? You (the teacher) are wrong to separate us on the basis of White racial identification. Your demand for us to self-identify is a form of racism. You are a bad teacher for making us feel uncomfortable. This classroom is unsafe."

This response reveals several issues. First, it demonstrates Said's idea of Orientalism as a form of knowledge production about the Other.[14] Students of color come into the frame only as a reflection of what the White self desires for itself. Second, racism must not be named; White people have no racial identity, and to insist that they do by calling on this identity as the basis for grouping is morally wrong, politically incorrect, and hurtful. Third, as a minority female teacher, I do not have the authority to challenge the unwritten code of classroom behavior. Responsibility for discomfort is projected onto the minority female instructor. In the classroom, White student solace trumps minority professor authority.

I believe this incident was unusual because minority students spoke back. The reasons for their vocality are complicated. First, we had been reading bell hooks's work and they had access to her elegant, precise prose; second, they correctly read the possibility for professor-sanctioned disruption of the unwritten classroom code; and, third, they were given time and space to form a "nonwhite" space wherein they could *collectively* embody difference outside of hegemonic whiteness.

Ringrose suggests that one of the main challenges of critical antiracist pedagogy comes from White defensiveness in feminist antiracist spaces and classrooms.[15] But, in this instance, the usual White defensiveness—including shutting down, silence, anger, tears, denial, and disavowal—was momentarily suspended. Instead of a withdrawal into silence, instead of disruptive outbursts, students felt free to vocally express their feelings of denial and resistance.

I believe the White students were less guarded than usual in this instance because we had earlier explored poststructural, postmodern, and intersectional understandings of identity formation through the works of Stuart Hall[16] and feminist scholars. With a conceptual understanding of identities as strategic, relational, and shifting, the students did not feel they needed to defend a fixed notion of White identity as overdetermining their sense of self. They found a way to momentarily depart from enacting rules that advocate color blindness as morally superior and preferred. They addressed their emotional response stemming from a fear of being perceived as racist if they acknowledged racial difference and White privilege.

In this regard, I would argue that the recent attention to White defensiveness and White guilt and shame as responses to learning about critical White identity reflects modernist understandings of identity formation. Postmodern, post-structural views of identity formation liberate students from believing that they have to defend their one true self from attack. Through these views, students learn of the social construction of whiteness as historically variable and ongoing rather than an essential, fixed identity position. The transparency and honesty I witnessed in the classroom were not simply a result of my facilitation skills in building a climate of inclusion; they also had to do with the critical content of the material I was teaching. Both pieces were necessary.

Yet, I do not want to dismiss too quickly my own positionality or the challenges I face in facilitating antiracist learning. For minority women faculty, the antiracist classroom is a confusing, conflicted, and unstable space. As one of the few female faculty members from an Asian Canadian background in a women's studies department, I am experienced at accommodating to the demands of belonging to White institutions. As earlier observed, I have been disciplined to fit in; consequently, I have had to work hard at unlearning, at making internalized and external whiteness problematic. This means contesting White, liberal norms of good pedagogy in an antiracist feminist classroom.

Fairness and equity are central tenets of liberal philosophies of "good teaching": all students should be treated the same. Any differences among persons should not result in differential treatment that results in inequality. This is an admirable ideal, but the reality that people are not equal tends to be ignored. The ideal and the real that are conflated in liberal principles of equality are enacted in colonial nation-states. Liberal principles of multiculturalism and pluralism are linked to fairness and equity. Together, these principles effectively obscure and silence the reality of teaching in a racially diverse classroom where all students are not equal. Institutional discourses perpetuated in technologies of ruling, such as routine teacher and student evaluations, help to enforce these assumptions about good teaching. Such technologies force teachers to consciously and unconsciously conform to liberal norms and to "fit in." Good pedagogy does not include challenging students to acknowledge and confront whiteness as the absent center or the assumed invisible presence. To deliberately practice a decentering, critical pedagogy that sets out to disrupt some students' settled notions of who they are and how they have been formed is dangerous practice. It will not win popularity contests or teaching awards. For minority women scholars working in the humanities and social sciences, we are the token, the special equity appointment, and, rarely, the exotic star. Being unappreciative and ungrateful of such "generosity" by doing oppositional work in the classroom makes one a target.

To explicitly challenge the normalized, structured inequality of classroom interactions among and between students and students and professors, one must be ready to be perceived as the angry woman of color. Perceived in this way, minority women faculty doing oppositional work are robbed of the power that is usually assigned to university professors. Furthermore, our presence in antiracist feminist classrooms paradoxically embodies threat and questionable authority because we do not perform as expected. Not performing as expected elicits feelings of anxiety among students. And thus we are caught in an endless feedback loop: others' unconscious displacement of anxiety onto our bodies creates anxiety within our bodies and vice versa. When I look out at the class, I observe the students' discomfort. They fix me in their gaze.[17] When I return the gaze, they avert their eyes, avoiding mine, perhaps sensing my uneasiness. I, in turn, feel unsure and uncomfortable, and together we are caught in re-performing inherited racialized scripts. I want to stop this carousel of racial mimicry.

Henry and Tator observe the pervasiveness of racism in postsecondary institutions, which they assert is:

> manifested or reflected in a multiplicity of ways, including: the teaching of a basically Eurocentric curriculum; the paucity of research and courses on racism; the absence of an anti-racist pedagogy; incidents of racial harassment and overt racism; the lack of resources allocated to implement effectively equity and anti-racism policies and practices; the power relations between White majority and minority faculty and staff; the polarization

between White students and students of colour, and the resistance to social change processes designed to eliminate racism.[18]

My antiracist feminism course is almost never fully enrolled; it typically hovers around 60% of full enrolment. I see this low enrolment as a reflection of systemic whiteness, where students do not take the course because they think it will not be about them. My colleagues perceive these numbers as a negative reflection of my teaching, which I then have to work hard to not internalize. I accept that teaching about racism will never be popular or in high demand since university classrooms are an extension of attitudes in society at large. The Canadian taboo against talking about race and racism, the assumption about the moral superiority of color blindness, extends into the university culture and its classrooms. It takes a certain kind of student to want to spend money on an elective course that they are "not ready to take on" or that may make them feel guilty. Furthermore, some colleagues see this course as just another course on difference and identity, and/or they think that, because gender and sexuality are the core concerns of women's studies (a discourse that is officially contested, but unofficially sanctioned), this course is indeed optional.

The White Settler Classroom Stands In for the Nation-State

We live and work in colonial institutions that have been designed to support White settler ascendancy in Canada.[19] The Canadian state education system is a colonizing apparatus intended to promote the natural superiority and dominance of the colonizers. It transmits the cultural knowledge deemed to be important to the White nation. It is intended to produce citizen-subjects who willingly consent to and fully participate in the ongoing project of nation-state formation. Canada's national cultural identity as a neutral third party in global politics is symbolically interconnected, without irony, to its geocultural representation as the natural, great, White North.[20] These geographic and cultural tropes draw on long-existing myths of moral superiority, civility, goodness, and whiteness in European cultural representations.[21] The Canadian national cultural engine has refined these ideals and myths by equating northern climate and geography with moral superiority stemming from physical and social hardiness and self-reliance. Many White Canadians believe in popular narratives that link Canadian-ness to our geographic location in "the Great White North." These narratives endow Canadians with a superior sense of justice and racial neutrality that is naturally derived by living so close to the purity of the natural environment. Canadian geography and climate are harnessed to signify whiteness.[22] In the global arena, according to Razack, Canadian citizens perceive themselves as exceptions who are exceptionally equipped to act as world peacekeeper.[23]

Notwithstanding the erasure of Indigenous inhabitants of the North in such discourses, such Canadian ideals are reflected in students enrolled in women's studies classes. Most have an explicit or implicit desire to make a difference, to do good, and to work towards social justice. In this regard, they actively perform White liberal Canadian goodness. For most, their good intentions are also bound up with their identities as economically and culturally privileged. In coming to critical White consciousness in the women's studies classroom, many White students quickly move past the guilt and shame stage in Helms's staged model of White identity formation,[24] pausing briefly as they "race to innocence."[25] According to Fellows and Razack, political solidarity often fails because of "competing marginalities" where women do not see themselves implicated in other people's subordination.[26] Racing to innocence disconnects one's liberation from others' oppression and prioritizes one's own subordination over others'. Because they themselves are oppressed, women are not complicit in anyone else's oppression. In other words, not only can one claim innocence, this stance allows redemption even if one is implicated. In racing to innocence, activists are confined to a limited hierarchical and additive model of oppression and, ultimately, a race to victimhood on the hierarchy of pain. Fellows and Razack further argue that Canadians believe in their innocence as national subjects in the global arena. This innocence means they do not see themselves as complicit in morally suspect actions of other countries, such as the United States.[27]

The White Settler as Antiracist Ally

In my classes, I observe among many students a desire to live up to the White settler ideal of the colonizer bringing civilization and civilized order to unruly natives. They want to be Janey Canuck, an image of the White Canadian adventurer: plucky, intrepid, adventuresome, and naïve.[28] They aspire to the myth of the White woman's burden—to save poor victims from harm and ignorance. The contemporary White settler female subject encountering critical antiracist whiteness wants to be redeemed to that position, to be restored as the good subject. Many of my students have traveled widely and believe themselves to be knowledgeable multiculturalists. They have internalized the Western girl subject as world ambassador, bringing social justice and betterment to a disadvantaged world. These young Canadian women—innocent, pure, and clean—view the world as open for them to explore, to recreate, to experience; in turn, these international experiences will assist them to self-actualize. The perception that the world exists for them to learn from takes for granted every-thing that brought them to this time and place. Entering my class shakes their stable sense of self as knowledgeable about difference. How quickly they recover! The class helps them to think about themselves and their experiences more critically. They impatiently ask, "But what can we do?" They hunger for the hope that is offered in the White ally subject position.[29] Their relief is almost palpable when the ally option for White subjectivity is presented. Their desire to do good, to be seen as good, to be perceived as nonracist, to be transformed from a White settler, colonizer, oppressor into an ally, helper, de-colonizer is honorable and well intentioned, but also problematic.

The discourse of the ally is widely circulated among social justice groups on my campus. Tatum suggests that White allyship should be offered to students as an alternative model of whiteness that offers hopefulness after the disassociative state of trauma that follows coming to critical consciousness about whiteness.[30] The ally role is thought to offer psychic relief to soothe emotions of guilt and shame.

In the cities and towns of the Pacific Northwest, where White cultural hegemony has seldom been countered, becoming an ally is a relatively easy move, because few White students have ever directly engaged in or witnessed explicit racism. Most White students understand racism and colonialism temporally as located in the past and spatially as located elsewhere, not here. In my White-dominant city, unlike multiracial, multicultural metropolitan cities, students' everyday embodied experiences with people of color are distant and remote. Even if students live, work, and play next to a First Nation reserve, or attend the same schools as Indigenous children, racist cultural practices and segregationist policies ensure that they will have little contact and interaction. White students grow up believing themselves unaffected by racism, ignorant of difference, and fully enclosed in a homogenous bubble of White culture. They are taught little about historic racisms in the formation of the Canadian nation. They believe, at best, that they are in a neutral relationship to the Other. Thus, in the minds of most women's studies students, becoming a White ally against racism when they are untarnished by racial violence and oppression and when they are completely (so they believe) objective and neutral in any encounters with those who are "different" is reasonable, attainable, and achievable.

Moreover, to cognitively align themselves with those who have direct lived experience with racism, women's studies students draw on their lived experiences with gender oppression and heterosexism and academic theories that explain these oppressions. The ally subject position offers these students a further means to legitimize their objective yet empathetic response to racism even when they have never directly experienced racism. It allows them to act, to shift out of the immobility that comes with trauma. But learning about racism through abstraction and metaphor does not equal direct lived experience. And this is the danger of allyship—it creates an illusion of equality and a false belief that "allies" are indeed taking antioppressive action, when, in fact, being an ally is a conceptual identification and little more. Although I empathize with students' trauma when their foundational beliefs of untarnished virtue, truth, and beauty are shaken, the ally subject position only serves to falsely and ideologically inoculate them against further critical learning about the ongoing realities of discrimination, poverty, and violence in many communities.

The difference between nonracism and antiracism is an important distinction in judging the ally subject position. When the ally script is adopted, the self is deluded into believing it is being antiracist when it is really being nonracist; that is, someone who is most concerned with *not appearing* to be racist. As an ally who supports and "stands in solidarity" with racialized people, one is not asked to speak from a place of personal experience, or to be accountable for the aftermath of direct confrontation in the face of discrimination, or to directly dismantle systems of unearned privilege and domination. One retains the role of outsider and eagerly returns to White innocence and moral virtue. The ally role permits White-identified students to assuage their guilt, shame, and remorse without requiring accountability for unearned privilege.[31]

Where Helms is concerned with White students' desire to regain a positive self-identity of whiteness,[32] and where Tatum offers allyship as a remedy to the immobilizing despair that both White and minority students may feel,[33] I view White ally subjectivity differently. In my experience, the possibility of redemption in the subject position of the ally offers a too-easy return to White innocence and to whiteness as the invisible norm. Allyship becomes a mask or a veil that can be taken off and put on depending on context. The ally subject position offers a salve to heal a wounded sense of self, but it fails the test of critical antiracism—which is the full dismantling of White dominance as the ultimate, albeit unattainable, objective.

White allies imagine themselves as neutral and unaffected by White racisms, and thus the only role for them in antiracism resistance is to stand alongside (and outside) those whose struggle it "really" is. White allies return to the place of disengaged neutrality and objectivity. They are reconfirmed as morally superior and innocent.

For these reasons, I do not offer allyship to students as a remedy for hopelessness. Instead, the ally is identified, described, analyzed, critiqued, and deconstructed. Together, racialized minority and dominant White students explore the fantasies, myths, trickery, and deviousness of being "the ally." From these narratives, we conclude that allyship satisfies a yearning for positivity and hope, but it fails to deliver on the criterion of stopping racism. When presented as an alternative model for being White, as Tatum suggests, becoming an ally seductively re-inscribes a romanticized and idealized nonracist White subject position.[34] Although I agree with Beverly Tatum that restoring in students a hopeful vision for their future is important, it is even more critical to ensure that students are not let loose with a false sense of having "got it." I have seen too frequently the smugness of identity policing in young activists that ends up doing more harm than good. For example, White allies may deem activists of color more committed and therefore more worthy of attention than White activists, regardless of the work they have invested in unlearning racism. Some activists monitor who can speak authentically about racism and oppression on the basis of color. Ultimately, these practices rework and reassert hierarchies of pain: the darker the skin, the more convincing and authentic the voice.

Yet students—quite rightly, as individuals interested in bringing about social change—want to know what they can do to help make a difference. As an alternative to allyship, I present the idea that White students desiring to do "good" must begin by asking themselves what antiracist feminism really wants. Antiracist White activists must move towards a model of co-implication, co-involvement, and co-accountability in antiracist feminist struggles.

My goal in undermining discourses of the White ally is to deflect objectification and distancing on the part of White students and some minority students who want to see themselves as always and already morally untarnished and "good." I do not want them to recuperate too easily from the pain of coming to consciousness, because, until they truly comprehend the realities of oppressed, marginalized, and minoritized groups in ways that do not simply relegate these groups to objects of pity or sympathy, as victims in need of saving, letting these students loose with the mistaken belief that they have somehow become enlightened and reborn as antiracist feminists is unethical pedagogy on my part. Deep self-interrogation and self-reflexivity about one's historical pathways that have led to automatic benefits from nation-state systems of White privilege cannot be achieved in ten to twelve weeks of three-hour weekly classes. This is a project for lifelong learning.

As a minority teacher, I do not stand outside hegemonic regimes. In many ways, each of us consciously and unconsciously performs and plays the White hegemonic game that keeps whiteness ascendant. I, too, have been disciplined by informal institutionalized rules of White social relationships: never name white-ness, never place White-identified students in a place of non-safety or discomfort, never speak about the rules.

When we speak of safe classroom spaces, whose safety are we talking about? To the credit of the students in the class I wrote about above, who were shocked and dismayed by my instructions to form groups based on racial identification, the discussion took a positive turn. Many students confessed their shame and guilt at falling so easily into a place of entitlement. They immediately recognized their assumption about university classrooms as *their* safe space, as spaces meant *for them.* They recalled the guidelines I had presented at the start of the class, when I told them that I do not promise a "safe" space for learning. I had said that safety is not a right; it is a construct. I cannot promise safety to each and every student when we are discussing difficult topics that are considered taboo in social circles. Safe spaces have to be made every day in every relationship by each participant in the classroom.

Women's Studies Classrooms as Unhappy Spaces

Feminist pedagogy wants to produce safe, happy classroom spaces so that young (White) women can emerge from silence learned from years of masculinist education in heterosexual-normed classrooms. Young women are supposed to experience happiness by coming to know themselves and their place in the world. There is nothing wrong with this goal. Critical self-reflection about one's positionality is thought to have a positive, uplifting, feel-good effect, and good teaching is supposed to result in positive evaluations. These ideals can be attributed, in part, to the strength of second-wave feminist comprehension of gender oppression as the primary determinant of gender inequality; second-wave feminism also fabricated a myth of feminist safety premised on universal sisterhood.

Some students may find the women's studies classroom a happy space, but, if happiness is unevenly distributed along racial lines, as well as lines of sexuality, language, class, religion, and other socially constructed identifiers of difference, then it is only a happy space for some students. And if some minority students are unhappy, then can it truly be claimed that women's studies classrooms are happy spaces? This is not merely a rhetorical question, because, if antiracist women's studies classrooms produce unhappiness as well as happiness, then these can only be aspirational, not actual, feminist classrooms. Furthermore, I and my women's studies colleagues are complicit in reproducing myths surrounding feminist pedagogy as distinct and superior to regular forms of teaching, as being better spaces than regular classrooms for women's and girls' learning.

Discordancy in the women's studies classroom is rarely acknowledged as normal or affirmative, however. Instead, the happy women's studies classroom is presented as the norm and the ideal where young women find themselves, secure their feminist identities, and speak in their own authentic voices. But antiracist feminist classrooms are necessarily unhappy spaces, because they are sites where racism, colonialism, sexism, homophobia, classism, and ableisms are played out. Rather than turning away from this reality, rather than pretending these experiences don't exist or that they are wrong, negative, or bad, I agree with Ahmed, who asserts that it is necessary and important to expose unhappy effects *as an affirmation*, because doing so offers a different set of imaginings.[35] If social justice produces unhappy effects, she argues, "the story does not end there. Unhappiness is not our end point, being outside the ideals that produce the good life still gets us somewhere."[36]

Ahmed observes that, in general, happiness is thought to be experienced when one is with like-minded people.[37] This version of happiness does not bode well for diverse, multicultural classrooms. Following the logic of similarity and affinity, the presence of diversity and difference will necessarily bring about unhappiness. Ahmed points to the feminist killjoy as an example of the destruction of normative happiness. The feminist killjoy brings about unhappiness when she points out moments of sexism during which things are not good for women. Similarly, the angry Black feminist is a killjoy when she names White racism. I, the antiracist Asian Canadian feminist activist teacher, become a killjoy when I draw attention to historic and everyday exemplars of racism, sexism, classism, and other oppressions as they are enacted in my classroom and when I fail to perform my historically designated role as obedient, docile, grateful Asian woman. Given the pain my body and affect endure in the antiracist feminist classroom, I find the name "killjoy" perversely appropriate.

Fluidity in the Classroom

In this chapter, I have discussed some of my challenges and observations in many years of teaching antiracist feminism to White settler subjects. Much of what is written about White students' resistance to knowing themselves critically in relation to racism presents individual students as having the ability to choose, after coming to critical consciousness, to give up White privilege and entitlement by working actively to dismantle structures of White privilege. Yancy argues that one of the ways Whites delude themselves into thinking that they can transcend racism and their racist selves is by believing that they are autonomous, transcendent subjects.[38] Through a number of cognitive maneuvers, they fail to see themselves as implicated and embedded in systemic racism. Yancy also identifies the White antiracists' failure to acknowledge themselves as opaque White racists. Most of his students, he observes, "assume that the process of ascertaining the limits of one's White racism is guaranteed by an 'all-knowing' consciousness that is capable of peeling back, as it were, various levels of internalized racism and at once discovering a non-racist innocent White one."[39] In other words, they are free, if they choose, after introspectively coming to critical consciousness of their White racist selves, to give up being racist. But, as racism and White hegemony are historically embedded and always-changing aspects of modern societies, is free choice possible? How does one choose to voluntarily give up membership in White culture? That would be akin to voluntary suffocation. Further, individualistic accounts minimize the systemic nature of racism and ongoing colonization that have operated to perpetuate White ascendancy. The whole education system is culturally designed to transmit the lesson that White, middle- and upper-class, able-bodied, heterosexual, Western, Christian students will naturally inherit the earth if they do nothing but comply with the rules. In the hallowed halls of academia, naming colonialism, sexism, and racism and acting as though they mattered are two different things.

I agree wholeheartedly with Yancy when he passionately pleads for antiracist students to linger, to tarry longer with their newly revealed embedded and opaque White selves. He argues that yearning for relief from the trauma of the burden of the racist self is an existential dilemma for Whites that cannot be easily remedied. Just at the moment they believe they are free of their racist self, they are ambushed by the return of the repressed—unbidden and unconscious thoughts of derision, stigma, refusal, pity, fear, and so many other negative emotions connected to their encounters with the abject Other. The phenomenon of ambush re-traumatizes, places limits on "self-knowledge of one's own racism," and "discloses profound uncertainty of the White racist self."[40]

In my teaching, I point out that one way of keeping the status quo in place is through normalizing whiteness in the classroom through codes of silence. Only recently have I become aware of the toll that teaching White subjects in hegemonic White classrooms has taken on my body and soul. I have unconsciously defended myself from White students' discomfort and trauma, which they address by displacing and projecting their anxious feelings onto me, their minority teacher. I have survived by denying and disavowing the emotional impact their projections have had on me. In sharing my experiences here, far from being a "killjoy," I hope this chapter offers hope and possibilities by acknowledging that antiracist teaching is often not happy. Moment to moment, though, class to class, unhappiness can transform into rare moments of pleasure and joy—sometimes accidentally and unexpectedly, depending on relationships between groups of students, and sometimes deliberately and consciously through the methods, content, and skills of the teacher. These moments are rare, because, for all our planning and thinking, antiracist feminist teachers are attempting to dismantle the whiteness in the invisible wallpaper of our classrooms—a monumental task. For minority women faculty, these moments of joy can better emerge when we acknowledge and address our own disavowals and denials in relation to critical whiteness pedagogy.

Through the politics of emotion, I have grown in understanding my experience in teaching antiracist feminisms to mainly White settler subjects. In a hegemonic White classroom, happiness and sadness are episodic moments that rise, fall, and pass. Resistance coexists with affirmation, angry rejection with joyous embrace. I might wish for more moments of joy, but, given the systemic racism that permeates the academy, our communities, our nation, and our world, there is a need to comprehend the absolute enormity of this impossibility at the present moment. Better, I believe, to affirm moments of transition and fluidity and to work towards greater frequency of happiness as an alternative to aspiring and affirming a fixed and constant ideal state of happiness as the already existing norm that negates minority women's realities.

Notes

1 Richard Dyer, *White* (London, England: Routledge, 1997); Stephanie M. Wildman and Adrienne D. Davis, "Making Systems of Privilege Visible," in *Critical White Studies: Looking Behind the Mirror*, eds. Richard Delgado and Jean Stefancic (Philadelphia, PA: Temple University Press, 1997), 314–319.
2 Kathy Hytten and Amee Adkins, "Thinking Through a Pedagogy of Whiteness," *Educational Theory*, 51(4), 2001: 433–450; Cynthia Levine-Rasky, ed., *Working Through Whiteness: International Perspectives* (Albany, NY: State University of New York Press, 2002).
3 Dyer, *White*.
4 Peggy McIntosh, "White Privilege: Unpacking the Invisible Knapsack," *Independent School*, 49(2), 1990: 31–36.
5 Paula S. Rothenberg, ed., *White Privilege: Essential Readings on the Other Side of Racism*, 4th ed. (New York, NY: Worth Publishers, 2012).
6 Zeus Leonardo, *Critical Pedagogy and Race* (Malden, MA: Blackwell, 2005).
7 Himani Bannerji, *Thinking Through: Essays on Feminism, Marxism, and Anti-Racism* (Toronto, Canada: Women's Press, 1995); Ena Dua and Bonita Lawrence, "Challenging White Hegemony in University Classrooms: Whose Canada Is It?", *Atlantis*, 24(Part 2),

2000: 105–122; Roxana Ng, Pat A. Staton, and Joyce Scane, *Anti-Racism, Feminism, and Critical Approaches to Education* (London, England: Bergin & Garvey, 1995).

8 Frances Henry and Carol Tator, "Racism and the University," *Canadian Ethnic Studies,* 26(3), 1994: 74–90.

9 Ibid.

10 Virginia Lea and Erma Jean Sims, eds., *Undoing Whiteness in the Classroom: Critical Educultural Teaching Approaches for Social Justice Activism* (New York, NY: Peter Lang, 2008); Beverly Daniel Tatum, "Teaching White Students about Racism: The Search for White Allies and the Restoration of Hope," *Teachers College Record, 95*(4), 1994: 426–476.

11 Gloria Ladson-Billings, "Silences as Weapons: Challenges of a Black Professor Teaching White Students," *Theory into Practice, 35*(2), 1996: 79–85; Carol Schick, "'By Virtue of Being White': Resistance in Anti-Racist Pedagogy," *Race, Ethnicity and Education, 3*(1), 2000: 83–101.

12 bell hooks, *Reel to Real: Race, Sex, and Class at the Movies* (New York, NY: Routledge, 1996); bell hooks, "The Oppositional Gaze: Black Female Spectators," in *Black Looks: Race and Representation* (Boston, MA: South End Press, 1992), 115–131.

13 John T. Warren, "Doing Whiteness: On the Performative Dimensions of Race in the Classroom," *Communication Education, 50*(2), 2001: 91–108; quote on p. 106.

14 Edward W. Said, *Orientalism* (New York, NY: Vintage Books, 2003).

15 Jessica Ringrose, "Developing Feminist Pedagogical Practices to Complicate Whiteness and Work with Defensiveness," in *Working Through Whiteness: International Perspectives,* ed. Cynthia Levine-Rasky (Albany, NY: State University of New York Press, 2002), 289–318.

16 Stuart Hall and Media Education Foundation, *Race: The Floating Signifier* (Northampton, MA: Media Education Foundation, 2002).

17 Frantz Fanon, *Black Skin, White Masks* (New York, NY: Grove Press, 1982).

18 Henry and Tator, "Racism and the University," 2.

19 Martin John Cannon and Lina Sunseri, eds., *Racism, Colonialism, and Indigeneity in Canada* (Don Mills, ON: Oxford University Press, 2011); Carol Schick, "Keeping the Ivory Tower White: Discourses of Racial Domination," *Canadian Journal of Law and Society, 15*(2), 2000: 69.

20 Andrew Baldwin, Laura Cameron, and Audrey Kobayashi, *Rethinking the Great White North: Race, Nature, and the Historical Geographies of Whiteness in Canada* (Vancouver, Canada: University of British Columbia Press, 2011).

21 Dyer, *White*; Sherene Razack, *Dark Threats and White Knights: The Somalia Affair, Peacekeeping, and the New Imperialism* (Toronto, Canada: University of Toronto Press, 2004).

22 Baldwin, Cameron, and Kobayashi, *Rethinking the Great White North*; Razack, *Dark Threats and White Knights.*

23 Razack, *Dark Threats and White Knights.*

24 Janet E. Helms, *A Race is a Nice Thing to Have: A Guide to Being a White Person or Understanding the White Persons in Your Life* (Topeka, KS: Content Communications, 1992).

25 Mary Louise Fellows and Sherene Razack, "The Race to Innocence: Confronting Hierarchical Relations Among Women," *Journal of Gender, Race and Justice, 1*, 1998: 335–352.

26 Ibid.

27 Ibid.

28 Helen Harper identifies Emily F. Murphy's novels *The Impressions of Janey Canuck Abroad* (1902) and *Janey Canuck in the West* (1910) as the source of the "Janey Canuck" character, the female equivalent to "Jack Canuck." Both characters are overtly Canadian figures. Janey Canuck, Lady Bountiful, and the White lady traveler are historical

fictional figures that captured the public imagination in the nineteenth century. These subject positions have been reworked in contemporary cultural tropes and, according to Harper, their narratives can be identified in Canadian multicultural policy documents. Harper sees young White women teachers from the South desiring to work in the North reworking the Janey Canuck subject position. See Helen Harper, "When the Big Snow Melts: White Women Working in Canada's North," in *Working Through Whiteness: International Perspectives*, edited by Cynthia Levine-Rasky (New York, NY: State University of New York Press, 2002), 269–288.

29 Anne Bishop, *Becoming an Ally: Breaking the Cycle of Oppression* (Halifax, NS: Fernwood, 1994).

30 Tatum, "Teaching White Students about Racism."

31 Sara Ahmed, *The Cultural Politics of Emotion* (Edinburgh, Scotland: Edinburgh University Press, 2004).

32 Helms, *A Race is a Nice Thing to Have.*

33 Tatum, "Teaching White Students about Racism."

34 Ibid.

35 Sara Ahmed, "Multiculturalism and the Promise of Happiness," *New Formations,* 63, 2007: 121–137.

36 Ibid, 135.

37 Ahmed, "Multiculturalism and the Promise of Happiness."

38 George Yancy, "Looking at Whiteness: Tarrying with the Embedded and Opaque White Racist Self," in *Look, A White!: Philosophical Essays on Whiteness* (Philadelphia, PA: Temple University Press, 2012), 152–176.

39 Ibid., 168.

40 Ibid., 170–171.

6

PEDAGOGICAL CONTOURS OF RACE AND RACISM

Clarence Sholé Johnson

Introduction

Navigating the contours of race and racism in the classroom can be very daunting and challenging. This is because any such discussion ultimately involves an examination of the history of racism in modernity and the institutional enactment of racial injustice against people of color in contemporary society. And such discussions can be very unsettling and uncomfortable, both for White students and for students of color. For White students—or, at least, some of them—talk of racial injustice is seen as an indictment of Whites generally and they themselves personally. Some White students have considerable difficulty accepting the brutal fact of White racism and White racial privilege, and how their lives are (in)directly implicated in it. And, for students of color, especially Blacks, such discussions confirm and validate their beliefs about the ubiquity and all-pervasiveness of racial injustice to which they are subject, directly or indirectly, as a lived reality, and for which they are always demanding some form of rectification. How then does one teach about such a sensitive topic of race and racism without alienating White students, on the one hand, and without negating, invalidating, or minimizing the experiences of students of color, on the other hand?

The Story of Race—*or*, Race as a Pseudoscientific Endeavor

From a pedagogical standpoint, I begin the study of race and racism by historicizing the issue. By this I mean examining the idea of race, racial classification, and race discourse as such in modernity's scientific outlook. My aim in providing such contextualization is to invite the students to see and appreciate how the problem of race and racism came about in the first place, in the hope that such appreciation will guide them into confronting and addressing the problem as it exists in contemporary society. In this regard, I often begin by examining European modernity, the period roughly between the seventeenth and nineteenth centuries, variously described as the Age of Reason or the Age of Enlightenment. In particular, I highlight what I consider the distinctive characteristic of this period; namely, the endeavor of European man to subject nature to rational explanation using the laws of thought, and to seek to control nature. By recalling Francis Bacon's well-known aphorism that knowledge is power, I elaborate modernity's endeavor to classify all living entities into distinct categories in order to better facilitate human understanding of the environment. The underlying belief of this period was that humans *qua* rational beings can use reason to make sense of and acquire knowledge of the observable phenomena that comprise their natural environment, and thus to unravel the hitherto believed mysteries of nature. Among the observable phenomena with which humans are surrounded are different types of entities, ranging from minerals and vegetation to a variety of animal species that constitute the flora and fauna of the environment. Modern European man examined these various types of entities and endeavored to systematize/classify them, along the lines of Aristotelian taxonomy, according to certain distinctive and distinguishing features that he believed the different types of entities possessed.

This intellectual endeavor to systematize and classify entities, applied to the animal kingdom, led modern European man to distinguish between rational and nonrational animals using the possession or absence of rationality as the criterion to determine into which category an entity fell. But this enterprise itself begs a further question: How was rationality or its absence determined in the first place? Here, the answer was given in terms of the neurological development an entity was believed to have. In other words, according to European man, an entity's rationality (or lack of) and, hence, the entity's humanity (or lack of) was a function of the degree of the entity's neurological development. This idea was at the core of the science known as "phrenology," the study of the cranial features of an entity. The presumption was that the cranial features of an entity provided an insight into the features of the entity's brain, and, hence, of the entity's cognitive endowment or deficiency. Of course, all this was supposedly based on observation; that is, scientific methodology. What is of note, however, is that, even within the category of rational animals, some members were deemed inherently more neurologically endowed than others, and so were inherently more human than others. In short, humanness admitted of variation and degrees.

But how did the scientists account for the varying distribution of neurological endowments among the various subsets within the rational category in the first place? The answer, oddly enough, was skin pigmentation: black, brown, yellow, red, and White. The darker the pigmentation of an entity, the lower the entity's degree of neurological endowment, and, hence, the entity's cognitive development, degree of rationality, and the lower the entity was in the human scale. On the other hand, the lighter the pigmentation of an entity, the greater the degree of the entity's neurological endowment, and, hence, its cognitive development, degree of rationality, and the higher the entity was in the human scale. It is this idea that is articulated in the concept of race, with the terms "black," "brown," "yellow," "red," and "white" being invented to serve as racial names for the various degrees of humanness.

If this is the short story about the inception of race and racial categories, however, it is also the short story about the inception of racism in the human circle. This is because European man did not just create the aforementioned racial categories, but he also correlated each racial category with certain psychological attributes that he considered inherent to the category. Thus, we have Blackness identified with caprice, whimsicality, laziness, and carelessness; whiteness identified with rule-governedness, inventiveness, confidence, and optimism; and redness (the Native American) identified with slavishness to custom and obstinacy. Added to all this, European man tagged on and correlated value predicates (moral and aesthetic) to each racial category thus constructed, and structured these racial categories in a hierarchy.[1] For example, he ascribed moral and aesthetic beauty to Whites and moral and aesthetic deformity to Blacks; gentleness to Whites and deviousness to Blacks; and covetousness to "yellow" (read: Asians). It was these psychophysical and axiological correlations that engendered the belief in racial superiority and inferiority and the expression of this belief in social practices.

Of course, all such correlations were purely arbitrary, even though they purported to be scientific. And I call attention to this arbitrariness by characterizing the supposedly "scientific" endeavor as pseudoscientific. This characterization is deliberate because I want the students to take a very critical look at science and at the study of race itself. It is to make the students aware that there is good science and bad science, and to enable the students to try and determine what is wrong with the supposedly scientific methodology employed in the study of race. In short, what makes the supposedly scientific study of race *bad* science? Because then the construction of racial categories and what I consider its attendant racism is well documented in canonical sources such as the writings of Carl von Linné, Georges-Louis Leclerc, and other eighteenth-century thinkers, it is therefore with these canonical sources that I begin my study of race.[2] We methodically go through these standard writings and engage in textual analyses, and, as we do so, draw upon contemporary articulations of such characterizations of race and exhibition of racism in our sociopolitical settings.

Manifestations of Racism in Contemporary Setting

For example, in 2012, we witnessed the first of three presidential debates between the incumbent Democratic candidate President Barack Obama and his Republican challenger Mitt Romney. By all accounts, Obama failed to perform as expected, much to the chagrin and dismay of his supporters, and Romney handily won the debate. But no sooner had the debate ended and the polling results were in than John Sununu, former Governor of New Hampshire, and a Romney surrogate, took to the airwaves characterizing Obama as "lazy." The blog of Think Progress, a project of the Center for American Progress Action Fund, lists the following declarations as part of Sununu's "history of racial remarks" aimed at Obama: "Obama is foreign" (7/17/2012); "Obama doesn't know how to be an American" (7/17/2012); "Obama is a lazy idiot" (10/4/2012); and, "Obama has no class, [he] just wants to be cool" (10/25/2012).[3] I bring to the students' notice that no other U.S. president or presidential candidate had ever been described in such a manner—that is, as *not* being an American and that he had to learn to be one, or as lazy, and the like—even candidates of either party who had no chance of securing their party's nomination. Using such comments, then, but especially Sununu's characterization of the President as "a lazy idiot," I go on to demonstrate to my students that there is nothing new here being said about Obama because of his race. Sununu's characterization is merely a contemporary articulation of a narrative about Blacks that is traceable to Carl von Linné and others, such as Hume and Kant, routed through both the 1751–72 edition of the French *Encyclopédie* and the 1798 edition of the *Encyclopedia Britannica* and related sources.[4] I also invoke popular culture, supposedly fictional works such as Joyce Cary's *Mister Johnson* (first published in 1939) and minstrel shows of the 1950s in which Blacks are caricatured as stupid buffoons and infantile beings, to illustrate the ubiquity of racism that trades upon the characterizations of Blacks in supposedly intellectual sources of the highest order.

But it is not only in explicit vitriolic forms, such as Sununu's descriptions and similar sources, that we find expressions of racism. I direct my students' attention to the Democratic party's 2008 primary debates in which then candidate Hillary Clinton asserted that her main rival, candidate Obama, was "not electable." Be it noted that, at the time, there were other candidates, such as then Congressman Dennis Kucinich and Senators John Edwards and Joe Biden, among others, who, for all practical purposes, were unlikely to be selected as the party's nominee, so the contest was essentially between Hillary Clinton and Barack Obama. This was the setting in which Clinton made the remark. But what did she mean in declaring that Obama was "not electable" when she did not make such a declaration about any of the other candidates? And how did she arrive at that conclusion about Obama? I get my students to appreciate the import of Hillary Clinton's declaration in construing the proposition "X is not electable" to mean "X is not *of the kind* to be elected." In other words, Hillary Clinton was saying that, given the racial politics and racist attitudes of the United States, Obama, being Black, was not the kind of individual who could be elected to the presidency. But this begs the question: What kind of individual qualifies for electability to the highest office of the land given America's racial politics? The answer, obviously, is a White individual. Clearly, Clinton was invoking and committing herself to the prevailing belief then that one had to be White to be electable to the highest political office of the nation. Put another way, she was subscribing to the racial norms that privilege whiteness and marginalize other races, especially Black people.

Bill Clinton, too, gave expression to a similar attitude, in the South Carolina primaries of the Democratic party when the polls were showing a tight race between Hillary Clinton and Obama. Despite the fact that the race was close, Hillary Clinton was poised to win South Carolina until Bill, in campaigning for her, was said to have commented that in 1988 the Reverend Jesse Jackson, the first Black candidate to run as the flag bearer of the Democratic party, had won South Carolina but that that did not get him anywhere in the race. This reference to Jackson's failed 1988 bid for the Democratic party's nomination was considered insulting to many Blacks who were already supporting Hillary Clinton, with the result that many Blacks switched sides and this caused Hillary Clinton to lose South Carolina to Obama.

For our present purpose, what is the significance of Bill Clinton's reference to Jesse Jackson's 1988 win in South Carolina? And why did many Blacks consider Clinton's comment an insult? The essence of Clinton's remark seems to have been that *even if* Obama won South Carolina it would not get him anywhere in the nomination contest because as in 1988, the United States was not ready for a Black president. Thus, the Democratic party would not nominate him. In this regard, such a win would have been a waste of time, effort, and resources. I explain to my students that Bill Clinton, like Hillary, was invoking and exploiting racist attitudes in the United States to further his endeavor to secure the nomination for his wife. And this was why many Blacks considered his remarks insulting.

Whether or not this makes both Clintons racist is arguable. At least, it can be said that they espoused racist beliefs and attitudes while *explicitly* disavowing racism. This view may seem puzzling, perhaps even paradoxical, when one considers that during his presidency Bill Clinton mainstreamed the concerns and interests of Black people to the point that many African Americans had considerable economic success under his administration. Clinton initiated policies such as offering tax incentives to businesses to relocate and operate in the inner cities in order to stimulate economic development. For these reasons, then, many African Americans genuinely like the Clintons, and, in this regard, one can invoke Toni Morrison's characterization of Bill Clinton as "the first Black President."[5] So, how, then, can Clinton subscribe to racist beliefs and attitudes? Perhaps the answer lies in what George Yancy would describe as an "ambush."[6] The Clintons, like a good many liberal, self-avowed antiracist Whites, get ambushed by their own very racist attitudes and beliefs that lurk in the subconscious until forced out by circumstances. And so they are shocked by the reality of their own internalized racism.

The internalization of racist attitudes and beliefs is well expressed in a documentary entitled *The Color of Fear*, in which a diverse group of men from various racial backgrounds—White, Black, Mexican, Chinese, Japanese,

Puerto Rican—explore the effect of racism on them.[7] I get the class to watch this DVD, as it crystallizes several of the issues I cover in the course: White supremacy, White dominance and the marginalization of people of color, White privilege and the invisibility of the so-called "Other." I get the class to examine not only the various perspectives that are represented on these issues on the DVD, but also, and more importantly, how White supremacy has structured social location in terms of a racial hierarchy in the society, and how that hierarchical structuring has created an intra-race hierarchy within each subaltern racial group. It is in this way that I try to get the students to see how their own very existence is implicated in the racial dynamics of the society, and how some of them are privileged because of their race and others disadvantaged because of their race. The subject of race and social location is then given a detailed treatment through readings that address the issue of White privilege.

Race, White Supremacy, and White Privilege

Having laid out the hierarchical structuring of the various races in the society, with White at the top and the various shades of color in descending order, I go on to challenge my students to visualize how this structure is reflected in the media, in corporate organizations, and in similar cardinal institutions in society, such as the Supreme Court. Concerning the media, I call attention to the line-up, at least during the 1990s, of the CBS news program *60 Minutes*. In particular, I call attention to the order in which the journalists were introduced to the viewing public. At the time, the only Black journalist on the program was Ed Bradley (now deceased). The standard line-up used to be along the following lines or a variant thereof: Harry Reasoner (White male), Morley Safer (White male), Mike Wallace (White male), then Ed Bradley (Black male) and Diane Sawyer or Lesley Stahl (White females). As is obvious, this order reflects White male privileging, then an overall male gender privileging (by including the Black male), and then the White female at the bottom of the structure. It is evident that the missing component in this structure is a female of color. This structure is essentially reproduced in *Fortune* magazine's "Fortune 500" list of corporations in the society. Prior to the appointment of the late Justice Thurgood Marshall in 1967 to the Supreme Court of the United States, the Court had consisted of all and only White males. And even later, with the appointments of Justice Sandra Day O'Connor (now retired) to the Supreme Court in 1981 and Justice Clarence Thomas in 1991, the Court has traditionally been dominated by White males.

Such empirical evidence provides a basis to elaborate the twin concepts of White supremacy and White privilege. Concerning White supremacy, the tendency among many Whites, students included, is to understand it in terms of membership of neo-Nazi groups, skinhead organizations, and the Ku Klux Klan. Thus, such Whites reason that, since they are not members of any of these groups, and they even disparage and disavow all such groups, they therefore are not White supremacists. To illustrate this point, some of my students even share personal stories about some of their family members (grandparents, parents, or other relatives) who they say were (or are) blatantly racist, and how they would even make fun of those family members' beliefs.

Such personal stories often bring comic relief to the class and make the class very entertaining and interesting. But while it is refreshing to hear such candid admissions about their family members, I point out to the students that they themselves subscribe to and participate in White supremacy without their knowledge and without their deliberate consent (to adapt a phrase from Bertrand Russell).[8] I demonstrate this point by getting them to see that White supremacy means, essentially, the normativity of whiteness in the society and its resultant White dominance and White privileging, and how these are enacted in society at large. So, even though they themselves may not be doing or saying anything overtly racist, and they may be challenging such racist and White supremacist beliefs, nevertheless (and paradoxically), they are participating in White supremacy by virtue of the fact that they are beneficiaries of a social system built on White supremacist architecture.

And, to illuminate this point, I analogize my view with male privileging in society, a society structured on patriarchal beliefs, perspectives, and values. I illustrate how the males in the class, including myself, are beneficiaries of a social structure that privileges us in terms of the assumptions made about men, simply by virtue of us being men: as authority-figures, intelligent, and commanding. Given these assumptions, therefore, in any relation between a male and a female, the male's viewpoint, belief, or judgment generally is given pride of place regardless of how nonsensical it might be, and the female's is given a subordinate status in spite of the fact that it may be the better of the two. It is precisely such assumptions that privilege men in society by giving them advantages over women, assumptions that benefit us simply because we are male, and that feminists are challenging. *Such benefits that we accrue as a result of this dynamic are undeserved or unearned.* They are undeserved both because we haven't done anything to earn them and because we have got them by participating in a social structure that is configured, among other things, to dominate and oppress women. By virtue of the fact that we are participants in and beneficiaries of those assumptions and values, therefore, we are all engaged in male dominance and female gender oppression. *White privilege, similarly, bears all of the hallmarks of male privilege (and other forms of privilege in society), but, obviously, with a racial stamp.*

Returning to the subject of White privilege, we then examine particular texts written by renowned White scholars, such as Peggy McIntosh and others, on the topic.[9] Although Black scholars since W. E. B. Du Bois have been talking about this phenomenon in one form or another, I use contemporary White scholars' acknowledgement (better yet, "confessions") of this reality *to introduce* the topic because these are admissions by Whites of the all-pervasiveness of a phenomenon about which people of color have always been complaining and protesting.

In addition, I use the "confessions" and personal testimonies of contemporary White scholars to make the point about the subtlety, complexity, and immanence of racism, White supremacy, and White privileging in contemporary society. In so doing, I get the students to see how their lives are implicated in White supremacy and that "racial problems" are not a thing of the past, as some tend to think.

Another pedagogical benefit of foregrounding the "confessions" of White scholars about White supremacy and White privilege is that these "confessions" nicely lead to a discussion of the myth of meritocracy. The essence of this myth is that personal success is owing to individual effort. An individual who fails therefore has not expended enough effort to succeed in society, and so he or she is responsible for his or her personal failure. Since Whites generally are more successful in society than people of color, their successes are a result, according to this view, of their individual efforts. To counter this myth, I redirect my students' attention to the DVD mentioned earlier, *The Color of Fear*, because the myth of meritocracy is one of the central issues examined in the documentary. To get the students to understand why this is a myth, I ask them to reflect once again on male privilege in our society, noting, particularly, that, just as male success in society is generally a result of male privilege, so the general success of Whites is owing to White privilege—a point well demonstrated by able scholars such as Iris Marion Young, Peggy McIntosh, and others. On the basis of this discussion, we then proceed to an examination of the nature of oppression by reading selections from Iris Marion Young's *Justice and the Politics of Difference*.[10] By so doing, we theorize oppression to understand its essence and thus to appreciate how one can be a participant in a structure of oppression without knowing that, and also how one can be oppressed without being aware of it.

Classroom Dynamic: Students' Reaction and Interaction

It may be wondered how White students react to some of the views on race and related issues (as exemplified above), especially when they are challenged to see themselves as participants in a White supremacist structure of oppression and domination? And what is the nature of the interaction between White students and students of color in such a setting, when they are in close physical proximity to one another and are made to view their existence through the lens of such a racial dynamic as is brought out in the course?

Before answering these questions, let me begin by saying a word about the kind of climate I create in the classroom in order to facilitate discussions as part of the course. Right at the beginning, when I am going over the course syllabus and structure of the course, I make it categorically clear that the course is not a forum for indictment (or guilt-tripping) and recrimination. Rather, it is a forum for edification, so that, at the end, we all would come away different and much improved from how we started, and that such difference, hopefully, will be reflected in our actions and attitudes towards others who are racially and otherwise different from us. I direct the students' attention to Plato's dictum in the *Republic* that the value of education is to turn the soul around.[11] In other words, the purpose of education is *to transform the self into a better self*—and this is the primary objective of the course. Keeping this primary objective in mind, I can say that, in general, I have been encouraged by the responses I have been receiving from all of my students, but especially the White students. I say "in general" because, as is to be expected, there are always exceptions. So, let me begin with one such exception.

About three years ago, two White male students whom I had previously taught in other courses signed up for this course. They were generally good students and, at the risk of sounding immodest, they liked my teaching skills and told me how much they had enjoyed my classes. Indeed, this was their very reason for signing up for the course. One of my pedagogical techniques is to encourage class participation through discussion of issues, and to require every student to give a mandatory class presentation on an assigned topic. Unlike in previous classes, however, where each of these students had been very active and enthusiastic, in this class they were rather quiet and unenthusiastic—even when we read the thought-provoking views of canonical figures such as Locke, Hume, Kant, and Hegel, among others, on race; views that generated a lot of lively discussion. I began to sense that they were uncomfortable with the topic itself. And their discomfort was intensified further when I showed the class the DVD, *The Color of Fear*. As I stated earlier, this DVD vividly illustrates some of the key issues addressed in the course, and challenges each of its viewers to see how their life is influenced by racial dynamics, whether as beneficiaries of White supremacy or as recipients of the oppression of White supremacist architectonic. I believe these two students were unable to accept the brutal fact of racism and White supremacy that the DVD depicts, but, more so, the implicit idea in the DVD of a person's involuntary involvement in the practice of racism by virtue of being White. This was too much for them, so they dropped the course and I never saw them again.

Undoubtedly, I was disappointed, especially because one of these students had actually sought me out for academic guidance following his taking my Introduction to Philosophy, and, because of his experience in that course, he came and took my Ethics course. Furthermore, he even encouraged his girlfriend to take my Ethics course later still. In any case, after it became very noticeable that these young men were no longer attending the class, the remaining students, both White and students of color, jokingly commented, "They can't handle the truth"—an adaptation of the well-known line from the movie *A Few Good Men* (1992) starring Jack Nicholson, Tom Cruise, Demi Moore, et al.

I was gratified by this reaction of the rest of the class because it showed that some of the students were willing to confront and engage the issue of racism, White supremacy, and race, gender, and other forms of oppression in which we all participate in one manifestation or another. Indeed, the atmosphere in the class was convivial, and the majority of the White students showed a keen appreciation of the experiences of students of color, especially when those students spoke about the parental guidance they received at a very young age to navigate the treacherous terrain of overt or covert racist forms of behavior. In fact, a good many of the White students saw themselves as allies in the fight against racism and White supremacy. I only hope that this was not mere youthful idealism.

In this regard, I provide here an example of a most revealing and rewarding response, in the form of an email, that I received from a White male student as recently as spring 2012.

> Hi, Dr. Johnson,
>
> I would like to offer my sincere and heartfelt thanks to you for letting me audit your class, and including me in the official email postings and curriculum (festivities, if you will).
> Your class is of the utmost importance to me, for many reasons.
> First, as a member of the ACLU [American Civil Liberties Union], I am a strong supporter of civil liberties. But, more significantly, I think the racial divide in this country is and has been conveniently exploited by the Caucasian plutocracy for political and financial gain. The demonization of the suppressed is the main impediment to racial equality.
> Secondly, as a musician, artist, and songwriter, I want to make a difference in people's lives. I long for the betterment of society by way of humanity, equality, understanding, and fruits of "the examined life."
> What is most interesting, after attending only two of your classes, I realized I was raised a racist. I'm not talking about overt racism like White sheets in the trunk of the car or members of the KKK burning crosses on church lawns or even voting for segregation—I'm talking about the essence of the unspoken. Even growing up poor in the foothills of the Appalachian Mountains, the unspoken was always in the air: racial superiority bolstered by small-town religion, gossip, social status, privilege, and the Caucasian good-old-boy system still prevalent throughout the South. Much of this thought bears warrant by way of divine revelation.
> Racism can be vulgar, but it can also be subtle. This is the type of racism that we all should be more aware of. Only a well-examined life can shed light on the many dark shadows perpetually dancing for the mentally chained.
>
> My best,
> Dean

I think this realization is important for everyone because the Aristotelian idea of "maintaining the truth" gets lost in the subtleties.

To which I responded as follows:

Hi Dean,

Thank you for your very complimentary remarks about the course. I honestly like the fact that the course has struck a chord with you, especially given your artistic and personal interests. In this regard, it is an absolute pleasure to have you in the course. Many a time, some of us feel that we are neither sexists nor racists because we have not done anything overt and personal toward a member of other races or genders. But, if we understand how racism and sexism are deeply implicated in the power structures of society in very subtle and complex ways, from which we somehow benefit even without our knowledge, then we will understand that we are participating in the values that uphold oppressive practices without knowing so. And that is one of the things I want to bring out in the course. To that end, I shall be analogizing various forms of oppressive practices—race, gender, disability, age, to name a few—of which we should be conscious in society. But, above all, I wish to highlight the perspectives of various philosophers in shaping oppressive structures in society. By so doing, I am trying to encourage students to read all philosophers very critically and not to deify or idolize any.

Again, many thanks for your interest in the course and for your wonderful observations. Let's keep on trying to make a difference in the world.

See you on Monday.
Cheers,
Dr. Johnson

And a final email from Mr. Hall at the end of the semester:

Hi Dr. Johnson,

I wish to extend my sincere appreciation to you for allowing me to audit your class this semester. It has been a wonderful and enlightening experience, and I have thoroughly enjoyed every moment of your lectures and class discussion.

My apologies for having to miss the last few classes. My work has suddenly consumed my Monday evenings as well as Fridays. If it's any consolation, I am finishing all the required reading for the class and seeking out further academic authorship on racism and Eurocentrism.

The reading, assignments, and work I have done for this class will prove invaluable in my writing and discussion of my song *Old Jim Crow*. I plan on referencing Eze, West, Yancy, Du Bois, and your *Cornel West &*

Philosophy: The Quest for Social Justice in my upcoming blog posts about the song.

Hopefully, if I am fortunate enough [to] attend school full time next semester, I can take your class again in an official capacity. The engaging class discussions always turn to current events, and a deeper understanding on this subject could only improve anyone's understanding of a culturally diverse society.

All my best,
Dean

Dean Hall is a professional singer, songwriter, and musician in Nashville. He can be looked up on Google and/or on YouTube. As can be seen from my reply, Dean, as a non-traditional White male student, was an invaluable source of insight and inspiration to the diverse body of younger students, and an invaluable member of the class. This, in a nutshell, addresses the issue I posed earlier about the nature of the interaction among students.

Professorial Involvement

I will conclude by elaborating on my role in the classroom. Cognizant of the sensitivity and volatility of discussions about race and racism in the media and similar kinds of settings, which oftentimes degenerate into shouting matches, I consider my role in the classroom to be both an expositor of the evolution of race, and its concomitant which is the practice of racism. I also see myself as a facilitator of healthy and productive analyses and interchange of ideas among interlocutors. As expositor, I direct the students to the standard literature on the topic of race and racism, and challenge them to engage in critical textual analyses of the sources, both scientific and philosophical, in order to get a handle on the intellectual foundation of racism. As facilitator, I encourage the students to draw upon autobiographical and biographical materials that instantiate the standard narratives about race and racism. Since racism is an institutional phenomenon, meaning that it is embedded in the very interstices of the social fabric of society, I therefore try to challenge the students, both victims and beneficiaries of racism alike, to see how their disparate experiences derive from institutional structures not of their own making but in which their very lives are implicated. I do this to get them to appreciate the point that the very complexity and intractability of racism is precisely because of this fact about its embeddedness in the social fabric.

As professor, then, but more so as a Black professor, I consider my primary goal to theorize racism and show how the discrete or episodic experiences that constitute the personal autobiographies and biographies brought to bear upon the discussions are concrete instantiations of the phenomenon theorized. In short,

I view my role in the classroom as that of a Socratic intellectual midwife in birthing the concrete to illuminate the abstract and using the abstract to give cogency and coherence to the concrete.

But a major challenge I have faced in this enterprise pertains to the theorization itself, and the challenge is largely from students of color. Some students of color seem to want to *reduce* racism to personal autobiographies, and the challenge is to get them to go beyond such personal experiences to determine why such disparate experiences are of a kind. The challenge, in other words, is to get them to abstract from their personal experiences in order to be able to provide a theoretical basis for those experiences. Incidentally, some of my female colleagues who do feminist studies speak of a similar challenge they have with some female students. According to those colleagues, some female students tend to reduce feminist studies to the experiences they personally have had by virtue of the fact they are women. The challenge for professors, then, is to disabuse such students of that narrow conception of feminist studies.

My challenge is of a similar kind. I try to meet it by getting my students to realize that, while their personal narratives are very vital and useful to interrogate racism, the critical question is left unanswered; namely, what is it about all such experiences that make them *experiences of racism*? And that, in the absence of any such answer, the experiences they invoke might appear to be merely coincidental. But, given the ubiquity of racism, as they all tend to agree, their disparate experiences therefore cannot just be coincidental. It thus behooves them to be able to account for its ubiquity, and they can only do so by theorizing racism. In other words, I point out to them, as well as to the rest of the class, that, unless they can theorize racism, they cannot explain why their experiences are as they are. Some of them are reluctant to take the challenge, so they drop out of the course. Others, however, are willing to undertake it, and they continue. And that is fine with me.

For me, then, the classroom is a venue for intellectual heavy-lifting, and, as a Black professor, I take it as a personal and professional obligation to challenge all of my students, both White and students of color, to undertake the heavy-lifting that I believe will enable us to appreciate the gravity of the problem of race and racism in our society. I do so in the hope that only by undertaking such heavy-lifting can we begin to nibble at the problem and then try to propose some solution or other as best we can imagine.

Notes

1 See, for example, Carl von Linné "The God-given Order of Nature," in Emmanuel Chukwudi Eze (ed.) *Race and the Enlightenment: A Reader* (Cambridge, MA: Blackwell, 1997), chap. 1.

2 The canonical sources in question are in Eze, *Race and the Enlightenment*.

3 Igor Volsky, "John Sununu's History of Racial Remarks About Obama," ThinkProgress.org, October 26, 2012, http://thinkprogress.org/politics/2012/10/26/1094491/john-sununus-history.

4 For the entries in these encyclopedias, see Eze, *Race and the Enlightenment*, 91–94.

5 Toni Morrison, The Talk of the Town: Comment, *New Yorker*, October 5, 1998; rpt. Toni Morrison, "Clinton as the first Black president," *New Yorker*, October 1998, in http://ontology.buffalo.edu/smith/clinton/morrison.html. See p. 2 in particular. Granted, the sense in which Morrison made this reference is different from the one I am considering. Morrison is referring to an affinity she sees between Clinton's experience and that of most African American males: born poor; grew up poor in a single-parent home; working class background; plays music (in his case, the saxophone); loved junk food; and his un-policed sexuality made him the object of humiliation, hatred and vilification by his political opponents to the point of metaphorically body-searching him. (This last point is a reference to the Monica Lewinsky sexual scandal over which the Republicans tried but failed to impeach Clinton.) Even so, there is no denying that African Americans thrived under Clinton's administration because of deliberate policies he initiated, and in this regard it is germane to call him the first Black president, following Morrison.

6 George Yancy, *Black Bodies, White Gazes: The Continuing Significance of Race* (Lanham, MD: Rowman & Littlefield, 2008), 229. As Yancy goes on to note, "[B]eing antiracist does not mean that the White self has arrived. There are many good whites who continue to participate in structures of racial power from which they benefit" (*Black Bodies, White Gazes*, 232).

7 Mun Wah Lee, Monty Hunter, Robert Goss, Jr., and Richard C. Bock, *The Color of Fear* (Oakland: CA, Stir-Fry Productions, 1995).

8 Bertrand Russell, *The Problems of Philosophy* (London, England: Oxford University Press, 1912). Russell is elaborating the value of studying philosophy, and, in this context, he says that the person with no philosophic exposure "goes through life imprisoned in the prejudices derived from common sense, from the habitual beliefs of his [or her] age or nation, and from convictions which have grown up in his [or her] mind without the co-operation or consent of his [or her] deliberate reason" (*Problems of Philosophy*, 91).

9 Paula S. Rothenberg's *White Privilege: Essential Readings on the Other Side of Racism* (New York, NY: Worth Publishers, 2012) is a beautifully arranged anthology that contains writings by Peggy McIntosh, Tim Wise, Charles W. Mills, and others.

10 Iris Marion Young, *Justice and the Politics of Difference* (Princeton, NJ: Princeton University Press, 1990).

11 Plato, "The Republic," in *A Plato Reader: Eight Essential Dialogues*, ed. Charles D. C. Reeve (Indianapolis, IN: Hackett Publishing, 1992), 518, c–d.

7

A LETTER TO MY KINFOLK ON THE ONE HUNDRED AND FIFTIETH ANNIVERSARY OF THE EMANCIPATION[1]

A. Todd Franklin

My Dear Brothers and Sisters,

The space that you and I occupy is, in many ways, rather disconcerting. As faculty of color on predominately White campuses, our presence at faculty meetings, at the lectern, or in any space reserved for the professoriate is often looked upon with suspicion. On the one hand, there are suspicions concerning our intellect, and, on the other, there are suspicions concerning the nature of our scholarship. These suspicions are not unique to our campuses. Sadly, they are simply local expressions of the deep-seated racial prejudices that have historically run rife throughout the academic world.

Accounts of these racial prejudices abound, and one need only look through the archives of *The Chronicle of Higher Education* to discover a litany of lamentable experiences of disparagement. Although the dimensions of racial prejudice in the academy are multiple and the dynamics are accordingly quite complex, the aspersions cast upon Black scholars and Black scholarship always have been and continue to be quite pronounced. Writing one year after celebrating the 30th anniversary of several prominent departments and programs devoted to the critical study of the African diaspora, Nell Irvin Painter bemoans the fact that she and other Black scholars still find themselves faced with the "struggles of perception."[2] Having devoted more than 25 years of her scholarly career to the development of Black studies, as well as having served as the director of Princeton's program in African American studies, the degree to which Black scholars and Black studies remained in disrepute was driven home for Painter when, in virtue of her association with the program, a Princeton student journalist asked her whether she had a PhD. The problem, as Painter surmises, is that, even after the emergence of a long and laudable line of Black scholars and the evolution of Black studies into a paragon of interdisciplinary sophistication, "the silent, even unconscious assumption still prevails that Black studies and Black faculty members suit each other perfectly, because the field is simple and the people are not so smart."[3]

Although new generations of Black scholars continue to emerge and new programs in Black studies continue to blossom, the struggles of perception remain rather pronounced. One of the most odious indications of this fact is a recent characterization of the dissertations of Northwestern University's first cohort of African American studies PhDs as nothing more than "a collection of left-wing victimization clap-trap."[4] Genuinely annoyed by the fact that up-and-coming scholars would have the audacity to link the overlooking of Black experiences and the devastation of Black communities to the continuing legacy of White supremacy, one of *The Chronicle*'s White, paid bloggers used her platform as an opportunity to viciously lampoon their scholarship, defame their intellectual integrity, and summarily declare that, whatever the problems of Blacks in America may be, the only real solutions are ones "that don't begin and end with blame the White man."[5]

Like me, and many others, you are already well aware that such smug and condescending attempts to ridicule and revile us are nothing more than palpable testaments to the imbecility of their authors. Sadly, however, the persistent struggles of perception that we face as scholars highlight the significance of the fundamental struggles of perception that we face as teachers. Following in the footsteps of James Baldwin, I write to you today in the same vein as he wrote to his nephew, James, some 50 years ago. Recognizing the challenges of dealing with Whites who are deeply immersed and deeply invested in certain perceptions, Baldwin was determined to try and tell his nephew "something about how to handle *them*."[6] Similarly, all too familiar with the challenges of teaching their progeny, I want to share a few things about how to handle the newer generation as well.

What do our White students see when they look out upon the racial landscape of American society? In general, they see a society that is racially stratified in innumerable ways—a society in which, by and large, Whites are on top and Blacks are on the bottom. Looking out upon the hills and valleys of social status and social location, they see Whites who are widely known and respected for their accomplishments in the domains of intellect and industry and Blacks who are primarily noteworthy for their ability to athletically perform or entertain. There upon the hills, they see themselves surrounded by other hard-working and respectable Whites and fellowship with them regularly as members of various organizations and clubs. Down below in the distant valleys of the ghettoes, they see Black folks as dangerous and self-destructive "gang bangers" and "welfare queens" who do nothing but get high, get pregnant, get killed, or get incarcerated. Looking out upon the rivers of educational and economic opportunity, they see waves of White faces as they walk across college campuses and intern throughout corporate America. Occasionally, however, they will see a black face or two.

More often than not, the black faces that they do see mix right in and flow with the currents of whiteness. Although some of these folks form irksome little eddies that beat against the levees that control the channels of access, those levees nevertheless stand firm as safeguards that protect the so-called quality and integrity of the waterways by rendering vast reservoirs of black faces socially still and stagnant. Finally, as most of our White students look out upon the horizon of the future, they see themselves as generously endowed with all of the talents of mind and attributes of character that pave the way to success, and pity what they see as the shameful lack of such abilities and attributes among so many Blacks.

In sum, most of our White students see freedom of association and take no notice of segregation. They see the ravages of social pathologies, but they fail to recognize the social antecedents. They see instances of disparity, yet they fail to discern evidence of discrimination. At base, although they see the hallmarks of America's racial hierarchy, they fail to perceive the pervasive presence of racism.

Curiously, raising the specter of racism gives them little to no pause, for most of them remain comfortably ensconced in a socially codified sense of racial innocence. Taught from an early age that racists are people who burn crosses in front of homes and drag people to death behind pickup trucks, the aversion that they feel towards such actions is regarded as a clear indication of their racial innocence. As they grew older, they were immersed in a host of philanthropic programs and organizations. They collected clothes and organized food drives that offset the deprivations of poor people of all colors, and the earnestness with which they continue to engage in such efforts is taken as a sure sign of their "racial innocence." Now that they have reached adulthood and stand poised to assume the duties of citizenship, many of our White students are enamored of the fact that ours is a nation whose leaders not only tap Blacks to serve as high-level government appointees, but one whose people demonstrate a willingness to popularly elect a Black person to serve as their president. Determined to give concrete expression to the modern-day American credo that the operative factor is not the color of a person's skin but the content of their character, many of our White students actively support mainstream Black political candidates, and their effort in doing so is widely celebrated as indisputable evidence of their "racial innocence."

In contrast, we who stand beyond the boundaries of whiteness see and know the matter rather differently. Properly understood, racism is not only a matter of reprehensible individual attitudes and actions, it's also a matter of reprehensible social outcomes. More specifically, racism is not simply a matter of the thoughts and behaviors of people who despise racial Others. Rather, as you and I so clearly see, racism is much more prevalently a matter of the systemic and disproportionate allotment of social benefits and advantages on the basis of race.

For most of our White students, however, the prospects of them readily perceiving racism along such lines are slim. That which stands out as the greatest obstacle to them doing so is their reticence to truly reconcile themselves to the social ramifications of their whiteness. At base, this reticence is simply symptomatic of the way in which many of our White students are mired in a socially pernicious cycle of bad faith; a cycle, moreover, in which Whites flee not only from the fact that they explicitly benefit from a system of racial advantage, but also from the fact that their posture of indifference perpetuates it. Trapped, as it were, in a very seductive and coercive form of bad faith in which their ability to comfortably enjoy all of the surreptitious social advantages that they accrue in virtue of their whiteness is predicated on their ability to carefully avoid problematizing it, few, if any, Whites will ever instinctively develop the wherewithal to actively contest the operative forces and structures of racism. Faced with this realization, it's natural for us to resent the idea that it is our responsibility to liberate them. However, given that we have utterly no hope of radically transforming America's racial landscape unless they somehow become active allies, it is imperative that we who stand beyond the pale of whiteness reach out to the students who are ensnarled within it and struggle with all of our pedagogical might to effect their liberation.

Stationed, as it were, at various outposts within the heart of whiteness, we are palpably aware of the chasm that exists between us and the vast majority of White students who roam the pathways of our campuses. A novelty to most, many of these students have never had a Black teacher or professor before, and few, if any, have ever worked closely with one. Doubtful of our abilities and suspicious of our motives, lots of these White students steer clear of our courses and drift beyond our reach. For one reason or another, however, some of them end up in our midst. Most of our interactions with these students occur within the context of the classroom. Although the classroom provides us with an excellent opportunity to introduce them to radically new ways of perceiving the nature of racism and its relation to the realities of America's racial landscape, classroom interactions alone prove insufficient as a means of radically transforming the ways in which they perceive themselves in relation to any newly gained insights.

There within the classroom we can introduce them to all manner of data, analyses, and narratives with respect to the pernicious role of race within American society. Most of this material will lead to intense and thought-provoking class-room discussions. More often than not, however, these discussions will be sorely lacking in terms of critical self-reflection on the part of White students. Inevitably, the issue of whiteness will come to the fore, and, just as inevitably, most of the White students will begin to shutdown. Those who do have the where-withal to continue the conversation will usually couch their comments in terms of an indefinite "us" or "we," but rarely, if ever, will they put themselves out there and frame what they have to say in terms of a self-implicating first person form of reference such as "I" or "me."

Much of their reticence to do so, however, is fundamentally a matter of the pedagogical medium. Regardless of how conscientiously you strive to make your classrooms respectful and tight-knit learning communities, students will always be somewhat, if not greatly, inhibited by the inherently public nature of it all. In contrast, you'll find that students are often much more inclined to take up issues of whiteness in more personal terms when they are given the opportunity to do so within the confines of a private class journal. True to form, the private journal encourages the students to make the shift from the plural to the singular, and, once they do, some of them actually begin to frame their own whiteness as problematic.

At times, however, some of the students scarcely get farther than oblique acknowledgements of their role in relation to racial oppression and expressions of sympathy for those who unfortunately endure it. One recent case in point is a student of mine named Anna.[7] Anna characterizes herself as a "White middle-class woman" who hails from a rural White community in upstate New York. Ironically, Anna claims in her journal that one of her favorite quotes is a line by Audre Lorde that reads, "The oppressors maintain their position and evade responsibility for their own actions."[8] Although she credits class discussion with opening up her mind to "the struggles faced by others" and claims that "we need to listen and pass on what we've learned so that the next generation doesn't make the same mistakes as us," she never expressly acknowledges any role she may have in relation to various "mistakes" pertaining to issues of race. Instead, Anna conveniently foregrounds relations of class and casts herself as someone who admittedly oppresses the poor, but also endures being oppressed by well-off Whites. Stressing her role as oppressed rather than her role as oppressor, Anna details how it "kills" her to see rich White girls enjoy all sorts of advantages "without a care in the world" while she, on the other hand, finds herself forced to struggle her way through life. Ultimately, as Anna sees it, she and these girls have "completely different situations," and, in the end, she freely confesses that thinking about it makes her "a little bitter."

Although students like Anna lay claim to their whiteness, they evade its racial implications by cloaking themselves in relations of class. Opportunities to directly challenge their tendency to do so rarely emerge. In Anna's case, however, the fact that she shares her sentiments with me via the medium of a private journal provides me with a chance to applaud her appreciation of the fact that oppressors tend to "evade responsibility for their own actions" and press her to think more deeply about how focusing on class might constitute one way of doing so. Furthermore, it also allows me to assure her that she is not alone in her utter disdain for the fact that some folks are unduly privileged, and ask her if she's ever thought about the various advantages that those rich White girls would still enjoy even if they weren't rich.

For some, feedback of this nature will be rather off-putting. Those who cling the tightest to their sense of "racial innocence" will probably be very reluctant to respond to it; but, even if they don't, there's always the hope that jarring allusions to the need to engage in further self-reflection will effectively serve as a catalyst that causes them to do so.

In contrast to students like Anna, other White students emerge from the journal writing process much more critically self-aware. Take Sarah for instance. Sarah was so powerfully struck by what we were reading and discussing in class that she seized upon the journal as an opportunity to spell out what she learned about oppression and declare how determined she is to do something about it. Highlighting an essay by Patricia Hill Collins, Sarah wrote as follows:

> The title, "Toward a New Vision: Race, Class, and Gender as Categories of Analysis and Connection," is analogous with the title of our class: Race, Gender, and Culture. I read Collins's piece as a synthesizing account of this semester. It seems to draw on almost every author we have read in one way or another. She questions "truth," highlights "circumstance," poses questions, etc. Her emphasis on "new ways of thought and action" through "reconceptualization" and "transcendence" articulates the aims that our class strives towards. The problem with race, gender, and class struggle is that there are so many deeply entrenched power dynamics and misguided beliefs that society, at large, accepts without question. These prescribed notions hinder our ability to connect with people who are different from us. As students in the classroom, we are engaged in philosophical, sociological, and intellectual discussions about texts. I know that sometimes I get caught up in the reading and in my own thoughts and forget that what I am reading is the same reality that I am living. The works we have read have ranged from centuries, to decades, to years old. But what is different? Like Collins points out, most janitors are still Black. Most secretaries are still women. Hamilton is still stuffed with predominately White, upper-middle-class students. Nothing has changed, we (and I stress "we" because I have an active part in this) have just learned to mask the oppression in different ways. It's disgusting, frustrating, and debilitating.

Here, Sarah clearly characterizes racism and other forms of oppression in terms of power and perception, and emphasizes the importance of contemplating them in the context of lived experience. Once she herself does so, she becomes painfully aware of the fact that, despite centuries of analysis and critique, "nothing has changed" when it comes to the prevalence of disproportionate allotments and outcomes predicated on difference. Making matters worse, Sarah also becomes painfully self-conscious of herself as someone who actively perpetuates many of the social arrangements that mar the American landscape, and the thought that she does proves "disgusting, frustrating, and debilitating."

Fortunately, however, Sarah then thinks back on why she took the class, and reframes things more optimistically:

> This reading really made me reflect on why I am taking this class. As I have stated, sometimes I do get caught up in the reading and forget that these are real issues. However, then I remember why I took this class. I wanted to learn, to discuss, to grow, and then take all of that and go out and change something.

Years ago, I would have been happy as can be to have a privileged White student express such awareness and determination; however, years of experience have taught me that such newly self-conscious students rarely have the wherewithal to follow through with their intentions in relation to matters of race.

Nowadays, students like Sarah prompt me to think back to a former student of mine named Jack. Smart, athletic, popular, and passionate, Jack hailed from a well-to-do family and grew up outside of Boston. One of the first White males to ever enroll in one of my courses on race, Jack was to my mind the great White hope. Jack never missed a class and he was always an active participant. Although he got a bit defensive when we would take up works that were explicitly hostile toward Whites, he eventually came to appreciate why someone like Malcolm X would have no qualms about characterizing the White man as a "devil." As the issues became more and more contemporary, and the focus shifted more toward the structural and the systemic, Jack became more and more interested in the idea of making a difference. Once the class ended, however, Jack lost his resolve; instead of following through and actively challenging racial inequalities, he quickly fell back into the fold of whiteness and focused his energies on reaping the social and economic benefits of fitting in with those of a similar hue.

Oftentimes, when we have students like Jack, we like to think that we've done such a great job of opening their eyes and getting them to see the racist ramifications of certain ways of living one's whiteness that, once they move forward, their actions will naturally follow suit. Unfortunately, however, their promise proves fragile. Looking back at what happened to Jack, one of the most important lessons I learned was the importance of personal engagement as well as intellectual engagement. It's important to plant the seed for change, but simply doing so is not enough; for, unless you take the time to nurture it, there's little hope that it will actually grow and bear fruit.

As a scholar, I've always known what to teach my students when it comes to matters of race; but, as a teacher, it took me a number of years to figure out how to help those who yearn to break free of the oppressive attitudes and inclinations of whiteness to do so decisively. Students like Sarah prove promising, but they still stand in need of a lot of guidance and support. One of the things these students need most is someone to help them find ways to remain true to their insights and strengthen their antiracist resolve. When Sarah tells me that she's disgusted with the fact that she and other Whites are responsible for racial oppression, I ask her to tell me about the people in her life who actually experience it. Rarely, however, do students like Sarah have personal relationships with those who suffer racial oppression; and, when they do, they are typically far fewer in number and much more tenuous than the relationships they have with racially inattentive or insensitive Whites. At this juncture, Sarah's heart is certainly in the right place, but, unless she finds a way to anchor it, there's little hope that she'll be able to resist slipping back into socially deleterious ways of living her whiteness.

Getting those who have just begun to grapple with their whiteness to see this can often be rather difficult, but one of the best ways to do so is to share a few stories. The first thing I do in a case like Sarah's is tell her the story of Jack. I tell her how Jack was also very perceptive when it came to racist social outcomes and very passionate in his desire to do something about them. I tell her how pleased I was at the progress he made over the course of the semester and how crushed I was when he later faltered. I tell her how Jack's story is the all too common story of a passion devoid of personal attachments to those beyond the pale—and then I tell her the story of David and explain how forging such attachments makes all the difference in the world.

Unlike Jack, David became actively engaged in the struggle to transform America's racial landscape. Deeply troubled by inequalities in terms of educational outcomes, David now strives to help frame the focus of educational reform on ways to address the real deficiencies of the system as opposed to the presumed deficiencies of the students. For David, however, contesting misconceptions of the intellectual aptitude of Black children, and arguing that we need to take measures to better serve them, isn't simply a matter of heeding the wisdom of the latest research. For David, doing so is much more a matter of standing up for the little ones he teaches, tutors, and mentors for 10 to 11 hours a day; the ones who give their best because he gives his best; the ones who eventually excel because he refuses to allow them to believe that they can't. It's these little faces that come to David's mind when he encounters Whites who disparage the character and capabilities of children who are Black; and it's the thought of these faces that emboldens him to challenge and chastise such people, regardless of whether they are strangers, friends, or family.

Once I finish telling Sara about David's triumphs, I tell her about his trials. I tell her that, despite his activism, David still continually struggles with the temptation to fall back into the ways of whiteness, and that, if it weren't for his connections to others beyond the pale, he might eventually do so. Moreover, I tell her that one of David's greatest virtues is his critical awareness of the complex relation in which he stands to racism, and that another is his recognition of the critical importance of intertwining his life within the lives of those who experience racism in order to truly empathize with their situation and continually reinforce his resolve to change it.

Hopefully, Sarah will do likewise and bond with racial Others in ways that will secure her liberation and bolster her resolve to rise up and establish herself as part of an urgently needed new generation of unflinchingly antiracist Whites. For far too long, others who've been situated like Sarah have stood idle as those of us beyond the pale have struggled to undo the racist gerrymandering that has rigidly and reprehensibly stratified America's racial landscape. Thoroughly ensconced within the delusion of "racial innocence," many see no need to take issue with what, to their eyes, is nothing more than a consequence of practices and systems that are fundamentally neutral. Unfazed by the way we are ridiculed for daring to suggest that much of the responsibility for our fate is not our own, many of these same Whites see no need to protest when others cast aspersions upon our character and our intellect. Fortunately, my dear brothers and sisters, with care, many of the young Whites we teach can be pulled free from the snares of this delusion and firmly placed upon the path to becoming loyal antiracist allies. One by one, we will liberate them, and, one by one, they will join us in the struggle to liberate other whites. Although the numbers in need of liberation are daunting and the task of doing so is difficult, you and I both know that this is a task that we must nevertheless doggedly undertake; for, given the ways in which the delusions of racial innocence perpetuate the nightmares of racial oppression, you and I both certainly know that "we cannot be free until they are free."[9]

Yours in solidarity and hope,

Todd

Notes

1 In homage to James Baldwin's 1963 letter to his nephew on the one hundredth anniversary of the Emancipation Proclamation, published as "A Letter to My Nephew," *The Progressive*, December 1962; and "My Dungeon Shook—Letter to My Nephew on the One Hundredth Anniversary of Emancipation," in *The Fire Next Time* (New York, NY: Dial Press, 1963).

2 Nell Irvin Painter, "Black Studies, Black Professors, and the Struggles of Perception," *The Chronicle of Higher Education*, December 15, 2000: B7.

3 Ibid.

4 Naomi Schaefer Riley, "The Most Persuasive Case for Eliminating Black Studies? Just Read the Dissertations," Brainstorm blog, *The Chronicle of Higher Education*, April 30, 2012, http://chronicle.com/blogs/brainstorm/the-most-persuasive-case-for-eliminating-black-studies-just-read-the-dissertations/46346.

5 Ibid.

6 James Baldwin, "My Dungeon Shook—Letter to My Nephew on the One Hundredth Anniversary of Emancipation," in *James Baldwin: Collected Essays* (New York, NY: Library of America, 1998), 292.

7 All student names have been changed in order to safeguard their privacy.

8 Audre Lorde, "Age, Race, Class, and Sex: Women Redefining Difference," in *Sister Outsider: Essays and Speeches* (Berkeley, CA: Crossing Press, 2007), 115.

9 Baldwin, "My Dungeon Shook," 295.

8

RACIALIZED CONSCIOUSNESS AND LEARNED IGNORANCE

Trying to Help White People Understand

Arnold Farr

Racism and the Need Not to See

The system of racism/White supremacy and all that goes with it—from slavery, to Jim and Jane Crow laws in the South, to northern forms of segregation called "districting," to recent forms of institutionalized racism—represents America's greatest embarrassment. The embarrassment is so great that most self-respecting White Americans would like to put this history as far behind them as possible. The mechanisms for forgetting are so powerful and pervasive that Michael Eric Dyson has referred to the U.S.A. as the "United State of Amnesia" and, following Joseph Lowery, "the 51st state, the state of denial."[1] Many White Americans would like to think that racism was the product of past generations, and that they no longer benefit from racial discrimination. They think that the racists today are groups such as the KKK. Since they neither belong to nor support such groups, and since they are on friendly terms with several Black people (and perhaps they even voted for Obama), they are not racist.

White students in predominantly White colleges and universities are the recipients of this "I'm not a racist" mentality. This is taken a step further to include the view that we are all now, or should be, colorblind. This alleged colorblindness is indeed a form of blindness itself. The claim that one does not see color or race unfortunately puts one in the position of not seeing the racism that is still present in our society. The refusal to see race is the refusal to see the long-term effects of racism on Black people. It is a refusal to see the social, institutional, legal, and economic mechanisms that are in place to keep a large portion of the Black population from achieving the same optimal form of life as their White peers.

The purpose of this chapter is not to explain or examine the various forms of racism that continue to exist. The task here is to simply explore forms of pedagogy deployed by Black professors who teach and explore issues regarding race and racism on predominantly White campuses. For me, a proper and effective pedagogy requires some understanding of the psychological and social mechanisms that may create resistance to talking about race. Let me say at the beginning that, in this chapter, I will not be talking about White students who are consciously and intentionally committed to some form of racism or White supremacy. My concern here is with those White students who really do believe that we are beyond racism.

The "Habitus" and Racialized Consciousness

One of the biggest impediments to fruitful discussions about race in predominantly White institutions is the belief that racism has been reduced to the conscious intentions of the individual racist. So, if a person is not consciously committed to overt racism and discrimination, they are inclined to see themselves as not racist. Further, since most of the people that they know are like them, they are further inclined to think that racism no longer exists. This view is reinforced by an overemphasis on individual intentions and will in our society, and not enough attention paid to the effects of certain social structures on individuals and their life prospects. For this reason, I have used the term "racialized consciousness" instead of "racism." The term "racialized consciousness" actually represents a form of the unconscious. However, I use "consciousness" here because even our conscious choices are racialized. What is unconscious is the fact that many of our decisions and life choices are informed by racialized social positions. The sociologist Pierre Bourdieu's notion of "habitus" is a useful tool for understanding how racialized consciousness works.

> The objective homogenizing of group or class *habitus* that results from homogeneity of conditions of existence is what enables practices to be objectively harmonized without any calculation or conscious reference to a norm and mutually adjusted in the absence of any direct interaction or, a fortiori, explicit co-ordination. The interaction itself owes its form to the objective structures that have produced the dispositions of the interacting agents, which continue to assign them their relative positions in the interaction and elsewhere.[2]

Although Bourdieu's focus is socioeconomic class, his analysis of the concept of "habitus" works just as well for race. In the case of economic class and race, people are continually put at a disadvantage through a process of social development and organization that conceals the mechanisms of social domination. Multiple forms of oppression work according to different logics of domination, but are subject to the same structuring principle. It is this structuring principle that goes unnoticed in class- and race-based oppression.

In the above passage, what is clear is that the practices of social groups do not require conscious reference to a norm. Norms are already deeply embedded in the habitus and, therefore, can exercise influence behind the back, as it were, of consciousness. We may describe the habitus as a field of social interaction with pre-established webs of meaning, social positions, norms, identities, group membership, forms of discourse and discursive practices, and so on. Hence, social interaction does not occur in a vacuum.

Bourdieu continues:

> The *habitus* which, at every moment, structures new experiences in accordance with the structures produced by past experiences, which are modified by the new experiences within the limits defined by their power of selection, brings about a unique integration, dominated by the earliest experiences, of the experiences statistically common to members of the same class. Early experiences have particular weight because the *habitus* tends to ensure its own constancy and its defense against change through the selection it makes within new information by rejecting information capable of calling into question its accumulated information, if exposed to it accidentally or by force, and especially by avoiding exposure to such information. One only has to think, for example, of homogamy, the paradigm of all the "choices" through which the *habitus* tends to favor experiences likely to reinforce it (or the empirically confirmed fact that people tend to talk about politics with those who have the same opinions). Through the systematic "choices" it makes among the places, events and people that might be frequented, the *habitus* tends to protect itself from crises and critical challenges by providing itself with a milieu to which it is as pre-adapted as possible, that is, a relatively constant universe of situations tending to reinforce its dispositions by offering the market most favorable to its products. And once again it is the most paradoxical property of the *habitus*, the unchosen principle of "choices," that yields the solution to the paradox of the information needed in order to avoid information.[3]

The concept of habitus is useful for understanding the ways in which racism perpetuates itself (intentionally or unintentionally), and it also aids us in understanding the resistance to candid conversations with White people (within this context, particularly students) about race. The habitus is not only a structure; it is a structure that is perpetually structuring. That is, it rearranges social relations and data in such a way that the old is preserved in the new. Hence, even in the aftermath of social movements that were designed to overcome racism (and quite a bit of progress has been made), racism and its long-term effects remain. For example, Bourdieu claims that the habitus structures new experiences in accordance with structures produced by past experiences. One of the main and enduring motifs of racism in the United States is that Blacks are not as intelligent as Whites. Whites have a way of maintaining this view, even in the face of counterevidence. The notion of Black exceptionalism is one of their most effective tools. On campuses across the country, there is always the "smart Black." However, how often are Whites told, "You are a credit to your race"? The Black person who is a high achiever stands out as an exception to the rule. This allows Whites to recognize intelligent Blacks while maintaining that Blacks in general are intellectually inferior.[4] The habitus functions in such a way that new data does not contradict old racist assumptions. Habitus also blinds us to social processes and forms of social organization that give members of certain social groups an advantage over others. Bourdieu explains this in terms of the social distribution of four forms of capital.

He says:

> I have shown that *capital presents itself under three fundamental species* (each with its own subtypes), namely, economic capital, cultural capital, and social capital. To these we must add symbolic capital, which is the form that one or another of these species takes when it is grasped through categories of perception that *recognize* its specific logic or, if you prefer, misrecognize the arbitrariness of its possession and accumulation. I shall not dwell on the notion of economic capital. I have analyzed the peculiarity of cultural capital, which we should in fact call *informational capital* to give the notion its full generality, and which itself exists in three forms, embodied, objectified, or institutionalized. Social capital is the sum of the resources, actual or virtual, that accrue to an individual or a group by virtue of possessing a durable network of more or less institutionalized relationships of mutual acquaintance and recognition.[5]

The multiple forms of capital discussed by Bourdieu are useful for helping us and our White students understand the perpetuation (intentional or unintentional) of White privilege, and the way that White students are the recipients of White privilege. One of the things that triggers White students to become angry and defensive when race is introduced as a topic in the classroom is that they think that they are being blamed for the sins of past generations. Since they were not advocates of slavery or Jim and Jane Crowism, they believe that they are not affected by racism, and, therefore, should not be bothered with a critique of a system that they were not a part of creating.

The habitus, in addition to structuring forms of discourse, values, practices, identities, and so on, also structures the accumulation and distribution of economic capital (financial resources, property, etc); cultural capital (education, information, etc.); social capital (social connections); and symbolic capital (the social value placed on the other three forms of capital as well as the value placed on group membership). Past practices, social interactions, social relations, and experiences have structured the four forms of capital and their distribution in such a way that the members of certain social groups have more at birth than others. We might say that the four forms of capital are bargaining chips that are made available for individuals at birth.[6] One does not have to be conscious of these bargaining chips to make use of them or to benefit from them. Consider a Black person and a White person walking into a store. Due to symbolic capital, the White person is not as likely to be followed as the Black person. On predominately White campuses, the vast majority of administrators and faculty are White. This normalized White power structure is invisible to White students due to its normalization. On such campuses, the Black professor may be mistaken for a janitor or a cook. Consider the role that all four forms of capital play in determining where children get to go to school and the quality of education that they get.

The Disarming Power of Preemptive Forgiveness

The phenomenon of racialized consciousness combined with epistemologies of ignorance,[7] and atomistic individualism, makes it very difficult to explain, discuss, and teach about race in predominantly White institutions. In the above section, I have tried to explain this difficulty by examining some of the social mechanisms (e.g., habitus and racialized consciousness) as constitutive sources of learned ignorance and resistance. Much more could be said about these mechanisms, but that would take us beyond the conspectus of this chapter. My purpose in discussing them at all here is to reveal the social and psychological disposition of the White student who is the recipient of the disclosure by the Black professor of ongoing racism in the United States. Understanding the social and psychological mechanisms that shape White, racialized consciousness and learned ignorance is important for developing strategies for teaching White students about race.

My first teaching strategy I call "preemptive forgiveness." Preemptive forgiveness is not the traditional Christian form of forgiveness, as in turning the other cheek or pardoning someone after they've harmed you in some way. This traditional form of forgiveness has been overused, and I would suggest that oppressed people be less inclined to forgive. The purpose of preemptive forgiveness is to open a space for free and honest conversations about racism and other forms of oppression. In spite of Bill Clinton's call, in the 1990s, to have a conversation about race, our society has not yet learned to talk about race, due to White America's obsession with comfort. How many times have we been in conversation with well-intentioned, liberal White people who become angry or claim to be uncomfortable when things get a bit too deep vis-à-vis race. These people are fine with talking about race as long as we do not go deep enough to challenge their own identity and privilege. Hence, even when we talk about race, the conversation ends up being truncated and very superficial. There is a fear of offending someone or of saying the wrong thing.

When conversations about race begin to move beyond the superficial level, people often back out. Conversations about race and racism are so difficult for White people because of the pervasiveness of White denial; the reduction of racism to conscious, intentional, individual forms of hatred and discrimination, and our failure to think structurally. The result is that our students are completely unprepared to discuss or listen to discussions about race. Even well-intentioned students who might be open to a discussion about race often freeze up because they are afraid that they may say the wrong thing.

Preemptive forgiveness opens the space for a candid conversation about race. Before we enter the conversation, we recognize that, due to decades of denial, we have be ill equipped for candid conversations about race. Due to our lack of preparedness, it is a given that some people hold false assumptions about race and racism. It is also a given that we will make mistakes and perhaps offend someone (unintentionally) during the conversation. Preemptive forgiveness is the act of forgiving one another in advance for the inevitable mistakes that will occur during the conversation. I forgive my students, they forgive one another, and they forgive me. With forgiveness in place, we are now free to enter a conversation about race that goes well beyond the typical superficial level.

Preemptive forgiveness has a disarming effect with regard to students and faculty who might get defensive because they feel that they are being blamed for a form of oppression that they may not be consciously committed to. With preemptive forgiveness, all participants are put on an even playing field due to the recognition that we have all been ill prepared by our society for a serious and honest conversation about race.

The Oppressed and the Oppressor in Malleable Subject Positions

I believe that a critique of racism must take place within an examination of the larger context of multiple struggles for social justice. As an African American, it is to be expected that I bring race and racism to the academic table for critique. However, due to White denial, what is a real, objective problem is reduced by White students to the mere venting of a personal problem. Addressing the problem of race within the larger problem of struggles for social justice disarms students a second time, because it takes away their ability to reduce the professor to an angry Black who is simply venting a personal problem. This approach is the first step in my second strategy for discussing race in the classroom.

For this second strategy, I make use of Ernesto Laclau and Chantal Mouffe's concept of "subject positions." The term "subject positions" allows Laclau and Mouffe to talk about identity and the struggles of oppressed social groups without the reduction of the oppressed to some essentialized notion of identity. They write:

> Whenever we use the category of "subject" in this text, we will do so in the sense of "subject positions" within a discursive structure. Subjects cannot, therefore, be the origin of social relations—not even in the limited sense of

being endowed with powers that render an experience possible—as all "experience" depends on precise discursive conditions of possibility.[8]

Subject positions are the products of certain discursive structures. This discursive structure is very similar to the concept of habitus. Therefore, I will not spend time discussing it. The term "subject positions" indicates that human subjects or individuals are shaped by their place within a habitus or discursive structure. For example, racial identity is a function of a racialized narrative (which is a function of a particular discursive structure). However, no "subject position" is simply fixed and final. They are malleable insofar as each subject position has certain limitations (which are also features of the discursive structure) that preclude the complete determination of the subject.

Subject positions shift as social and political practices and discourses shift. These shifts are due to several factors. For example, the meaning of race and racial identity will shift as one moves from one geographical space to another. Another shift is caused by one's attempt to manage the social contradictions by which one has been constituted. For example, in the United States, Blacks were made to feel morally inferior to Whites. However, to maintain order, Whites forced Blacks to accept their moral code of conduct which seems to suggest that Blacks were capable of understanding and conforming to the White moral code of conduct.[9] Finally, subject positions tend to shift because one occupies a multiplicity of social positions, which, from time to time, are in conflict with one another and tend to shift as public opinion about these positions shifts. Therefore, it is possible, and often is the case, that one may be an oppressor and oppressed at the same time. For example, as a Black male in the U.S.A., I occupy the subject position of the oppressed (in terms of my relation to Whites), or, at least, as a member of an oppressed group. However, as a heterosexual in an antigay society, I occupy the position of oppressor. Even though I support gay rights, I still benefit from heterosexual privilege. I have never had to fight for the right to marry whom I love. So, our society is structured in such a way that marriage is not a problem for me. This is not the case for members of the gay/lesbian community. We can also break down subject positions in terms of class privilege, gender privilege, and so on. The acquisition of the four forms of capital that I discussed earlier also has an effect on one's subject position regarding group membership. Hence, although I might be pro gay rights or pro women's rights, I still share privileges with those who may be sexist and antigay.

The recognition of various subject positions and their malleability is very important for my second teaching strategy, and it complements my notion of preemptive forgiveness. It keeps the conversation within the larger discussion of struggles for social justice by requiring the students to reflect on their on multiple subject positions, and where they may be a member of an oppressor group and where they may be a member of an oppressed group. It also takes away their ability to reduce my critique of racism to a mere personal problem, as I, too, must critique my own subject position as unintentional oppressor in relation to women, gay people, and so on.

The two strategies that I have discussed, and the necessary understanding of the social and psychological position of Whites, have brought me great success in getting White students to discuss race and see it as a real problem. The success has been so great that, years ago, some of my colleagues suggested that I publish something on this approach. I never had the time to sit and reflect on my approach for the purpose of writing until now. I can only hope that others may try this approach and have the kind of success that I have had with it for almost two decades.

Notes

1 Michael Eric Dyson, "Giving Whiteness a Black Eye: Excavating White Identities, Ideologies, and Institutions," in *Open Mike: Reflections on Philosophy, Race, Sex, Culture, and Religion* (New York, NY: Basic Civitas Books, 2003), 112.

2 Pierre Bourdieu, *The Logic of Practice*, trans. Richard Nice (Stanford, CA: Stanford University Press, 1990), 58–59.

3 Ibid, 60–61.

4 For a more detailed examination of Black exceptionalism and its racist implications, see Arnold Lorenzo Farr's "The Smartest Black Man in Union, South Carolina: Complimentary Racism and the Dialectic of Marginalization," in *Marginal Groups and Mainstream American Culture*, eds. Yolanda Estes, Arnold Lorenzo Farr, Patricia Smith, and Clelia Smyth (Lawrence, KS: University Press of Kansas, 2000), 111–119.

5 Pierre Bourdieu and Loïc J. D. Wacquant, *An Invitation to Reflective Sociology* (Chicago, IL: University of Chicago Press, 1992), 118–119.

6 For example, in South Carolina, a law was passed, in 1740, that made it illegal for Blacks to learn to read or write. This allowed Whites to accumulate various forms of capital (especially education) that they could pass on to their offspring while Blacks could accumulate no capital whatsoever to pass on. Hence, very early on, an advantage was bestowed upon White children that gave them long-term advantages over Black children and their offspring. See Henry Louis Gates, Jr., "Writing 'Race' and the Difference It Makes," in *"Race," Writing, and Difference*, ed. Henry Louis Gates, Jr. (Chicago, IL: University of Chicago Press, 1985), 9.

7 I borrow the term "epistemologies of ignorance" from Shannon Sullivan and Nancy Tuana. See their edited volume *Race and Epistemologies of Ignorance* (Albany, NY: State University of New York Press, 2007). The term "epistemology of ignorance" was actually coined by Charles W. Mills in his *The Racial Contract* (Ithaca, NY: Cornell University Press, 1997), 18.

8 Ernesto Laclau and Chantal Mouffe, *Hegemony and Socialist Strategy: Towards a Radical Democratic Politics*, 2nd ed. (London, England: Verso, 2001), 115.

9 See Arnold Farr's discussion of the critical function of marginalization in *Marginal Groups and Mainstream American Culture*, 111–119.

9

ON WHY RACE MATTERS

Teaching the Relevance of the Semantics and Ontology of Race

Clevis Headley

This chapter defends the philosophical importance of teaching the semantics and ontology of race in opposition to those thinkers who are dismissive of race on the grounds that race is semantically and ontologically derelict. In sanctioning the philosophical respectability and credibility of race, I draw upon some of the ideas and strategies I have utilized in teaching race, some of the recurrent assumptions about race that students bring into the classroom, and some of the substantive insights emergent from my teaching regarding the philosophical status of race.

Before I drive headlong into the body of this chapter, it is important to register a few brief observations about the status of race. There exists a mythology about race in our culture. This mythology, among other things, consists of clusters of assumptions, presuppositions, conceptions, practices, rituals, metaphors and beliefs. Like other mythologies, our mythology of race facilitates ways of making sense of diverse and often chaotic social, cultural, historical, and political phenomena. And, although questions about the truth or falsity of this mythology itself are philosophically idle, a condition characteristic of all mythologies, we use this mythology to determine the truth condition of individual statements about race. Our mythology makes possible styles of thinking about race; indeed, we modify our style of thinking about race in relation to the foundational and structural shifts in our cultural mythology of race.

Like all mythologies, our mythology of race claims no hegemonic consistency. Perhaps it would be more accurate to describe this mythology as schizophrenic rather than as contradictory. Nevertheless, the basic conservative epistemological inclination of human agents to avoid making radical changes to their belief system functions to maintain overall epistemological stability. This much is obvious, since this human characteristic gradually and very slowly integrates ideas or experiences that would severely disrupt the stability of our mythology of race.

Currently, there are at least four major features of our mythology of race worthy of recognition. First, it is almost axiomatic today to hear the effortless repetition of the idea that appeals to race constitute a new racism, or, rather, that such activity is racist if not by design then as a consequence of such activity. In other words, uses of race, appeals to race to interpret or to render meaningful contested aspects of our political, social, and/or economic practices are declared racist. Second, within the discipline of philosophy, the reigning consensus is that race is an illegitimate concept, a concept deformed by impeachable semantic and ontological imperfections. Third, even as there are great pressures, ranging from the cultural to the scholarly, to transcend race, racism remains a persistent feature of daily life. So entrenched is racism that basic indicators of social well-being indicate greater and greater disparities in health, education, housing, and wealth between Whites and Blacks. And, fourth, despite the above claims, race remains a potent cognitive reality infused in the everyday lives of individuals, a persistent structural feature present in every aspect of daily existence. It seems that, as the calls for the end of race become more repetitive and aggressive, race takes on the ontological profile of an apparition. Indeed, it would not be too much of a stretch to draw an analogy here between the calls for the demise of race and Nietzsche's observation regarding the death of God. We recall Nietzsche's poignant observation that, although God is dead, the shadows of God still remain. So, God's presence remains even if it is the case that belief in God is no longer sustainable. Similarly, even as we witness obituaries of race, as it were, the shadows of race persist, indicating that we are far from being done with race.

The general structure of this chapter is as follows: the first section tells the story of an encounter with a student; the second section focuses on some of the challenges Black philosophers confront with regard to teaching philosophy; the third section investigates issues related to the notion of false clarity with regard to race; the fourth section concerns strategies to promote racial literacy as an antidote to notions of color blindness; section five concerns the importance of enabling students to appreciate how an appropriate understanding of race is beneficial for understanding their everyday existence; section six tackles the semantics and ontology of race, focusing on the constitutive status of race; section seven inserts race into the contested context of political philosophy, with the aim of establishing the analytical veracity of race in illuminating our political reality; and, finally, section eight examines some of the concerns emergent from the relation between race and the discipline of philosophy.

Why Race Matters

Cornel West recently visited my university to deliver a lecture to a mixed audience of faculty, students, administrators, community leaders, and the general public. Due to the hybrid nature of the audience, West delivered a lecture that, he hoped, would resonate with the various groups constituting the audience. West, being probably the most gifted orator in the United States, did an amazing job of underscoring, among other things, the importance and relevance of philosophy, the importance of civic engagement and responsibility, and the importance of carrying on the infinite struggle against all forms of hatred, prejudice, and bigotry. He also called specific attention to the enduring legacy of slavery and the persistence of racism in American history and society, and sought to explain the importance of critically confronting the past in the attempt to build a better world. And, finally, he underscored the relevance of race as a category of analysis, as well as an existential mode of being. West enunciated this latter point by referencing the African American blues and jazz musical traditions.

I have mentioned West's visit and lecture in order to underscore the haunting problematics of critically engaging race and racism in the American academy. About two days following West's visit, one of my more advanced students, a White male in his early fifties, approached me. He had previously owned a business, fell on hard times, and decided to earn his college degree. This student very politely expressed his exasperation about the lecture, for, according to him, talk about slavery, racism, and race was very unhelpful; indeed, he added that it is this kind of discourse that contributes to the persistent blemish of racism. While speaking with a sense of unmitigated confidence, and seemingly convinced by the progressive thrust of his thinking, he effortlessly declared racism and considerations of race as best located in the past, an irrelevant past precisely because we now have a Black president. Obama's election to the presidency, according to him, is evidence enough to establish a collective societal maturity in transcending the vile limitations of race. Indeed, this student quickly informed me that, when he observes both West and me, he does not constitute us as Black men. Somehow, our level of education has miraculously rendered us "raceless." Hence, as my student proceeded to convey to me that to describe myself as Black, to race myself, is to reduce my standing as an individual.

I have mentioned my encounter with this student precisely because he is a paradigmatic representative of the liberal view of race. Liberalism urges each individual to adopt a posture of color blindness. Not seeing race is a very important and effective way to preclude treating individuals on the basis of irrelevant physical characteristics. Furthermore, as liberalism instructs us, racism persists to the extent that talk of race remains a prominent feature of our social and political discourse.[1] Indeed, liberalism formally frames, as well as substantively determines, the content of our mythology of race. Hence, liberalism encourages us to join in the celebration of a postracist society; we have reached the telos of antiracist struggle in actualizing a society where race, at best, qualifies as a semantic and ontological fiction.

As previously stated, I discuss some of the strategies I use to defend the importance of understanding race not as some unfortunate concern, capable of gaining only the support of those unlucky and uneducated individuals who are seduced by its promiscuous appeal. I defend race as a legitimate category of interpretation and analysis. Furthermore, I also defend race as a lived reality that cannot be eliminated, abolished, or transcended, either because it is as a matter of personal choice or through the utilization of a sterile logic, which exposes its unsavory contradictions, confusions, and ambiguities.

Race and Racism in the American Academy

Teaching philosophy in predominately White North American universities offers great professional opportunities to Black philosophers. At the same time, many obstacles confront Black philosophers engaged in this professional undertaking.[2] The "disability" is acute for the Black philosophy professor precisely because of the transcultural embedded stereotypes regarding the analytical "incapacities" of African peoples. We are told that philosophy requires high levels of abstract and analytical thinking, and, since Blacks are predisposed to be highly emotional and excessively sensual in their basic mode of being, they are incapable of reaching the requisite degree of cognitive detachment and logical distance from raw emotion and subjective experience, as required by the conceptuality and universality of philosophy. While Blacks easily succeed in music and in other "softer" academic fields, they struggle in the more analytically demanding disciplines, such as philosophy.

There is a certain double jeopardy, perhaps a species of Du Bois's notion of double consciousness, which already frames the vocation of the Black philosophy professor. First, the Black professor of philosophy must also contend with what Miranda Fricker identifies as testimonial injustice. Fricker variously defines testimonial injustice as the harm or wrong a speaker suffers because of the prejudice of a hearer who believes that the speaker lacks epistemic credibility. In Fricker's own words, testimonial injustice is "[t]he basic idea ... that a speaker suffers a testimonial injustice just if prejudice on the hearer's part causes him [or her] to give the speaker less credibility than he [or she] would otherwise have given."[3] This projection of epistemic incapacity imposes upon the Black professor of philosophy unsavory burdens that his White colleagues need not contemplate or confront as serious challenges. Fricker also maintains that an individual can similarly suffer if one is granted too much epistemic credibility. For even when Black professors of philosophy are recipients of epistemic credibility, they are still severely restricted to serving only as experts on race and judged as insufficiently competent to excel in other areas of philosophy with the requisite degree of analytical rigor and competence.

The Black professor of philosophy must contend not only with hermeneutical injustice, but must also navigate an additional burden. The dissonant call to denounce race as a fiction, totally devoid of cognitive validity, and also as incapable of serving as a legitimate category of analysis, inflicts hermeneutical injustice on the Black professor of philosophy. Fricker variously describes hermeneutical injustice as occurring when a group is disadvantaged by fact that it lacks the appropriate concepts to understand aspects of its social experience. Here, the focus is on the relative depressed and inadequate epistemic resources and productive potential of a subordinated group in comparison to other groups that control greater disproportionate epistemic resources. Clearly, nullification of the use of race by Blacks to make sense of their being-in-the-world is tantamount to imposing an insurmountable epistemic burden on them. Indeed, this idea is really an invitation for Blacks to impose upon themselves a crippling epistemological crisis, for, in surrendering the analytical as well as the existential capabilities of race, Blacks would, thereby, render a significant portion of their existence, particularly their identity and history, epistemologically opaque and existentially fraudulent.

Teaching Race: The Notion of False Clarity

As previously stated, I describe the various strategies I employ to promote relevant epistemic issues and normative values when teaching race. Put differently, I teach about race partly to unsettle the racial illiteracy that prevents most students from entertaining or expressing ideas that cannot be adequately expressed in the cognitive system of assumptions, principles, and categories that make possible the dominant paradigm of race. I also teach about race to encourage students to think beyond the reigning dominant mythology of race in order to imagine alternative styles of thinking that would be more conducive to a rethinking of the reality of race, as well as appreciative of its analytical force. We should note that, according to the dominant view, it is not permissible to describe individuals as belonging to a race. Rather, our challenge is to treat individuals qua individuals as moral and political equals. This dominant view holds that race is not real because, among other things, it is not an essential feature of what makes a person the person that he or she is; hence, race is an illegitimate concept. Since race is not really real, talk about race promotes racism or else cynically encourages efforts to "play the race card" and inflame racial hostility. Another aspect of this dominant view is the effortless exploitation of the metaphor of color blindness, urging that we should all struggle not to see the accidental features of individuals such as skin color. Race, accordingly, is an irrelevant external feature of individuals, best relegated to the status of an accident of one's private history.

There is a false clarity underpinning the dissemination of the dominant liberal view of race. The admonition to view society as a collection or aggregate of isolated individuals, occupying a level plane where diverse opportunities and goods await distribution on the basis of merit, as determined by a fair and open competition, advertises a certain simplistic view of society that promotes a false clarity and confidence. A serious problem emerges from promoting false clarity. Instead of illuminating the complexities of the sociocultural world, false clarity distorts these dense complexities. Those who present a view of the sociocultural world as representative of the outcome of fair competition for resources among free and rational individuals invite us to accept existing economic and political outcomes as natural and fair. In this conception of things, race, as announced by many adherents of formal equality, plays no significant causal or explanatory role, since individuals compete as isolated individuals and not as representative members of particular races. However, this tendency to exile race from our understanding of things is, ironically, just another strategy to code racist motivations in the neutral language of formal equality, equal opportunity, and individualism. As will be made clear in this chapter, failure to recognize the materiality of race is to indirectly support the more sinister consequences of racial practices.

Another insidious feature of false clarity about race is the uncritical embrace of an epistemology of ignorance.[4] Among other things, the epistemology of ignorance actively promotes a false or distorted perception of reality, either because of the discomfort of acknowledging certain facts about the world or the willingness not to know certain things because of the fear that this knowledge would unsettle one's perception of the world. From another context, we can think of the epistemology of ignorance as a collective agreement not to know, an agreement to misinterpret the world by deliberately ignoring or discrediting knowledge that would cause us to face hard truths about the system that we live in. As is to be expected, dominant groups conspicuously benefiting from the strategic misinterpretation of things, or strategic blindness not to see certain things, usually consider these various distortions or one-sided descriptions as acceptable. Ultimately, even our dominant political discourse crystallizes around clusters of misinterpretations that structurally cohere with the functioning of a system of social, economic, and political arrangements that reinforce the power and vested interests of dominant groups.

Racial Literacy as an Antidote to Color Blindness

My antidote to color blindness—a cognitive condition that ultimately mutates into cognitive disorientation—is to promote racial literacy; that is, the critical ability to read and interpret the world through the category of race. Without assuming race to be an objective feature of the physical world, I emphasize the fact that the sociocultural world is a human construction, or, in Kantian language, constituted by a network of concepts, categories, social practices, and institutional arrangements. Consequently, since race is part of the sociocultural world, race too is a construction that is socially, culturally, and existentially real, even if race is not empirically real and observable in a manner similar to the perception of physical objects. The reality of race does not depend on whether or not race is an objective feature of the world, precisely because race acquires legitimacy as a root metaphor by which the sociocultural world, among other things, became a human achievement.

I develop the preceding claims by calling attention to the use of language. Here, I challenge the dominance of realism, the view that there is an objective world existing totally independently of our language and concepts. Furthermore, that an objective world exists and its ontological structure is totally indifferent to the structuring powers of human consciousness. Since the world is independent of language, the role of language is to passively mirror or represent the world as it is; the structure of language should be isomorphic with the structure of the world. A basic tenet of this realist conception of things is that the primary purpose of language is to state facts and to say what is true. Language's primary goal is informational. Within the context of race, I discuss the fact that language is not merely a passive medium or a blunt tool restricted to expressing true statements. Language also functions in nonliteral modes; specifically, a system of metaphors. We use language as a vehicle of semantic extension, a cognitive device to describe one thing in terms of another. Language is also performative, as described by speech act theory. In the slogan of speech act theory, we do things with words;[5] language is actional by virtue of the fact that it can alter the affectivity of place or space, and it also ontologically inspires the diachronic presence of various discreet entities. Language conjures beings into existence. For example, an individual, or a group of individuals, can mobilize racist language to harm (psychologically harm) or to dehumanize others. This use of language is not fact stating. Rather, in this case, it is utilized to bring about certain effects in the world. Consequently, the semantic validity of racist language is not contingent upon whether or not race claims an objective ontological status. Such language gains its semantic authority from the cluster of patterns of intentions, beliefs, practices, structures of feelings, and so forth of human beings.

Racial Literacy as an Antidote to Hermeneutical Injustice

Racial literacy also has the potential to enable students to avoid two incapacities: (a) the inability to correctly and effectively understand the everyday materiality, or reality, of race, and (b) a cultivated inability to meaningfully discuss the general semantics and ontology of race. I explain to students that these incapacities make them victims of hermeneutical injustice, the injustice of lacking the necessary concepts for understanding a significant area of their social experience.[6] This hermeneutical deficit prevents one from gaining access to crucial aspects of self-understanding. For example, we can imagine the existential and epistemic vertigo that can paralyze an individual who lives in a world in which race is persistent, but the individual lacks a competent understanding of the role of race in shaping the affairs of daily life. The trauma associated with the realization and awareness that one is indeed raced can be particularly troubling, especially if one previously lived in an environment that sheltered one from the practicality of understanding themselves as raced.

Michael Monahan, in his recent bold philosophical defense of the reality of race against the racial abolitionists and racial eliminativists, has enforced the inescapability of race and why attempts to transcend race are destined to fail.

Race, according to Monahan, is not an annoying, irrelevant, and insidious contingent property of persons that ought to be rejected. As he writes:

> One's racial being ... is not a fixed and given essence—it is neither a property that we simply possess, nor is it a strictly contingent activity that we can choose to abandon. It is ... more a sort of location or context, and it is in this way, as inevitably conditioning one's subjectivity, that racial reality must be understood. One's Whiteness, Blackness, Asianness ... is not something that can *be* purely in the way the politics of purity would have us believe, but it is also impossible for one to purely *not be* raced, or simply decide by voluntary fiat *how* one is raced.[7]

We are all raced in that we are born into a human reality infused by race. However, our race is not a dangerous fiction. And as Monahan states in a different context:

> Race is something that we *do* not something that we *are*, and it is, importantly, something that we always do in concert with others, whose ways of doing race inevitably shape the ways in which we are able to do (or *not* do) race.[8]

The claim that race is inescapable, as to be expected, is bitterly resented by many White students, mainly because of the perception that Whites are raceless and also because of the unquestioned normativity of whiteness. Indeed, White students often articulate their protest against race in terms of their not being responsible for the sins of the past. At these times, I often resort to the philosophical uses of history for the purpose of getting students to understand that, although they were not present at the founding of the United States as a sovereign entity, they have been born into a society in which White skin color has been privileged. The point is not that each and every White individual in the past and in the present has been successful in accumulating disproportionate amounts of wealth and opportunities, but that White skin color has historically been used as a marker for access to wealth and opportunities. Du Bois's "Psychological wages of whiteness,"[9] Cheryl Harris's notion of "whiteness as property,"[10] and George Lipsitz's notion of the "possessive investment in whiteness" are but three examples of this phenomenon.[11] It should be noted that I introduce these ideas not for the sake of alienating my White students, but to set them on the path of working through, as well as critically engaging with, their inherited historical traditions in the hope that they will gain a critical appreciation of how race has infused these diverse traditions.

With regard to hermeneutical injustice, I also address why a distorted appreciation of the relevance of race can aggravate interactions among groups that are racially designated as Black. Some individuals who are phenotypically Black resist racial categorization by announcing that they are not African American, and that, since they are not African American by birth, then they should not be classified as Black. The opposition is further amplified by the claim that those who consider all people of African descent as being of the same race are racist because they assume that all people of African descent are identical in all regards.

I intervene in this protest against racial classification by communicating to students the importance of understanding, as well as appreciating, the difference between race and ethnicity. On the one hand, I explain that race, despite being a social construction, is also vaguely correlated with the biological features of a person; that is, there is some degree of ontological reciprocity between the sociocultural and the biological. But I am careful to communicate to students that even this modest appeal to biology is not an appeal to biological essentialism about race. Rather, it makes race a biosocial concept. I also explain the appropriateness of appealing to biology in this context by invoking such notions as geographical isolation and biological mutation. I critically discuss how these notions clarify the tangled dynamics of biology, culture, and history, a tangled relationship that sustains the emergence of groups with different genetic histories.

On the other hand, I explain that ethnicity is a cultural category, dependent upon linguistic, religious, dietary, musical, and other differences between groups. For example, African Americans and Haitians are of the same race; namely, Black. However, they are of different ethnicities, precisely because of differences in religion, language, music, and tradition of food, among other things.

Another important point that I discuss regarding the difference between race and ethnicity is the legal imperative of racial classification. I have encountered many students, both Black and White, who are highly offended by requests for racial self-identification. Again, I explain to students that the main reason why this information is requested is not because the government has an interest in pressuring individuals to identify themselves racially even if individuals are in principle opposed to such self-identification. I explain that the purpose of racial self-identification is intimately connected with the enforcement of various regimes of civil rights and antidiscrimination laws. For example, plaintiffs in a class-action antidiscrimination lawsuit, among other things, must materially establish that they suffered harm caused by the racial discrimination of an employer, and that this harm in question was due mainly to their racial identification. An effective way to establish that harm has been done is to, among other things, review and critically scrutinize the history of the employer's interactions with the group in question. One way to obtain this information would be to review job applications to detect possible patterns of discrimination, and this method would certainly focus on racial identification.

Appreciating the difference between race and ethnicity enables students to understand why practices of racial classification need not suggest that all individuals so designated share a common culture, or religion, or even language. At the same time, I also critically discuss why it is unrealistic to expect that sociocultural concepts, such as race, will determinately possess clear and discrete boundaries. Indeed, I underscore the fact that race and ethnicity, as sociocultural concepts, are often contradictory, contested, indeterminate, and fuzzy. However, these characteristics neither render these concepts illegitimate nor do they nullify their application.

The Semantics and Ontology of Race

In underscoring the constitutivity of race—namely, its semantic and ontological contestability—I also endeavor to provide students with a dynamic understanding of racism, one that I hope would vastly equip them to better appreciate its contestability and contradictory profile. Put simply, racism is not merely or primarily a personal or individual issue; neither is racism an exclusively private phenomenon of isolated individual prejudice, the mere expression of individual preferences. Of course, it should be noted that there is individual-based racism, but this kind of racism need not be considered the paradigmatic case of racism. Nevertheless, the question is precisely how wide ranging are the effects of individual racist behavior compared to the effects of insidious institutional racism?

Nevertheless, in the attempt to distance racism from a strictly individual modality, I am careful to establish why racism exists even if there are no individual racists. Racism can persist and flourish without the existence of self-identified racists.[12] The common view is that racism is an individual incapacity such that a racist individual is an individual who holds insidious and vile beliefs about other individuals because of their race. Racism, in this view, is commonly framed as an internal, private state of consciousness; once again, considered primarily as an individual phenomenon. Instead of defending this individualistic model of racism, I attempt to lead students to appreciate racism as an institutional phenomenon in which people with good intentions can, through the apparently neutral functioning of institutions, engage in practices with crippling negative racial impact.[13] This institutional approach to racism underscores racism as an external phenomenon in the sense that, once again, racist structures are not located in the minds of isolated individuals, but are manifestations of deep and recalcitrant structures of inclusion and exclusion affecting the outcome of complex social, political, and economic interactions. In other words, racism is not the manifestation of some rational incapacity or an unfortunate psychological defect; rather, it is institutional in the sense that individuals do not exist in a void. Their behavior, values, goals, and so on are shaped and constituted by the various human practices that constitute the life-world of human existence. The basis of racism is not merely or primarily biologically determined, but is socially inspired and facilitated, and this fact underscores the intimate and dynamic connection between the individual and external normative structures.

In appealing to institutional racism, I make it clear to students that, unlike Jim Crow racism, which was visible, public, and legally sanctioned, institutional racism is not always visible and public in the same way, precisely because it often hides behind the rhetoric of neutrality. Furthermore, unlike individual-based racism, which is primarily motivated by intent, institutional racism is not necessarily motivated by racist intentions. Institutional racism is, among other things, the negative racial impact inflicted upon certain groups as a consequence of the implementation of racially neutral policies. For example, residential segregation resulting from the neutral operations of the real estate market—meaning the operation of the real estate market in accordance with the laws of supply and demands and freed of any legal barriers based upon accidental features of an individual—can have a devastating impact upon Blacks. This harm usually takes the form of Blacks not enjoying adequate access to educational opportunities and to the job market. Again, ample evidence confirms two significant facts about segregated, poor communities: they do not attract new businesses, and their schools are usually savagely underfunded and poorly staffed. Clearly, then, the negative racial impact resulting from neutral practices occur without there necessarily being individuals with malignant racial motives, seeking to distort the housing market to disproportionately favor Whites. But, again, it is important to note that to focus on institutional racism does not necessarily entail the rejection of individual racism.

Race and Political Philosophy

Another reason for emphasizing the semantic legitimacy of race and its onto-logical reality is to empower students to become more competent readers and interpreters of the political world. While political liberalism preaches the virtues of individualism, I encourage students to question this view of political reality. Again, I discuss how the gospel of liberal individualism obscures the structures of opportunities that excessively benefit dominant social groups while severely limiting the opportunities available to historically subordinated groups. Appeals to individualism and the relevant modalities of individual responsibility and individual merit give rise to the false notion that race does not matter and that there is a level playing field of competition. The problem, however, is that liberal individualism cannot explain the disparities in wealth, education, health, and opportunities between Whites and Blacks in terms of natural individual differences in talents and skills.[14] Liberal individualism invites us to embrace a false equivalence between Blacks and Whites as participating in a fair competition, while failing to confront the structural differentials that relegate Blacks to subordinate positions. In this context, in order to underscore the persistent reality of race, it becomes important to deflate excessive appeals to individual responsibility and individual failure, potent notions that serve the purpose of shifting blame to Blacks for failing to exercise the requisite initiative to take advantage of opportunities. We are often told that, since Blacks tend to view themselves as a collective political entity, they complacently depend upon the government to better their situation. However, this kind of collective political redemption will never materialize, precisely because American political ideology is grounded in a social ontology of individuals and not groups; only individuals are legitimate political actors.

Although it would be absurd to totally deny the limited relevance of individual accountability, I underscore the existence of enduring patterns of racial discrimination and inequality that render idle efforts to discount entrenched historical structures of racial discrimination.[15] Indeed, there is the risk of practicing blindness to history, which would prevent one from effectively perceiving how race remains a major factor in determining differences in outcome between Blacks and Whites.[16]

I also attempt to connect the plausibility of race to the collective behavior of groups. Far from society being a stage of dramatic individualistic competition, a competition open to all individuals regardless of race, it is, rather, a stage of competition among groups seeking to maintain group privileges across a wide spectrum of goods and opportunities. In this case, what emerges is that Whites, as a racial group, engage in the opportunity of hoarding resources.[17] This phenomenon can be explained in terms of the control of major institutions, on all levels of society, by Whites. This resort to the notion of hoarding, I argue, is necessary because it explains the constant condemnation of policies crafted to provide opportunities to Blacks. Such policies are said to involve programs that unfairly harm Whites by denying them equal access to opportunities; hence, the discourse of reverse discrimination.

Indeed, appeals to reverse discrimination unnecessarily amplify attempts to articulate an unbiased commitment to fairness and equality. I explain to my students that it is important to respond to dogmatic appeals to reverse discrimination by establishing that these appeals, even if unintended, are really attempts to privilege the notions of individualism and individual merit. A basic narrative emerges from when these notions are taken as foundational to our political discourse. This narrative takes the following form: If society is truly, or, at least, should be, an arena of fair competition among individuals, then the government should not create laws that privilege any racial group. And, if past discrimination against Blacks was wrong, to adopt laws favoring or granting Blacks special privileges that are not extended to Whites is also wrong. Hence, affirmative action, to the extent that it is a group-based program and that it privileges Blacks over Whites, it is a form of discrimination against Whites; affirmative action is reverse discrimination. I point out that the problem with equating affirmative action with reverse discrimination is the attempt to establish a false equivalence. Efforts to provide Blacks with opportunities and to eliminate the negative effects of racial discrimination are not equivalent to the historical project to establish White supremacy and the normativity of whiteness. Affirmative action is not intended to send a message of racial subordination or of inferiority to Whites, as was the case with the legally sanctioned practice of Jim Crow.

The discrimination Blacks faced was categorical and universal in scope. Furthermore, it was not some unfortunate deviation from the norm, but, rather, historically sanctioned as legal, even by the government of the United States. Blacks were denied opportunities to obtain education, accumulate wealth, secure decent housing, gain access to and even secure political power. Acts of discrimination directed at Blacks were meant to send a message, a message of inferiority. Affirmative action is radically different from antiblack discrimination because its main purpose is not to universally exclude Whites from participating as full citizens in society. Affirmative action is not a form of antiwhite racism. Neither is affirmative action an attempt to severely limit access by Whites to education, jobs, housing, health care, and so on. Far from demanding that Blacks should be hired in preference to Whites, it merely encourages employers to take affirmative steps to actively reach potential Black applicants when there are vacancies, specifically in light of the reality that Blacks were and continue to be discriminated against based upon their racial identity. And, even if an employer desires to hire a Black candidate, they must hire a qualified candidate and not the first Black applicant. Affirmative action communicates no message of racial inferiority to Whites.

Finally, in my efforts to weaken the attractiveness of appeals to individualism, merit, and personal responsibility, I introduce Charles Mills's notion of the racial contract to expose the hollow core of concepts such as formal equality of opportunity when such concepts are extricated from the flow of history.[18] We recall that the purpose of social contract theory was, among other things, to explain legitimate authority and why free, rational, and self-interested individuals have an obligation to obey the laws and commands of a group calling itself the government. The basic narrative of social contract theory is that individuals voluntarily entered into an agreement to assume the burden of obeying laws in order to enjoy certain mutual benefits. On the social contract view, since the government is an expression of the will of the people, the people are obligated to follow and obey the rules enacted by the government.

Mills challenged the basic methodological assumptions of the social contract theory, arguing that in its bleached philosophical guise, it does not convincingly explain modern society. Rather, Mills favors the metaphor of the racial contract, precisely because, as he claims, it does a better job of explaining what has been going on in modern society. In Mills's view, Blacks were not equal participants in the social contract; the contract was an agreement among Whites. To the extent that Blacks participated, they participated primarily as objects and not subjects of the contract. The agreement among Whites recognized Blacks not as persons but as property, as slaves and not as free, rational, and self-interested individuals. The importance of introducing Mills's conception of the racial contract to my students, among other things, is to deflate pretensions of individual accomplishment, to underscore the ontological prominence of race for an adequate understanding of modern society, and to expose the invisibility of whiteness as normativity.

Clearly, then, one goal of my efforts is to lead students to the realization that race is neither some idiosyncratic feature of one's private history nor a matter of personal, subjective preference that one can choose either to ignore or to recognize. Rather, race emerges as an objective phenomenon with its own autonomous ontological status. This development suggests that understanding race also requires situating race in the broader context of the historical narratives that constitute the structures of intelligibility that render our various practices, institutions, and conceptions of selfhood meaningful.

Finally, as previously stated, I teach that the concept of race, although an intersubjective construction, nevertheless enjoys a degree of autonomy. Concepts need not answer to some objective reality in order to possess semantic and ontological sovereignty. Consider the fact that although the name "Hamlet" does not refer to an actual individual, there exists in our culture a set of descriptions and even an identity that we associate with this proper name. The name represents a cluster of ideas about human existence and questions about the meaning of life that can provide an individual with some degree of cognitive guidance in the midst of an epistemological crisis. The literary tradition of teaching the play *Hamlet* does not excessively display an obsessive interest in determining whether or not an actual individual answering to the name "Hamlet" existed.

Consequently, just as the name "Hamlet" need not designate an actual individual in order to function in the multiple ways it does in our culture, similarly, concepts such as race are objectivities that exert a tremendous amount of power, totally independently of whether they refer to determinate objects in the world.

Race and Philosophy

I want to conclude by briefly discussing some of the philosophical points I share with students regarding the relationship between race and philosophy. With regard to the ontological status of race, I do not advocate either the elimination or the abolition of race. Although both eliminativists and abolitionists have denounced race on grounds of its semantic and ontological deficiencies, I approach race as a sociocultural concept and, therefore, apply different semantic and ontological requirements to race. One highly plausible theoretical approach to the ontology of race is dynamic nominalism, as formulated by Ian Hacking.[19] Hacking calls his position "dynamic nominalism" because he connects nominalism with our interaction with, and description of, the world. Hence, he maintains that categories of people come into being at the same time as the people falling under those categories, and that there is a reciprocal relation between these processes. Applying the insights of dynamic nominalism, we can infer that an individual's racial identity does not exist independently of socially constructed categories such as Whiteness or Blackness. Consequently, the status of these terms cannot be decided totally independently of human activities.

There are other issues warranting a brief consideration with regard to the relations between race and philosophy. Indeed, these concerns are methodological insofar as they relate to the question of method in philosophy. Here, I am limiting my focus to the practice of analytic philosophy and the amplification of logical analysis as the most effective style of philosophical practice. Of course, it should be noted that the point is not meant to repudiate the uncontested importance of logical analysis within philosophy. My concern is to expose the bad faith of philosophical practice when philosophy is reduced to the clarification of meaning, a task motivated on the questionable assumption that natural language desperately needs comprehensive logical overhauling in order to determine and conclusively fix the meaning of our concepts. This demand for necessary and sufficient conditions of the meaning of terms breeds a fascination with logical and linguistic analysis that ultimately lead to the denigration of certain concepts, concepts such as race, insofar as they cannot be tamed by the regimentation of either rigorous logical or linguistic analysis. The fetishizing of analysis geared towards the necessary and sufficient conditions for the use or application of terms leads to a search for concepts with sharp and definite boundaries. This rhetoric of meaning, which stipulates that legitimate concepts should possess sharp and clearly defined boundaries, prevents us from appreciating the extent to which certain concepts fulfill all the semantic and ontological work they are called to perform, even as they admit to being indeterminate, contested, and, at times, stubbornly ambiguous. What, in one view, qualifies as semantic blemishes, are, on another view, virtues that accommodate the flux and change of the everyday world, the sociocultural world, of existence. In other words, instead of seeking to determine the validity of concepts in terms of the pure, formal categories of logic, it seems that concepts such as race should be understood in terms of experience-centered categories; which is to say, naturalistically.

Closely connected to the fetishizing of analysis is the problem of scientism; that is, science as ideology.[20] In this context, the issue is to curtail the extension of a certain imperial practice of colonizing all areas of philosophy through the expansion of the methods, the semantics, and ontological presuppositions of the natural sciences. The proponents of this kind of naturalism confidently advocate that science provides the most plausible methods for ascertaining meaning, truth, and knowledge. Armed with these assumptions, many philosophers adopt the conceptual framework of natural kinds that stipulate such terms as the paradigmatic case of legitimate concepts. Fiercely parading the notion that natural kinds terminology designates entities existing independently in the world and that are identified by virtue of possessing a molecular essence, race is declared semantically counterfeit and ontologically fictitious precisely because there are no essences that determinately identify unique races. Again, we see the tendency to denounce race as philosophically suspect, for, in this case, race is declared unreal because it does not satisfy the standards stipulated for a concept to be a bona fide scientific concept. Race fails to be a natural kind term.

A final disability of philosophy's failure to deal with race, a failure that I attempt to communicate to students, stems from the tendency of some philosophers to denigrate the sociocultural world, as well as the contingency of human existence itself. In emphasizing the importance of objectivity, universality, and the a priori status of consciousness, these philosophers encourage a defiling of the materiality and sociality of human life. The point here is not that we should naïvely and uncritically attach ourselves to the prejudices, biases, and unreflective frames of mind that dominate our complacent mode of existence. Rather, as reflective agents, we should seek to overcome the various distractions that compete for our attention and that seek to compromise the quality of our thinking. Nevertheless, the assumption that we can only successfully achieve these tasks by decisively escaping the reality of our being embedded in networks of human practices, discourses, rituals, and so on is to invite the picture of human life as a life from a God's-eye perspective. This picture of unencumbered human consciousness, a transcendental consciousness hovering above the realm of being, as it were, must inevitably dismiss the lived reality of race.

George Yancy has called attention to the otherwise concrete, existential status of race as a lived reality. Yancy focuses, among other things, on the issue of Black subjectivity and investigates the extent to which the black body has traditionally served as the site of various condescending and dehumanizing stereotypes that the dominant culture has traditionally associated with Black existence. Excavating the dense layers of stereotypes that have crushed visions of Black subjectivity cannot be accomplished through the execution of a philosophical practice antagonistic to the concreteness of human existence. In other words, philosophical method dogmatically invested in abstract analysis and the invisibility of the human subject cannot do justice to the existential reality of race as a lived actuality. George Yancy brilliantly captures the regressive thrust of this philosophical method regarding race. He writes:

> A great deal of important scholarly work argues that race is semantically empty, ontologically bankrupt, and scientifically meaningless. In short, many philosophers posit that race is an illusion, that there is no factual support for a racial taxonomy. Since race has no referent and does not cut at the joints of reality, so to speak, it is said to be a fiction. Thus we are told to abandon the concept of race just as we abandoned the concepts of phlogiston and spontaneous generation. A physicalist's rejection of race is logically compatible with acceptance of racial eliminativism. "The eliminativist argues that races do not exist, either because they fail to be objective or because they've been falsely posited by hopeless theories of human difference." The problem with this, however, is that the phenomenological or *lived* intelligibility and reality of race (as it is *socially ontologically* lived) exceed what is deemed "real" within the framework of physicalist ontology. Indeed, one can reject the concept of race from a

physicalist perspective and yet engage in various forms of social performance that are racist. In other words, one can live/embody the *fiction* of race in such a way that generates *real effects* in the social world. It is also important to note that to believe that there is nothing more to say about race because it is impossible to reduce it to a naturally occurring object in the spatiotemporal world is to engage in a form of disciplinary hegemony.[21]

In another context, Yancy comments on the tendency within philosophy to valorize the perspectiveless perspective as a philosophically ideal location of thought:

> I theorize from a place of lived embodied experience, a site of exposure. In philosophy, the only thing we learn to "expose" . . . is a weak argument, a fallacy, or someone's "inferior" reasoning power. The embodied self is bracketed and deemed irrelevant to theory, superfluous and cumbersome in one's search for truth. It is best, we are told, to reason from *nowhere*.[22]

When we turn our attention to the concrete exigencies of lived reality, instead of pursuing strategies of existential erasure, Yancy maintains that we acquire a better understanding of the existential dynamic of the black body as a White construction and, consequently, gain an appreciation of the historical career of race in the contradictory and ambiguous role of thwarting Black subjectivity as well as sustaining notions of Black subjectivity, grounded in acts of resistance to White normativity.

This chapter neither defends an original thesis nor is it a nest of consistent theses. Rather, it functions as a gathering of interpretive insights garnished from critically confronting the mythology of race in the classroom. I have done so not from some perspectiveless perspective, but from the standpoint of a Black professor of philosophy, actively resisting the scourge of epistemic suspicion, and one who actively engages his students, especially White students, to become philosophically and historically literate vis-à-vis the concept of race. This willingness to defile the artificiality of attempts to cast doubt on the legitimacy of critically working through the challenges of race requires the courage to embrace alternative conceptions of philosophy, as well as different styles of thinking about race. It is with these alternative conceptions that I invite my students to engage.

Notes

1 For a solid discussion of this kind of reasoning, see Avery Gordon and Christopher Newfield, "White Philosophy," *Critical Inquiry*, *20*(4), Summer 1994: 737–757.
2 For a very interesting account of this phenomenon, see Bruce Kuklick, *Black Philosopher, White Academy: The Career of William Fontaine* (Philadelphia, PA: University of Pennsylvania Press, 2008).
3 Miranda Fricker, *Epistemic Injustice: Power and the Ethics of Knowing* (Oxford, England: Oxford University Press, 2009), 4.

4 See Charles W. Mills, *The Racial Contract* (Ithaca, NY: Cornell University Press, 1997) and Shannon Sullivan and Nancy Tuana, eds., *Race and Epistemologies of Ignorance* (Albany, NY: State University of New York Press, 2007).

5 John L. Austin, *How To Do Things With Words* (Oxford, England: Oxford University Press, 1971).

6 Ibid., 149.

7 Michael Monahan, *The Creolizing Subject: Race, Reason, and the Politics of Purity* (New York, NY: Fordham University Press, 2011), 204.

8 Ibid.

9 W. E. B. Du Bois, *Black Reconstruction: An Essay Toward a History of the Part Which Black Folk Played in the Attempt to Reconstruct Democracy in America, 1860–1880* (New York, NY: Harcourt, Brace and Co., 1935).

10 Cheryl I. Harris, "Whiteness as Property," *Harvard Law Review*, *106*(8), June 1993: 1709–1791.

11 George Lipsitz, *The Possessive Investment in Whiteness: How White People Profit from Identity Politics* (Philadelphia, PA: Temple University Press, 1998).

12 Eduardo Bonilla-Silva, *Racism Without Racists: Color-Blind Racism and the Persistence of Racial Inequality in the United States* (Lanham, MD: Rowman & Littlefield, 2003).

13 For a fine discussion of institutional racism in terms of negative racial impact, see Gertrude Ezorsky, *Racism and Justice: The Case For Affirmative Action* (Ithaca, NY: Cornell University Press, 1991).

14 Douglas S. Massey, *Categorically Unequal: The American Stratification System* (New York, NY: Russell Sage Foundation, 2007).

15 For a recent philosophical investigation and discussion of the institutional nature of discrimination, see Elizabeth Anderson, *The Imperative of Integration* (Princeton, NJ: Princeton University Press, 2010).

16 For more on the idea of "blind to history," see Peter Charles Hoffer, "Blind to History— The Use of History in Affirmative Action Suits: Another Look at City of Richmond v. J. A. Croson Co.," *Rutgers Law Journal*, *23*, 1992: 271–296.

17 For more "opportunity hoarding," see Michael K. Brown, Martin Carnoy, Elliott Currie, Troy Duster, David B. Oppenheimer, Marjorie M. Shultz, and David Wellman, *White-Washing Race: The Myth of a Color-blind Society* (Berkeley, CA: University of California Press, 2003).

18 See Mills, *The Racial Contract*.

19 Ian Hacking, "Five Parables," in *Philosophy in History: Essays on the Historiography of Philosophy*, eds. Richard Rorty, J. B. Schneewind, and Quentin Skinner (Cambridge, England: Cambridge University Press, 1984).

20 Susan Haack, *Defending Science—Within Reason: Between Science and Cynicism* (Amherst, NY: Prometheus Books, 2003)

21 George Yancy, *Black Bodies, White Gazes: The Continuing Significance of Race* (Lanham, MD: Rowman & Littlefield, 2008), 33.

22 Ibid, 65.

10

UNVEILING WHITENESS IN HIGHER EDUCATION

Scholars of Color and Double Consciousness

Zeus Leonardo

Being a scholar of color in predominantly White institutions of higher education is a peculiar sensation. It comes with the realization that, while university settings represent one of the valued destinies for what W. E. B. Du Bois once called the "talented tenth,"[1] they are a space where scholars of color struggle to reconcile two warring ideals in one body. In fact, historically White colleges and universities heighten the racial contradictions that scholars of color face when they insist on being *both* a person of color *and* a scholar. Like Du Bois' own fond but critical recollections of his time at Harvard as the first Black person eventually to earn a doctorate from one of the most storied universities in the world, scholars of color today face a double consciousness no less intense.[2] Although we face harsh conditions, from microaggressions[3] to intellectual guerilla warfares,[4] scholars of color in White institutions know that universities have much to offer in terms of dialogical spaces for deliberating the important themes of our time, as well as becoming agents within those public spheres as subaltern voices and alternative visions. In short, we necessarily color the university, forever altering it, and we are transformed by it in return. As peculiar bodies within the university, scholars of color exist in two worlds: the first within their lived knowledge of the racial world, and the second within the confines of a racialized epistemological standard in White institutions.

It is worth revisiting that haunting but lyrical passage from *The Souls of Black Folk*, for which Du Bois has become so well known.[5] He writes:

> After the Egyptian and Indian, the Greek and Roman, the Tueton and Mongolian, the Negro is a sort of seventh son, born with a veil, and gifted with second-sight in this American world,—a world which yields him no true self-consciousness, but only lets him see himself through the revelation

of the other world. It is a peculiar sensation, this double-consciousness, this sense of always looking at one's self through the eyes of others, of measuring one's soul by the tape of a world that looks on in amused contempt and pity. One ever feels his twoness,—an American, a Negro; two souls, two thoughts, two unreconciled strivings; two warring ideals in one dark body, whose dogged strength alone keeps it from being torn asunder.

This history of the American Negro is the history of this strife—this longing to attain self-conscious manhood, to merge his double self into a better and truer self. In this merging he wishes neither of the older selves to be lost. He would not Africanize America, for America has too much to teach the world and Africa. He would not bleach his Negro soul in a flood of White Americanism, for he knows that Negro blood has a message for the world. He simply wishes to make it possible for a man to be both a Negro and an American, without being cursed and spit upon by his fellows, without having the doors of Opportunity closed roughly in his face.[6]

Although Du Bois speaks specifically about a Black experience in the United States, for this short chapter, I would like to tap his insights in order to illuminate a *general* racial climate that scholars of color navigate. The specificities of Black experience include the history of enslavement, Jim Crow institutions, and implications of the Black–White binary in daily life. However, it is Du Bois' universal insights (as well as universalism) about the human condition under a racial predicament that touches the lives of all academics of color that I would like to highlight.[7] In particular, I would like to take advantage of his offerings of two concepts that explain this experience within predominantly White academic settings: the veil and double consciousness.

The institutional patterns speak loudly enough. In their introduction to a collection of essays centered on women of color in academia, Angela Harris and Carmen González show that, despite the rise of students of color in U.S. universities between 1997 to 2007, the number of professors of color only increased from 13% to 17% in the same period.[8] For women of color, the trends are more serious, with their representation decreasing as the rank rises and ending at 3.4% as full professors.[9] But, as Harris and González admit, this is only the tip of the iceberg, as faculty of color—specifically, women—face daily microaggressions, stereotyping, tokenism, divide-and-conquer tactics, minimization, condescension, intimidation, and stigmatization from their White colleagues and institutions. Sometimes, they face these chauvinisms from other scholars of color, who either have become what Paulo Freire once called "suboppressors,"[10] because their sense of humanity is based on the oppressor's standards, or who are positioned by their institution as (un)thankful beneficiaries of its grace. It is enough to turn a well-adjusted person of color into a destabilized cogito. Their argument supports Frantz Fanon's description of the psychic strain caused by White supremacy[11] and Patricia Williams' concept of "spirit-murder."[12] The editors sum up their observations of women of color's position in the academy as those who are "presumed incompetent," speaking to the racialization of relations of "ability" and the assumed abledness of whiteness.[13] Speaking against this dynamic represents an unwelcomed gesture from unthankful bodies in the eyes of whiteness that presumes itself "innocent." It is a predicament that subverts scholars of color's ability to teach in White classroom spaces where their perspective is minimized as self-interested or anti-intellectual. The upshot is that they are not fit for the rigors of objective academic knowledge.

Scholars of color are at once too much of color and yet not enough. For the university, they confound the whiteness of the institution. Particularly relevant for those who conduct race work, higher educational institutions tolerate, sometimes welcome, racial perspectives as part of their mission. But, it is often clear that this is not the usual business of academic life, and researching race is rarely uncontroversial—and not in the same sense as when a professor claims that Shakespeare was not the author of the great plays and sonnets we have come to associate with him. In fact, opening universities to women, people of color, and working-class students is a rather recent phenomenon, arguably resulting from post-WWII legislation. Be that as it may, "While many of the formal barriers have been lifted, academic institutions remain, at their core, profoundly inhospitable to the experiences and points of view of those formerly excluded."[14] That is, as an epistemic system, the university is ensconced in a Eurocentric mold out of which it is hard to break and unlikely to emerge from anytime soon. As peculiar, even "guilty," bodies in those spaces, scholars of color are reminders of the continuing racism in U.S. society; this time, within the realm of knowledge production.

Regarded with "amused contempt and pity," scholars of color who conduct race work are suspect because their *perspectivist* research agenda is more subjective, less objective, or more or less a form of advocacy. As instructors, scholars of color are frequently challenged by novice White students within domains in which the former are clearly experts. With respect to university norms, scholars of color's collaborative spirit, one informed by connection with their community writ broadly, goes against the pretenses of the "romance of the brilliant, lonely genius,"[15] or what I might here refer to as the "lone writer." We should note also that advocacy work, if that is indeed an accurate portrayal, is necessarily less valuable, less intellectual. Looked on with contempt from White conservatives like Allan Bloom or William Bennett, scholars of color's rootedness in the lived world is blamed for the falling standards of the academy since the glory days of "real" Harvard or Yale men [*sic*]. It does not seem to occur to them that they also take on a racialized perspective on the world and advocate for a group's interests. Their project is transcendent and intellectual, scholars of colors' project is ephemeral and political. Rather than evidence of a White double consciousness, a "double unconsciousness"[16] is evident where White denial creates a standard only to be exposed as a double standard.

Scholars of color also earn the pity of White liberals who value race as an academic idea, but have a difficult time with race as a lived, embodied experience. It may be said that, like the South, White conservatives "respect" individuals of color, but despise your race; like the West and East coasts, liberals "love" your race, but could do without the individual. Seeking safety from either one is a hidden tax on scholars of color, a *burden* that White academics rarely appreciate because the veil prevents them from seeing experiences of color on their own terms. The point is not that White colleagues across the political spectrum are unkind, intentionally or unintentionally. That would shift the problem to the inter-personal, rather than structural, plane. This would underestimate the dynamic and misrepresent the overall racial predicament. It is more profound than that. It is a structured interaction perhaps captured best by Raymond Williams' phrase, a "structure of feeling."[17] In this case, a certain relation of racial affect[18] underpins everyday exchanges between scholars of color and their White colleagues and students, all of which proceeds as rather natural and almost invisible. In classrooms that incorporate legitimate conversations around race, White feelings of decenteredness give rise to the insistence on "safe spaces" for race dialogue, a demand that usually means safety for Whites and continued violence for students of color.[19] Safety in the context of race dialogue is rarely for the benefit of people of color.

Meanwhile, scholars of color experience a disequilibrium that no tenure case is likely to consider as a condition that affects one's productivity. This process gets the better of some scholars of color, preferring instead to pursue other careers or moving from one institution to another searching for the "holy grail" of racial belonging. Of course, he or she is doomed to fail, but they knew this from the start. Most remain and survive; a select few thrive. Certainly, many White academics have their own complaints about the academy (and there are many legitimate ones), but they are not racial in nature. To agree with Bernal and Villalpando that this condition amounts to "academic apartheid"[20]—one standard for scholars of color (particularly those who study race), and another for Whites (even those who study race)—is met with suspicious eyes. Meanwhile, a "Herrenvolk" ethics makes for two experiences; one White, the other of color.[21] Shining an analytical light on it is likely to be received as plaintive complaint or excuse seeking. What is lost is that these observations may come just as often from highly successful, productive scholars of color who are at the top of their game.

Opposite Peggy McIntosh's helpful metaphor of the White knapsack,[22] from which Whites may draw at least more than 40 said racial privileges—from being liberated from the pressure to represent one's race to finding bandage that matches light skin color—scholars of color carry a proverbial albatross that weighs them down. And, whereas the White knapsack seems to lighten the social load for Whites, the albatross seems to burden people of color. Like Midas, the unbearable whiteness of the institution rests squarely on minority shoulders. But, consistent with Du Bois, this burden becomes a gift in terms of recognizing the value-laden nature of academic life. Rather than value neutral, it is, instead, normative—and racial, at that. Pointing this out does not devalue academic work as a purely subjective enterprise, but problematizes a certain way of conceiving it: as apolitical, as detached from participation in social life.[23] The albatross of color may weigh down minorities like bricks, but it also comes with the assurance of planting their feet on the ground when it comes to racial matters, rarely having the luxury to take the academic space for granted and hovering above the fray. It does not represent an injunction against White-dominated universities, but to help them realize the promise that many of them uphold regarding excellence and free exchange of ideas; this time, extending it to scholars of color.

In accomplishing this task, the inclusion of scholars of color also requires that they not be stripped of their racial specificity, aesthetics, and character. Because the "cultural arbitrary"[24] known as whiteness arguably drives communication and behavioral patterns in the university, minority scholars may begin to lose their "color." That is, because public comportment in universities articulates with White sensibilities, scholars of color experience deracination at one level or another the longer they stay. Too much of color for the institution, after spending enough time in higher education, they are too "pale" for their own community. It is less a commentary about their loss of "authenticity" and more about the way that the university works on them, both body (e.g., gestures and postures) and mind (e.g., habits and common sense). This does not suggest that scholars of color reject being altered by their educational experience or creating a more expansive understanding of themselves as they traverse White spaces. There is much about this experience of disjuncture that recommends itself as it transforms scholars of colors' standing with their own group, enabling critical reflection on what it means to live out a complex relationship with others we perceive to be like "us." The move toward cosmopolitanism requires an exilic positionality, in Said's sense of it as an intellectual choice one makes in order to remain an amateur (in the fight against professionalization) and maintain a perspective of critical distance (not to be confused with detachment).[25]

At stake here is not just scholars of colors' experience with double consciousness, but of double alienation. Too much of color for the university, they experience the imposition of a "tape" foreign to their self-concept. This dynamic could be exemplified by the simplest of self-expressions, such as handshakes and ways of addressing colleagues. But, it runs more deeply than that as scholars of color change not only the way they relate to others, but to themselves. After so many years, they may even wonder what they were like before entering institutions of higher learning, but are frustrated by the faint echoes of their previous selves. It is a bit like trying to remember one's childhood; some things remembered, much forgotten. Like the mask that Fanon invokes as a temporary persona that colonized Blacks put on and then remove once they return to the colony only to be horrified by the fact of their Blackness,[26] scholars of color have become masters at disguise. One does not have to go the distance with Fanon—that a person of color's destiny is whiteness—to recognize the importance of the attempt to blend in, if at least to avoid detection or protect oneself against violence, which assumes a coercive dimension to academic life.

Unfortunately, the temporary mask becomes ossified as a veil that is more or less permanent. Intellectuals of color who spend enough time in predominantly White institutions become estranged from their previous selves as they become habituated to the mask turned into a veil. Their previous self, which may be misrecognized as their *real* self, has become increasingly opaque. Something is gained, whether in terms of social mobility or job security in rarefied institutions, or maybe even access to the "good life," but admittedly something is lost. And perhaps there is something about emancipation from an essential life or primordial self that is worth embracing here, making any postmodernist smile from ear to ear. Be that as it may, the brutality of the process cannot be underestimated. Trying to recapture an originary self is like remembering the beginning of a story that one can only recall having entered in the middle. This feeling of loss may have its liberating moments for scholars of color who may choose to begin anew, but the echoes haunt him or her in the strangest moments.

Like Du Bois, who enjoyed his time at Harvard with the likes of William James and George Santayana, scholars of color in historically White universities and colleges appreciate participating in the progressive dimensions of academic life. But, like Du Bois, who was clear-eyed about the racial atmosphere of his surroundings, today's scholars of color function with both eyes open or risk perishing. It is their spirit of resolve, their insistence for inclusion, and their fitness to survive in a condition they realize was not meant to see them through, that we see the burden turn into a gift. But it is not a gift for them alone, as their presence unarguably enriches the experiences of their White colleagues and students. After all, the university's root word may be traced to that Eurocentric promise of universality that it has failed to deliver. Maybe its deliverance requires a different messenger.

Scholars of color enter the university bearing a gift. But it is not one they bring without sacrifices along the way. These are not sacrifices with a clear pay-off in the end, as Derrick Bell never tired of reminding us.[27] Over and again, they experience an inhospitable situation when they teach racial themes in the classroom and confront the problems of White supremacy. They find purpose, even happiness, in this otherwise hostile condition, just as they eke out a life within the structural limitations of racism. They learn that opting out is an option, but that disengaging would only lead to death of another kind. They have much to teach the world about racism and are lived reminders that the project of racialization continues. Teaching against it is not just an academic act, but an ethical one.

Notes

1 W. E. B. Du Bois, "The Talented Tenth: Memorial Address," in *W. E. B. Du Bois: A Reader*, ed. David L. Lewis (New York, NY: H. Holt and Co., 1995), 347–353.

See also *The Negro Problem: A Series of Articles by Representative American Negroes of To-day*, ed. Booker T. Washington (New York, NY: J. Pott, 1903).

2 See Eugene F. Provenzo, *Du Bois on Education* (Lanham, MD: AltaMira Press, 2002).

3 Rita Kohli and Daniel G. Solórzano, "Teachers, Please Learn Our Names!: Racial Microaggressions and the K-12 Classroom," *Race, Ethnicity and Education, 15*(4), 2012: 441–462.

4 See Geneva Gay, "Mirror Images on Common Issues: Parallels Between Multicultural Education and Critical Pedagogy," in *Multicultural Education, Critical Pedagogy, and the Politics of Difference*, eds. Christine E. Sleeter and Peter McLaren (Albany, NY: State University of New York Press, 1995), 155–189; Dale Minami, "Guerrilla War at UCLA: Political and Legal Dimensions of the Tenure Battle," in *The Asian American Educational Experience*, eds. Don T. Nakanishi and Tina Yamano Nishida (New York, NY: Routledge, 1995), 358–372.

5 W. E. B. Du Bois, *The Souls of Black Folk* (New York, NY: Penguin Books, 1982); first published in 1904.

6 Du Bois, *The Souls of Black Folk*, 5.

7 See also Zeus Leonardo, "Unmasking White Supremacy and Racism," in *Rethinking Race, Class, Language, and Gender: A Dialogue with Noam Chomsky and Other Leading Scholars*, ed. Pierre W. Orelus (Lanham, MD: Rowman & Littlefield Publishers, 2011), 31–51.

8 Angela P. Harris and Carmen G. González, "Introduction," in *Presumed Incompetent*, eds. Gabriella Gutiérrez y Muhs, Yolanda Flores Niemann, Carmen G. González, and Angela P. Harris (Logan, UT: Utah State University Press, 2012), 2–14

9 Mikyung Ryu, *Minorities in Higher Education: Twenty-fourth Annual Status Report—With a Special Essay on the U.S. Hispanic Population* (Washington, D.C.: American Council on Education, 2010).

10 Paulo Freire, *Pedagogy of the Oppressed*, trans. Myra Bergman Ramos (New York, NY: Continuum, 1993); first published in 1970.

11 Frantz Fanon, *Black Skin, White Masks*, trans. Charles Lam Markmann (New York, NY: Grove Press, 1967); first published in 1952.

12 Patricia J. Williams, *The Alchemy of Race and Rights* (Cambridge, MA: Harvard University Press, 1991).

13 Zeus Leonardo and Alicia A. Broderick, "Smartness as Property: A Critical Exploration of Intersections Between Whiteness and Disability Studies," *Teachers College Record, 113*(10), 2011: 2206–2232.

14 Harris and González, *Presumed Incompetent*, 7.

15 Harris and González, *Presumed Incompetent*, 4.

16 Ricky Lee Allen, "From sadomasochism to humanization: An abolitionist theory of White guilt," paper presented at the 2011 Annual Meeting of the American Educational Research Association (New Orleans, Louisiana, 2011).

17 Raymond Williams, *Marxism and Literature* (Oxford, England: Oxford University Press, 1977).

18 Zeus Leonardo and Michalinos Zembylas, "Whiteness as Technology of Affect: Implications for Educational Praxis," *Equity and Excellence in Education, 46*(1), 2013: 150–165; Sara Ahmed, "Declarations of Whiteness: The Non-Performativity of Antiracism," *Borderlands E-Journal, 3*(2), (2004): 1–22, accessed 11/17/10; Michael W. Apple, *Can Education Change Society?* (New York, NY: Routledge, 2013).

19 Zeus Leonardo and Ronald K. Porter, "Pedagogy of Fear: Toward a Fanonian Theory of 'Safety' in Race Dialogue," *Race, Ethnicity and Education, 13*(2), 2010: 139–157.

20 Dolores Delgado Bernal and Octavio Villalpando, "An Apartheid of Knowledge in Academia: The Struggle over the 'Legitimate' Knowledge of Faculty of Color," in *Critical Pedagogy and Race*, ed. Zeus Leonardo (Malden, MA: Blackwell, 2005), 185–204.

21 Charles W. Mills, *The Racial Contract* (Ithaca, NY: Cornell University Press, 1997).
22 Peggy McIntosh, "White Privilege and Male Privilege: A Personal Account of Coming to See Correspondences Through Work in Women's Studies," in *Race, Class, and Gender: An Anthology*, eds. Margaret L. Andersen and Patricia Hill Collins (Belmont, CA: Wadsworth, 1992), 70–81.
23 See Edward W. Said, *The World, the Text, and the Critic* (Cambridge, MA: Harvard University Press, 1983).
24 Pierre Bourdieu and Jean Claude Passeron, *Reproduction in Education, Society, and Culture* (Thousand Oaks, CA: Sage, 1990); first published in 1977.
25 Edward W. Said, *Reflections on Exile and Other Essays* (Cambridge, MA: Harvard University Press, 2000).
26 Fanon, *Black Skin, White Masks*.
27 Derrick A. Bell, *Faces at the Bottom of the Well: The Permanence of Racism* (New York, NY: Basic Books, 1992).

11

METACOGNITIVE RACLaGE REFLECTION

A Black Professor's Journey to Use the Master's Tools to Dismantle His House[1]

Karsonya Wise Whitehead

"We don't have a race problem, black people just have to stop blaming everything on slavery."[2]

"I think black people like being poor, that way they can always blame the system rather than take responsibility for their own mistake."[3]

In the days leading up to the end of the semester, I am always nervous about my evaluations. I try to calm myself by thinking of the worst things that my students can write about me, and then I work on convincing myself that they would never *actually* write them. I remind myself that, despite how difficult it is to teach race, class, and gender, I do know how to teach. Despite my anxiety, I know that I am not *really* afraid of what they are going to write. It is actually the things that they do not write, the things that they take away from my class, which concern me and are what I really want to know. This is what keeps me up at night and why I constantly tinker with my lesson plans and curricula.

I purposely organized my classroom to be a space where I practice feminist pedagogy and engage myself as a feminist scholar. I challenge my students to see our classroom as a place where they can be transformed because their presence is acknowledged, their ideas are recorded, and their voices are necessary tools that we can and will use to shape the type of environment where we want to learn. My students were initially resistant to this idea of being present and engaged in the classroom discussions. They had to change their thinking about the classroom so that they could see the assigned readings as necessary stepping-stones for active engagement, and see the classroom discussions as their first steps on a path to becoming engaged scholars. I wanted them to be free, even though I had no idea what freedom looked like or how to actually get it.

Feminist teaching is one of the few professions where you may never know if something you did or said actually made a difference in your student's life. If I taught math or science, I could give them a pre- and post test to determine how much they have learned under my teaching, or, if I taught English, I could ask them questions about Shakespeare or Angelou or Chaucer—but I teach race, class, and gender, and I am trying to change their hearts and their values. I am trying to change their misconceptions and their stereotypes, and, sadly, there is no "test" that can determine whether or not my class is transforming them or has transformed them. I ask myself, more times than I would like to admit, what true transformation even looks like, and, even more importantly, as a teacher and scholar, if I have been transformed. At the beginning of every semester, I envision my students situated at point A, where they are standing firm on what they have always been taught to believe about the world; and, by the end of the semester, they have reached point B, which is this new space where they question themselves and the world in which we live. This new space is where they commit themselves to being better than what they were and doing more than what they have been called to do as they seek to contribute their voices to the world. I see my classroom as the straight line that is, of course, the shortest distance between these two points. This then is the work of the feminist teacher; to make sure that all boundaries are pushed, all assumptions are changed, all ideas and voices are welcomed and challenged, and all new points are reached. My job is to teach them that silence is not an option, either in the classroom or in their lives.

I remember the first time I discovered the work of Audre Lorde. I was a sophomore at a historically Black college and one of my professors, Dr. Jane Bond Howard (cousin to Julian Bond and niece of former college president, Horace Mann Bond), gave me one of Lorde's books and challenged me to begin to think like a feminist rather than just a Black activist. She said I had to find a way to bring all of my points of contestation—my race, my class, and my gender—together and use them as keys to liberate me rather than as chains to restrain me. I read it and then devoured everything I could by Lorde. I used to recite Lorde's statement, "Your silence will not protect you," every time I thought about not speaking out against injustice.[4] I said it then as a student and I say it now as a professor: "My silence will not protect me, it will not help my students, and it will not help me to create a world that I want my sons to live in."

Transformation

The study of the intersection of race, class, and gender ("RACLaGE") is at the heart of feminist pedagogy and has shaped and nurtured both the field and the classroom. By finding ways to address and confront these complicated issues of power and privilege, the feminist in the classroom must critically examine lesson plans, curricula, and personal biases and prejudices. The goal is to transform the classroom into a safe space where these types of discussions and interactions can take place without judgment but with accountability. One of the first ways in which to begin to transform the discussion is by teaching our students how to use metacognitive reflection to examine their lives in an effort to pinpoint significant moments in their history that helped to shape how they see RACLaGE.

Metacognitive RACLaGE reflection is not easy because it forces the student scholars to be especially attentive to their own biases by asking themselves, over and over again, *"Where did I get this from?" "Why do I see people of color, or women, or people who are economically challenged in this way?" "Is my idea about this person based on what I know to be true or based upon a stereotype?"* The work is messy and hard, as it forces the teacher scholar to be both a facilitator and a participant. It also means that the classroom is conducted in such a way that students are held responsible for what they say. It is not enough to begin with "I feel . . ." if a student cannot then say ". . . and this is why I feel this way." This work becomes even more complicated when the teacher scholar is a woman of color, working within an all-white and extremely privileged environment, and is on her own path of self-discovery, inquiry, and introspection.

Challenges

It was in 2010, at the end of another long semester of teaching an adjunct graduate Critical Race, Image and Theory course, that I sat down and tried to figure out how I got to that point. I was frustrated with trying, every day, to use the master's tools and the master's language to dismantle his house and change his system.[5] I was overwhelmed spending my days teaching undergraduates at a predominantly White institution and my nights working with graduate students in another predominantly White environment. My authority was challenged more than once and I often felt that I was on the defense, trying to defend my ideas and, in some cases, my people. I had a very difficult time with my students who often began or ended with the words, "I am not a racist." There were times when I felt that I was making incredible strides in the classroom—hearts were being opened, minds were being expanded, and biases were being torn down—but then I would read their reflections on teaching Black students or their reactions to reading a series of articles about race, and I would realize that my work, though it did lead to having some interesting classroom discussions, did not change hearts. I needed something else and I needed my students to do something else.

Beginnings

My road to the hallowed halls of White academic privilege has been a long and winding one. I spent 10 years working as a documentary filmmaker in New York, being the only Black woman in a sea of White faces trying to find ways to tell the types of stories that would speak to my community. At every juncture, I was stopped and gently encouraged to focus on telling the American story and not "just the story of Black people" (as if the two stories were different). I was frustrated with production and felt that there were places I needed to work to try and disrupt the cycles of poverty and illiteracy that seemed to plague my people.

I then joined a new teacher residency program and, in less than two months, I was assigned to teach social studies at an overcrowded Baltimore City middle school that bused in students from seven different communities. Although the school was located in an upper-middle-class neighborhood, 95% of the students who were bused in were eligible for free and/or reduced breakfast and lunch. Leading up to my first day, I remember that I had dreams of how I was going to train the next generation, disrupt the classroom-to-prison pipeline, teach my students to imagine themselves beyond their current situations, and help them to raise their test scores. What I found, much to my dismay, was a generation of kids who were reading below their grade level and were unable to think critically. I taught Advanced Academics, a program that focused on saving the lives and preserving the futures of 64 students (16 from both the sixth and seventh grades and 32 from the eighth grade) out of a population of 1,200. "We must save the Talented Tenth," my principal explained when I expressed some concerns about the system, "because the rest are not going to make it and are not worth our time."[6] I once taped a note right next to my classroom door that said, "You are living your dream, so teach the kids you have right now how to dream and then how to live those dreams." One of my students wrote on the bottom of my note, "If this school is your dream, then you should probably wake up."

I did and I only lasted four years. Every day I walked into the building, I felt like I was walking into the belly of the beast. I had a headache that started on my first day and did not go away until a month after I quit. It was not just the lack of pencils or books (the usual complaints about life in an inner-city school) that bothered me, it was the bars on the windows, the lack of toilet tissue, the gap that existed between the front office and the classrooms, and the overwhelming feelings of hopelessness and helplessness.

I tried to teach my students about race and about why these issues were important, but it was hard to help them to see the bigger picture when their everyday lives revolved around getting to and from home safely. My students would ask, sometimes in frustration and other times with a genuine curiosity, "What does race have to do with it?" and "Who cares about racism, I just want to get through school without being forced to join a gang" and "My cousin was shot last night and the guy who did it was Black not White, so what does that mean?" I slowly began to realize that focusing on deconstructing RACLaGE did not work in every environment, that there was no one-size-fits-all pedagogy. At this school, I was in a sea full of people who looked like me, but whose lives and life experiences were worlds away from mine. My students challenged me to rethink my ideas about class and class privilege. I would say to them, "Black people are similarly oppressed," and they would say to me, "Black people who have houses and two parents *and* go on summer vacations don't know what we are going through." I would say, "The 'n-word' is racially charged and should not be used to describe Black people," and they would say, "I use the word 'nigga' all the time and so does my mom; that's what she calls my daddy."[7]

It was in this environment that I began to have my students do a mini version of what would later become my "metacognitive RACLaGE reflection journals." Students kept a daily journal and were told to record one to two incidents that happened throughout their day that gave them insight into or made them think about RACLaGE. They would then reflect on these incidents and bring them to class to discuss in their small groups. It was disturbing how many incidents occurred during the day that completely undermined what I was teaching in the classroom. I had them read "White Privilege: Unpacking the Invisible Knapsack" and then had them unpack their own "backpacks."[8] They were uncomfortable talking about poverty and privilege. Their reflections at the end of the class revealed to me that perhaps I was not doing a very good job of teaching them how to see themselves. In response to the question, "What did you learn today?" I found that they did not learn anything that I wanted them to learn: "Mrs. Whitehead, today you made me realize that I am poor and now I'm sad" and "I don't know what we were supposed to learn today, but I didn't learn nothing. I don't got a backpack and I don't know how to get one" and "I got a backpack and today I learned that it's empty. Thank you."[9] When I would talk about gender roles, my girls would talk about how women in rap videos were making the choice to be in them and that, if they had the chance, they would be, too. And as for race, I was teaching in an all-Black environment about the importance of race relations. There were many days when my work did not feel relevant.

Although my students spent months working on these issues, it became increasingly clear to me that this work in this environment would not change the system. If I wanted things to change, I believed that I needed to be in an environment where I was teaching other people's kids and not just my own. After four years of teaching, and after receiving the 2007 Maryland "History Teacher of the Year" award, I decided that, if I really wanted to see some changes in this area and in myself, then I needed to teach in an environment where I would be the "Other." I knew that, if I wanted to change the system, I had to do it on the ground. I needed to teach in those environments where I would have to learn how to traverse the dangerous and muddy waters where there was tension, frustration, guilt, anger, and complacency about these issues—the real spaces where RACLaGE work needed to happen. There are days when I think about the students that I used to teach, many of who are in college today, and I know that I made a difference. I also know the price that I paid in making that difference, and, though there are days when I regret my decision, there are other days, when I am quiet and still, that I know that the work of a feminist scholar can and should be done on multiple levels. There are scholars who thrive in the middle school environment, people who were born to do that work; and then there are people like me whose battleground is the ivory tower, whose weapons are a pen and some paper, and whose voice must never be lost or silenced.

The Master's House

In the fall of 2009, I started my journey as a woman of color working and teaching in a Northern teaching institution. I was one of a handful of tenured/tenure-track faculty members of color on a campus with close to 3,500 students and more than 200 faculty members. I remember my first day on campus, when a Black male colleague came up to me and said, "You must be new here because I know every Black faculty member on campus." My course, Stereotypes in U.S. Film and Television, was one that I had developed and had proposed teaching it every spring. It was offered as an elective that also filled the diversity requirement. In the course, I used multiple forms of media to critically examine how race, class, and gender as socially constructed ideologies intersect, inform, and influence our perceptions, biases, and behaviors. Since I was a new professor and I was not sure whether students were interested in exploring RACLaGE, I was pleasantly surprised to find that my course was filled and closed less than two hours after course enrollment began.

Out of all my courses (I teach a 3:3 load), Stereotypes in U.S. Film and Television was where I began to develop my skills as a feminist teacher and where I found my voice as a researcher. When I first began teaching the course, I felt that I had to work hard to establish myself as the authority figure. I did not know how to create both a safe space for my female students and an open environment for my male students. I was not sure how to speak about race or gender without inserting myself into the middle of the discussion, and I did not know how to "force" them to be honest with themselves and with one another. Since I wanted them to contemplate and be contemplative, to be both in the moment and critical of the moments, I decided to combine my metacognitive RACLaGE reflections with the Jesuit idea of contemplation, as defined by Walter Burghardt. He argued that contemplation required a "long, loving look at the real," and, in my class, the "real" was RACLaGE and how they have been taught to view these issues.[10] My students had to write in their journals three times a week in three different sections:

1.   Readings and Responses—using close reading strategies, students had to reflect on the assigned chapters and articles, highlight the key points, and then reflect on what it taught them about RACLaGE and about themselves;
2.   Diversity Moments—students had to record one or two significant incidents that happened and that either made them think about or that challenged their social values, stereotypes, and assumptions;
3.   Metacognitive Reflection—students had to critically examine and deconstruct a source of media (i.e., a newspaper, a movie, a music video, a song), paying particular attention to how the issues of RACLaGE were addressed and how it impacted them.

They completed weekly "think tanks" (where they researched a specific issue and wrote a White paper about it), presented mini-lectures with a "power point" and talking points, wrote a biweekly "talking points" paper, watched video clips, and participated in robust in-class discussions. I actually thought that they were learning and teaching one another in an open, safe, and free environment. I was wrong.

As the days turned into weeks and then into months, I slowly realized how disconnected my teaching was from their life experiences. They were participating in my classes, and, sometimes, saying everything they thought I wanted to hear, but the in-class work was not translating into action. During the semester, there were at least four issues that occurred that demonstrated the disconnect between my teaching and their lives: (a) hearing the "I am not a racist" statement more than once a week, usually followed by a heavily veiled racist statement; (b) having students challenge my grades and assignments over and over again, even though I provided them with a rubric and detailed instructions; (c) hearing students address me as "Mrs." rather than as "Dr.," which is the title they extended to all of the male and White professors; and, (d) receiving class evaluations that evaluated me as a person rather than as a teacher. These issues, in which my teaching and my freedom in the classroom were challenged or severely limited, reflect the points of conflict where racism and sexism were present in my lived classroom experiences.

The first issue began happening during the second week of class. I told the students that we needed to be careful with our language and we needed to agree upon the terms that were acceptable in our environment. We went through a number of terms, from "ladies" and "gentlemen" (too formal), "boys" and "girls" (too juvenile), "men" and "women" (too gender specific), "pearls" (only if their grandmother was present), and "ya'll" (which just made everyone laugh). We finally agreed upon Zora Neale Hurston's use of the term "folks."[11] I told them they were free to use any other words in the classroom as long as they could explain why they chose to use a divisive term rather than something else (i.e. the use of the word "nigga," which was very controversial, but, for a few of my Black male students, it was, they argued, a part of their normal vocabulary). I also outlined some general rules to help establish a safe space. They were told to "share" the airspace, to disagree without being disagreeable, to give people an opportunity to reach their own conclusions, to refrain from speaking for everyone, and to follow the "Vegas" classroom rule (so, whatever happened or was said in the space, stayed in the space). Even with all of these rules, and my push to be open, the students still framed a number of their very racially charged comments with the phrase, "I am not racist . . ." as if that term would excuse the sweeping generalizations they would then make about a select group. My goal was to create a space where they had a voice on both the internal level (which was where I wanted them to focus on confronting themselves) and on the external level (by being accountable to what they were saying to one another and to me).[12] Second, the students constantly challenged my grading system as if my rubric was unclear or I was not sure about what I wanted them to do. In many of the instances, the students used a very condescending tone, as if they were the instructors and I was the student. I began to dread my office hours and the student e-mails, as I was spending an inordinate amount of time explaining or, in some cases, rationalizing my grading system. It became so intense that I checked with a couple of White male colleagues about their system, and they explained that they did not use rubrics, did not post grades, did not entertain a long e-mail chain constantly restating the directions, and never had students challenge their grading systems. By providing rubrics and detailed instructions (sometimes more than once), I actually thought I was creating a space where students would have agency and then exercise mastery with the material.[13] I wanted them to see themselves as a primary source for the creation of new knowledge that could then be contributed to our learning space. I wanted them to own their experiences and challenge themselves when they found that they were relying on stereotypes and misconceptions. I wanted that instead of being questioned, challenged, or dismissed.

The third issue was that the students often failed to call me by my academic title. I introduced myself as "Dr. Whitehead." I had it on my voicemail, and I signed all of my e-mails with my name and title. When I began teaching, I did not think much about it. When I first started teaching, I actually wanted them to call me Dr. Kaye, and my advisor (a White woman, who is now a dean) told me that, as a Black woman going into a predominantly White male environment, I had to insist that the students call me Dr. Whitehead so that they would understand that I am on the same level as my White male counterparts. I was almost embarrassed when I had to correct them. I felt that I sounded like someone who somehow *needed* to hear her title. I noticed that, while they removed my title, they in fact extended the title to all of the White professors, even if said professors did not have their doctorates. The assumption seemed to be that all White men in academia were professors with doctorates and all Black women were not. My students were making decisions based upon how Black women have been positioned in this society and about whom they considered to be the authority in the classroom.[14] They expected White men to be educated and smart, leaders in the academy, and in the classroom. The expectation was that Black women were not, and that we were imposters who were typically in supportive roles rather than in positions of autonomy and authority. This dynamic is closely tied to the fact that my students challenged my grading system or felt free to "demand" (rather than request) my assistance. If they did not see me as having autonomy and authority, then they felt that they were emboldened and entitled to question, challenge, or dismiss me, over and over again.

Finally, there was the problem that my evaluations were not a true indication of how well the course had gone. Although the evaluation numbers were extremely high (much higher than my other two courses), the qualitative comments were extremely judgmental: "Dr. Whitehead spoke about race too much. There are other races out there besides hers," "She could have smiled more," "I felt like she didn't care about me," "She seemed angry when she talked about race," "She only wants you to think her way," and, "She's way too close to the issue." Despite my best efforts, it seems as if some of my White students were uncomfortable with having a Black woman teach them about issues that pertained to people of color, women, and people who are economically challenged. I found that it was hard to smile when I was talking about discrimination, poverty, homelessness, and rape. While it did not cloud my objectivity, I sometimes felt that I was *too* close to the issues. At the same time, I knew that this work was important and that my students needed to learn this material. They needed to be challenged by me about how they saw the world and their place in it. They had, for the most part, grown up in environments where they had very little contact with people of color and people who were economically challenged, and I could not, as a researcher and scholar, allow them to leave my classroom without passionately encouraging them to confront these issues.

Teaching Teachers

While I was teaching Stereotypes in U.S. Film and Television at my home institution, I also chose to teach a graduate diversity course for first-year teachers who were going through an alternative teacher certification program. I was excited about this course and about having an opportunity to teach the teachers. I felt that, if I could get them to see how important RACLaGE was, both as a teaching tool and as a form of empowerment, I could help them to change how they saw the world, and, ultimately, they would be able to transform their classrooms. This was a more difficult environment because these were White teachers who felt "called" to teach in the inner city and were really not open to exploring their own biases and misconceptions. This is not to say that they were disingenuous. Rather, the important point here is that it was more difficult for these teachers to confront biases and misconceptions in both themselves and in others. They also kept metacognitive RACLaGE reflection journals, but they were instructed to include the activities of their students and their reactions to them. I was secretly horrified on more than one occasion to find that my teachers had misconceptions about their students, and that they were teaching out of a space where they consistently had low expectations of their students. This environment was much more challenging because the stakes were much higher. My teachers had to be really forced (and, in some cases, pulled kicking and screaming) to confront their own racism and classism. "When it's hot," one teacher said, "and I want them to listen, I just turn all the fans on me. Those Black kids can't stand the heat, so they get quiet very quickly." Other comments included: "I told his mother that if she really cared about him she would quit one of her jobs to be home with him and help him with his homework," "I just skip right over talking about slavery because I don't know anything about the topic and it makes me feel uncomfortable," "The natives are restless, it must be time to send these animals on break," and "They have on $200 tennis shoes but they don't have a pencil or a notebook. It's like they're in training to be locked up someday." Most of these comments were usually made in jest and resulted in laughter, but I felt that it spoke to a number of issues that needed to be confronted.

In an effort to challenge their basic assumptions about inner-city children of color, I had the teachers read bell hooks' "Outlaw Culture: Resisting Representations," and brainstorm ways that they could transform their classrooms into active spaces where their students have agency and are actively involved in an ongoing pursuit of knowledge. They worked on changing their role from teacher to facilitator, and from teacher to learner. They participated in a 48-hour language activity where they wrote down every comment that they made that clearly identified a RACLaGE issue that needed to be addressed. They participated in role-playing activities, learned how to write culturally responsive lesson plans, and how to insert diversity moments into their daily lessons. They learned how to be transformative educators and how to impart this knowledge to their students.

Into the Light

Coming out of these experiences, I realized that my work with my undergraduate students must continue to focus on confronting these crucial issues. Despite what they wrote on my evaluations, I had to work harder to disrupt the culture of silence. I also realized that, for my teachers, the only way to help to break the cycles (of underachievement, of low test grades, of poverty, of illiteracy . . .) was to help them to confront, recognize, and draw attention to the biases, stereotypes, and misconceptions that they had about their students and that their students had about themselves. The same issues I confronted when I taught middle school. The problems that existed when I left had actually gotten worse, and, though I thought that the only solution was to change the teachers, I realized that I was wrong. The problems that exist within the inner-city school system have multiple solutions, and one of them is to help the teachers to see themselves and their students differently. Helping my teachers and my undergraduates to be more reflective and to hold themselves accountable when they rely on stereotypes as a way to judge their students does help to transform environments, even though it is not the only thing that has to change. I realized, during that semester, that it was the only thing that I could change, and, despite how difficult it was to get the training to "stick," I could not stop. My silence does not protect me, it will not help either my undergraduates or my teachers, and it will not help to create the world that I want my sons to live in. The world that I envision, the one that I believe that I am helping to create, builds upon the world that Dr. Martin Luther King, Jr. once talked about—a world where everyone will be judged by the content of their character and not the color of their skin, their gender, or the size of their bank account. [15]

Notes

1 In biology, "convergence evolution" occurs when unrelated animals occupy a similar environment and begin to develop a superficial resemblance. I believe that the same thing happens when one attempts to study race, class, and gender as separate fields. They begin to fuse together and a superficial resemblance begins to occur, except in instances when the researcher and the research cannot be separated. I study race because I am an African American, gender because I am a woman, and class because I grew in a home that, at some junctures, was very economically challenged. These points cannot be studied separately because all of them inform both what I choose to research and how I research it. "RACLaGE" is the word I use to define my research, as, for me, these are not three separate areas—race, class, and gender—but just one: RA(ce)CL(ass)andGE(nder). See Audre Lorde, "The Master's Tools Will Never Dismantle the Master's House," in *Sister Outsider: Essays and Speeches* (Berkeley, CA: Crossing Press, 2007), 110–113.
2 Author's class notes from personal journal (ACN), April 15, 2010.
3 Ibid.
4 Audre Lorde, *The Cancer Journals* (San Francisco, CA: Aunt Lute Books, 1980).
5 In Adrienne Rich's poem, "The Burning of Paper Instead of Children," which was about the Vietnam War, the ongoing war against children, relationships, and gender inequality, she writes of the "knowledge of the oppressor / this is the oppressor's language / yet I need it to talk to you." See *Adrienne Rich's Poetry and Prose: Poems, Prose, Reviews, and Criticism*, eds. Barbara Charlesworth Gelpi and Albert Gelpi (New York, NY: W.W. Norton, 1993), 40–43. (I remember how, when I first read this poem, I wish I knew another language through which I could express myself and be understood by those who I love. I found myself as entrenched in the oppressor's language as I am in the oppressor's system. There were times when I looked at the face of the oppressor and I saw myself.)
6 ACN, September 16, 2005.
7 Ibid, October 12, 2005, and January 19, 2006.
8 Peggy McIntosh, "White Privilege: Unpacking the Invisible Knapsack," in *White Privilege and Male Privilege: A Personal Account of Coming to See Correspondences Through Work in Women's Studies* (Working Paper No. 189) (Wellesley, MA: Wellesley Centers for Women, 1988). Available at http://www.isr.umich.edu/home/diversity/resources/white-privilege.pdf (accessed 28 March 2013).
9 ACN, September 14, 2004.
10 Walter J. Burghardt, "Contemplation: A Long Loving Look at the Real" in *An Ignatian Spirituality Reader: Contemporary Writings on St. Ignatius of Loyola, the Spiritual Exercises, Discernment, and More*, ed. George W. Traub (Chicago, IL: Loyola Press, 2008), 89–98.
11 See, for example, Zora Neale Hurston, *Dust Tracks on a Road: An Autobiography* (Philadelphia, PA: J. B. Lippincott, 1942). I went through a similar naming activity at the National Women's Studies Association's Women of Color Leadership Project (WoCLP), and was surprised that the same objections were made and that that group also chose the word "folks."
12 Carol Gilligan, *In a Different Voice: Psychological Theory and Women's Development* (Cambridge, MA: Harvard University Press, 1982).
13 Laurie Finke, *Feminist Theory, Women's Writing* (Ithaca, NY: Cornell University Press, 1992).
14 bell hooks, *Talking Back: Thinking Feminist, Thinking Black* (Boston, MA: South End Press, 1989).
15 During the 1963 March on Washington for Jobs and Freedom, Dr. King avowed, "I have a dream that my four little children will one day live in a nation where they will not be judged by the color of their skin, but by the content of their character." A full transcription of King's August 28, 1963, speech is available at http://www.usconstitution.net/dream.html (accessed 22 April 2013).

12

THE RACIALIZED FEMINIST KILLJOY IN WHITE ACADEMIA

Contesting White Entitlement

Benita Bunjun

This chapter draws explicitly on two different periods and cities of my teaching trajectory in British Columbia, Canada, by engaging with comments from student course evaluations in 2012 and my own self-reflective journaling in 2005/6. The "university" has two campuses in different cities where I taught. The first is a large urban city known for its "multicultural and diverse climate" that I refer to as "Port-Louis," and the other is a smaller, White, conservative, Christian city, which I'll name "Rosehill." The making and development of both campuses came to exist on occupied unceded Indigenous[1] territories. I will refer to both campuses as "the university". The university, itself a colonial development project for the White elites, teaches the naturalization of the field of whiteness and how racialized Others must be reproduced and regulated within Canada, a White settler society. My teaching for this university has been predominately in the areas of women's and gender studies and sociology.

The students' evaluation quotes that I draw from in this chapter not only exemplify my experience as a feminist politicized faculty of color teaching from a critical intersectional race and feminist perspective in sociology at the university, but also demonstrate the unsettling of White student settlers and their White "entitlement." This unsettling that I invoke in my pedagogy produces deep resentment, defensiveness, and unproductive guilt that construct me as the "feminist killjoy" as theorized by Sara Ahmed.[2]

Canada as a White Settler Society

I draw from the course evaluations of two sections of a sociology course on Canadian society that I taught at the university. My pedagogical entry point to teaching Canadian society centers the scholarship of Canada as a White settler society. According to Sherene Razack:

> A White settler society is one established by Europeans on non-European soil. Its origins lie in the dispossession and the extermination of Indigenous population by the conquering European. As it evolves, a White settler society continues to be structured by a racial hierarchy. In the national mythologies of such societies, it is believed that White people came first and that it is they who principally developed the land; Aboriginal peoples are presumed to be mostly dead or assimilated. European settlers thus become the original inhabitants and the group most entitled to the fruits of citizenship.[3]

Attached to these White settler mythologies, there exists White amnesia and the ongoing denial of conquest, genocide, chattel slavery, and the exploitation of racialized bodies for labor. The "White nation fantasy," as described by Ghassan Hage,[4] is enveloped in reproducing the myth that Canada was peacefully settled and not colonized through the process of *terra nullius* (empty uninhabited lands). Even though such lands were already inhabited nations, according to Dara Culhane, they "were simply legally *deemed to be uninhibited* if the people were not Christian, not agricultural, not commercial, not 'sufficiently evolved' or simply in the way."[5]

As a nation, Canada is contradictory and contested. Its colonial construction can only exist with the continuing dispossession of Indigenous peoples. The nation is able to imagine its community of those who "truly" belong by the constant dispossession of those who do not belong to the nation. Himani Bannerji explains that discourses of national belonging involve "certain ideas regarding skin colour, history, language (English/French), and other cultural signifiers—all of which may be subsumed under the ideological category 'White.'"[6] Europeanness is represented as whiteness, which translates into Canadianness. Furthermore, embedded in this construction of Canada is a particular notion of nation and state formation. Bannerji criticizes Anderson's[7] concept of imagined communities because he neither examines the contradictions and tensions that may exist in the imagined community, nor does he question the type of imagination at work. Ahmed (2000) also refines this concept:

> The production of the nation involves not only image and myth-making— the telling of 'official' stories of origin—but also the everyday negotiations of what it means "to be" that nation(ality). The production of the nation involves processes of self-identification in which the nation comes to be realised as belonging to the individual (the construction of the "we" as utterable by the individual).[8]

Linda Carty's (1999) scholarship on the construction of Empire and the creation of the Other also offers an understanding of such discourses of nation building. Carty explains that the Other emerged as a "stratification based on skin colour and exemplified through England's positioning of its inhabitants in relation to those of the colonies, particularly in relation to the Africans."[9] She asserts that "by the late 18th century, England, one of the smallest countries in Europe, would 'own' and 'rule' most of the world."[10] England's mission to civilize Indigenous and Third World peoples of its colonies through colonial encounters contributed to the social construction of the Other.[11] "Constructing the Other would give legitimacy to the belief in White superiority and its 'civilizing' mission."[12] Discourses of the uncivilized, heathens, savages, and pagans run parallel to those discourses of racialization and Christianity. The emergence of discourses of inferiority was reproduced within the colonial empire. Hence, the nation and nationalism are formed, imagined and sustained through colonial anxieties and encounters with the stranger as the Other.

Ahmed's (2000) ontology of strangers, as articulated in *Strange Encounters*, provides the theoretical framework for analyzing the presence and encountering of strangers in constructing the dominant "I" or "we" within national and institutional discourses. The making of the stranger is ultimately about the making of the self and how one embodies the self in relation to encounters and contact with strangers. It is through this theoretical understanding that she argues, "there are techniques that allow us to differentiate between those who are strangers and those who belong in a given space."[13] Ahmed analyzes how the stranger is recognized as stranger prior to its appearance as a body identified as not belonging and out of place. She examines how the dominant subject of the nation ensures that the boundaries are maintained and enforced in order to keep the stranger out. If the stranger appears to cross the line or come too close, fear accumulates, demanding that the stranger be expelled in order to secure imagined purity and spatial formation.

> We can consider how nations are invented as familiar spaces, as spaces of belonging, through being defined against others who are recognized, or known again, as strange and hence strangers. In some sense, the stranger appears as a figure, as a way of containing that which the nation is not, and hence as a way of allowing the nation to be.[14]

By already recognizing the stranger as not belonging and out of place, the demarcation and enforcement of boundaries crystallizes the place *we* inhabit as home. Such boundaries are to be maintained and enforced in order to ensure that those we recognize as strangers and who have been determined as not belonging do not contaminate or threaten property, space, and person. Ultimately, Ahmed affirms that "recognizing strangers is here embedded in a discourse of survival: it is a question of how to survive the proximity of strangers who are already figurable, *who have already taken shape*, in the everyday encounters we have with others."[15]

The Feminist Killjoy

The Canadian society course was a third-year full-year course taught at the university in Port-Louis by two different instructors; each instructor independently taught one term. The instructor teaching part one, whom I refer to as "P," was a White female tenured faculty, and was often described in the student evaluations as providing a much safer environment where information was presented as "less biased," "more objective," and "more neutral". In contrast, the following student comments articulate how my racialized invocation troubled and unsettled their White selves.

> I did not feel like this class was in any way a "Canadian Society" class. The entire focus was on racial and ethnic inequality, White supremacy, and colonisation and often without even a focus on Canada ... I felt insecure and attacked for being a White middle-class student in this class. I understand the value in what she was trying to teach, but the manner in which it was done made me defensive and far less receptive to learning ...
>
> *(Student G)*

> There are other issues that are important in Canadian society than just the White settler society. I signed up for the course to learn about culture, diversity, ethnicity, gender, government, race, religion ... She could have made an effort to stay more neutral and academic ...
>
> *(Student F)*

> I felt very uncomfortable in this class, as a White, middle-class person. I understand the long-lasting effects that colonization and Europeans have had on Canada, as I am a third year sociology major. However, I have never felt so attacked in a classroom situation because of my background. I felt very defensive, which was not conducive to a beneficial learning environment for me.
>
> *(Student E)*

Hence, the above comments articulate the view that to bring comfort and joy, Canadian society should be absolved of its history of colonialism and White supremacy and should only reproduce and naturalize the happy image of Canada. It is I who "should be" reinforcing such benevolent imaginations and perform as the grateful, joyful woman of color who MUST (re)produce happy national subjects of the nation by infusing the learning experience in the classroom of White academia with positivity, objectivity, and neutrality.

Ahmed offers the important theoretical framework of the "feminist killjoys." She explains that feminist killjoys do not present themselves as the happy and smiling Other, but, rather, as the feminists who kill the joy of the nation and its national subjects.[16] I refer to "killjoy moments" as pivotal events in the classroom where the faculty of color not only contextualize hegemonic relations, but further "unsettle" the happiness that has been fabricated in the making of a White supremacist nation. Ahmed specifically recognizes politicized women of color and Indigenous women who point out forms of racism and exclusion within as "feminist kill-joys."[17] hooks and Ahmed describe how the proximity of the racialized body causes tension and anxieties for White subjects by unsettling happiness.[18] Ahmed explains:

> Happiness becomes a condition of membership: you have to be happy for them . . . You cannot speak about racism; that's too unhappy as it causes them to lose their right to happiness, resting as it is on an ego ideal of being good and tolerant. You certainly should not speak of whiteness, which would implicate them in the force of your critique. You have to stay in the right place to keep your place.[19]

In the classroom, White students and racialized students who invoke whiteness learn to recognize and reject curricula that contest the reproduction of a White settler society and homonationalism. The response from my students during the first month was as follows: "Benita is racist towards White people," "this is uncomfortable," "there is too much content on First Nations," and she/the content "is so negative." Racialized and White students invoke the field of whiteness by defending imperialism and nationalist discourse of White entitlement, which revolves around the "hard-working pioneers" who developed and civilized the lands and its natives. Another student who demonstrated her frustration stated:

> Although Benita's intentions are good, I feel as though the material she presented both in class and as reading material for outside of class purely reflected her *own beliefs* as a proud member of the gay and lesbian community and as an immigrant. It is important for us as students to engage in information that provides BOTH sides of the story as literature is also subjective. Benita's choice for reading materials was clearly *biased*, while Prof. P's choice of material was much more objective and provided both "sides of the story" so to speak.
>
> (Student D)

The "killjoy" challenges institutional hegemonic academia and the hierarchies of power within knowledge creation and distribution. This disruption has taken place because the "killjoy" has accidently been welcomed as the "stranger" through multicultural benevolent discourses of a White settler society. The stranger now disrupts White, heterosexual, middle-class entitlement and happiness through the emergence and practice of anticolonial pedagogy, which produces her as biased, partial, and lacking objectivity.

The Field of Whiteness and National Power

December 4, 2005, Rosehill

The term has now ended and I am so relieved. It is hard to believe that I made it through the semester. The first few months were rough for many reasons. This place is very White conservative, right wing, and with little awareness of the world in a global context. Being the first racialized woman to teach women's studies in Rosehill, or even as the only racialized person in a room of 20, or the only racialized woman in a room of 100 ... what a lived experience of racial endurance and survival with White academia. How am I to claim any space here on stolen [Indigenous nation] land?

In the classroom, especially in the beginning, it was very tough; my pedagogy and my scholarship, as well as my curriculum, were always contested by at least two students who felt extremely threatened/vulnerable about what they were learning in women's studies. There were days where my mere presence, not even my voice, was contested. The hurtful or confusing gazes from the university administration, as well as the students and the community at large, damaged my spirit and my health deeply.

Ninety-nine percent of my classes were predominantly White students who had rarely seen a racialized woman stand in front of them to teach them about their history. To teach three courses, seven lectures, five days a week and be daily experiencing contestation was truly an unknown experience to me and terribly heartbreaking. I had read and I was told but I never felt. Having been immersed in such an environment has deepened my awareness and honoring of self while daily engaging in strategies of survival in colonial academic environments.

February 25, 2006, Rosehill

Reflections on end-of-term student evaluations—"Benita is a racist, she hates White people"

When a racialized instructor teaches the dominant White about (their) history, norm/Other, dominance, oppression, homophobia, racism, and ableism ... she is a racist. When a racialized instructor teaches the dominant White students about how the White race has/is:

- always welcomed/-ing all peoples globally;
- saved/-ing the Indigenous (native, Indian);
- developed/-ing the Third World;

- (has been) a savior to us all, a humanitarian aid in wars;
- civilized/-ing the world;

she is a good teacher ... she sustains and nourishes their White settler happiness.

The above journaling reflections demonstrate how my mere presence as a racialized, queer, South Asian, female instructor in the university's Rosehill campus produced national anxieties that contested the *field of whiteness*. Hage theorizes what it means to belong to the nation and national accumulated capital.[20] He explains that citizenship is the primary formal marker of national belonging, "the act of taking on citizenship has also been termed 'naturalisation,' implying a process of acculturation, of belonging to a national cultural community."[21] Some academics equate citizenship with national belonging, but Hage disagrees. He argues that all categories describing dominant groups denote the reality of "referring to cultural possessions which allow their holders to stake certain claims of governmental belonging relative to the weight of the capital in his or her possession."[22] Hage recognizes that the value of each capital is "constantly fluctuating, depending on various historical conjunctures as well as the internal struggle within the field of national power."[23]

Hage defines the useful concept of "the field of national power," which, he asserts, is the "field of Whiteness."[24] He explains that "whiteness" is not a fixed category, but, rather, "an ever-changing, composite cultural historical construct."[25] This construct originated in opposition to "blackness" and "brownness," fabrications of colonial relations, where "White has become the ideal of being the bearer of 'Western' civilization ... Whiteness is itself a fantasy position and a field of accumulating Whiteness."[26] Accordingly, Hage argues that "Third World-looking people" are then classified "with very low national capital and ... are invariably constructed as a 'problem' of some sort within all White-dominated societies."[27]

The following statements from students in Port-Louis affirmed their great disappointment when I did not reproduce the same pedagogical framework that nurtured a classroom climate of happiness and comfort as instructor "P" had provided.

I absolutely loved the first semester of this course [with P] and was excited to start another semester of it with Dr. Bunjun. However, I (and the rest of my classmates) quickly discovered that this was not going to be a good finish to this course ... Granted, the entire course is about European colonialist history and the suffering of the colonized; however, many students commented that they felt guilted and put down because of her comments and attitudes. It honestly felt like a *reverse racism* against White people. I have taken many sociology courses concerning similar material, and have never once felt the way I did in this class. *This is not the way to fix any problems, it only adds to them.*

(Student B)

This is probably the worst class that I have ever taken. In no way was it a class about 'inequality' in Canada. Rather, it was a class that focused on White supremacy and racial violence in Canada. I agree that this information is important, but Benita made me feel, as a White female, that I was responsible for such hate crime. Along with talking to other White students in the class, we agreed that we felt discriminated against. We felt that we were singled out and had fingers pointed at us. We didn't learn anything *positive* about Canada, just that we are a White dominating society ... *I understand the importance of taking a critical view towards Canadian society, but one that makes me feel discriminated against, in my opinion, goes too far.*

(Student V)

These comments explain how I made the students feel bad for who they were, how I discriminated against them, and, ultimately, how I have produced "reverse racism" upon their national bodies. I displaced their traditional comfortable selves in White academia. One critical student discusses these discomforts by explaining:

I heard some students in the class complaining that there was a sort of "feminist agenda" operating and that, even though they were White, they aren't settlers; however, I think that is nonsense. It seems to me that the issue for these people is that they had to confront their privilege and were made to feel uncomfortable.

In a sense, [P's] class was *safer* in that students were not forced to confront their privilege and their complicity in perpetuating systems of domination and inequality. However, I think that this semester [with Benita Bunjun] was much more useful for the very reason that people were made to feel uncomfortable. If people look at these issues without examining how they are complicit in the production of them, then they cannot become aware that they are part of the problem. This class had the effect of making people understand their social location and how their unique positionality plays into the different issues we examined. Therefore, students were (hopefully) able to see how they sometimes benefited from and contributed to systems of oppression. I think that this kind of awakening really forces people to at least examine their own social situation and is much more likely to contribute to larger social change.

(Student A)

Hence, throughout the term, I was consistently compared to P—an inevitable comparison between a White, heterosexual faculty with tenure and me, a racialized, queer faculty without tenure. Such comparisons created a hierarchy of scholarly legitimacy. How dare I engage in the process of projecting my full subjectivity as other White faculty members have done for decades? How dare I speak about the Other? It appears that I had committed a great crime by not only exposing Canada's colonial White supremacist history, but, even more devastatingly, I had invoked feelings of guilt and defensiveness in my students. This comparison between myself and P produced the "unhappy, ungrateful, queer instructor of color" who shed her unhappiness onto those who are either happy White settlers or happy grateful settlers of color; both invest in the invocation and deployment of the field of whiteness.

For Canada and its academic post-secondary institutions, the field of whiteness produces and facilitates the claim of legitimate White Canadianness and White academics. This field of national power is further complicated when "this dynamic of accumulation reaches its limitations … when it comes face to face with those whose richness in national capital does not come from a struggle to accumulate and 'be like' White Australians [Canadians], but who appear 'naturally' White Australians [Canadians].'"[28] *How* one accumulates such capital is an important determinant of its national recognition and legitimacy. Therefore, "no matter how much national capital a 'Third World-looking' migrant accumulates, the fact that he or she has acquired it, rather than being born with it, devalues what he or she possesses" in comparison to the "naturally" White Canadian national subject.[29]

Dismantling White Entitlement and Happiness

The mere presence of a racialized politicized body within White academia is itself a form of resistance that deeply disrupts spatial, symbolic, political, and affective White entitlements. In particular, as a racialized, South Asian, queer feminist, White liberal academia has defined my presence and pedagogy as an encroachment that threatens its every heteronormative, middle-/upper-class field of whiteness. By attempting to not reproduce such a landscape, we, as feminist killjoys, are constructed as the most threatening because we do not cater to White institutional and national entitlements as "natural" and "inevitable." It is our colonial encounters with administrations, students, and with one another within such bourgeois intellectual institutions that produce differently positioned strangers. Our influence as racialized strangers who were never meant to teach within White academia is deeply troubling. If we were meant to walk the halls of White academia, it was only through processes of servitude, such as as cleaners, cooks, and clerical staff. Through the processes of colonization and immigration, the imperial multicultural project faces many un-expectations. One of them has been our presence as Indigenous bodies and bodies of color who intellectually entered and carved out academic spaces within a White settler society. Ahmed emphasizes that *some bodies* are constructed as negative and are encountered as being negative.[30] Frye explains that "it is often a requirement of oppressed people that we smile and be cheerful. If we comply, we signify our docility and our acquiescence in our situation."[31] Therefore, those that are oppressed must show and demonstrate signs of happiness and gratefulness, and, hence, those that do not may be perceived as negative, angry, hostile, and unhappy.

Ahmed introduces the concept of "happiness duty".[32] She explains that happiness can be constructed as a duty that functions as a debt which is owed and must be returned in the form of happiness. We, as politicized faculty of color who experience processes of exclusion, while being policed, disciplined, and regulated, are taught to be thankful and to perform the happiness duty to predominately White academics, administrators, staff, and students. Ahmed emphasizes that bodies pass as happy in order "to keep things in the right place."[33] For those who become objects and symbols of the troublemaker or killjoy, it is because they are willing to speak out about their unhappiness or they refuse to make others happy. "The feminist killjoy 'spoils' the happiness of others; she is a spoilsport because she refuses to convene, to assemble, or to meet up over happiness."[34] Student Z articulates, below, how negativity is perceived by unhappy students while describing her transformation as a student engaging with critical thinking.

> I know Benita will most likely get plenty of negative comments, but I enjoyed her class. I think there was initial negative reaction because, compared to P, Benita is more "intense" and presents more critical and "controversial" views on society. Also Benita's course was heavier on theory (compared to P's, that is, since P's class barely had any), which contributed to the general dislike.
>
> I feel that students who took this course without a general interest in Canadian society (because it is a required course) generally ended up feeling negative about Benita's class because it is more rigorous and demanding. I liked it, however, and I found it worth my time since I learned a lot from this course, and it inspired me to become more active in social issues.
>
> *(Student Z)*

I not only destroy happiness and joy, but I am also believed to be responsible for students' bad feelings and unhappiness. Feminist killjoys are constructed as unhappy people who ruin the field of whiteness spatially, symbolically, politically, and affectively. But some students, those who dare to open their minds and hearts, experience the benefits from such scholarship and pedagogy.

When the feminist killjoy within academic spaces is seen to be disturbing the fragility of the space, spatial entitlements are then threatened because spatial happiness is undermined as it interacts with other forms of entitlement. Often what does not get noticed is what makes the feminist killjoy courageously perform and speak in the way that she does. What are the invocations and deployments of power relations that produce the effects of excluding her, denying her scholarship, and omitting her subjectivity? Ahmed also explains that feminist killjoys such as queer, working-class, women of color feminists are seen to get into trouble because they are already read as being trouble before anything happens. Hence, power relations of exclusion and representation are already invoked prior to the possible deployment of these power relations across difference.

Many evaluations from the sociology course demonstrated that a number of students were well aware of the attacks that I would experience from their own friends and classmates, not only for teaching critical content within an intersectional analysis, but for daring to teach, articulate, and speak about the field of whiteness. Student T provides an example of critical awareness and also of compassion:

> I am aware Benita will probably get many scathing reviews. From the time I have spent with my classmates, I believe that this is because they were not ready to have their ways of thinking changed by someone who comes off so strongly. This is very unfortunate in a sociology class. A major frustration for me was that a small selection of my classmates often discounted ideas brought up by Benita, probably just because it was Benita that was saying them. Benita's analysis of Canadian society went very deep, and I strongly appreciate this, although many of my classmates might not. I truly believe that everyone at [the university] should be taking this class with her and learning what she teaches.
>
> *(Student T)*

The killjoys are seen as disrupting unity and fracturing the climate of the classroom because they speak out against the intersectional racist, classist, transphobic, nationalist, and ableist talk and culture within White academia's everyday discourses. Ahmed articulates how certain bodies are encountered as being negative:

> Do bad feelings enter the room when somebody expresses anger about things, or could anger be the moment when the bad feelings that circulate through objects get brought to the surface in a certain way? Feminist subjects might bring others down not only by talking about unhappy topics ... but by exposing how happiness is sustained by erasing the very signs of not getting along. Feminists do kill joy in a certain sense: they disturb the very fantasy that happiness can be found in certain places. To kill a fantasy can still kill a feeling. It is not just that feminists might not be happily affected by the objects that are supposed to cause happiness, but that their failure to be happy is read as sabotaging the happiness of others.[35]

In this instance, the feminist killjoy faculty of color is defined as the cause of unhappiness, and her critical engagement is read as targeting the happiness of her students rather than what nonwhite subjects are unhappy about. She becomes what Ahmed describes as "affectively alien" because she affects others in the wrong way and her "proximity gets in the way of other people's enjoyment of the right things, functioning as an unwanted reminder of histories that are disturbing, that disturb an atmosphere."[36] Not only are different degrees and intensities of White entitlement and its relationship to space, land, and territory questioned, but the emotions, symbols, and politics attached to the making and sustaining of such White entitlement within the field of whiteness are also interrogated.

The Politicized, Racialized, Feminist Killjoy's Contributions to Transformation

Lastly, I argue that racialized feminist killjoys are pivotal to institutional academic sites as they *provide the motivating force for institutional change and the necessary source of energy to engage and transform knowledge and scholarship.* For Audre Lorde, it is the feminist killjoy who engages in cou(rage) and anger. As Lorde states, "anger is loaded with information and energy."[37] She further asserts:

> I cannot hide my anger to spare you guilt, nor hurt feelings, nor answering anger; for to do so insults and trivializes all our efforts. Guilt is not a response to anger; it is a response to one's own actions or lack of action. If it leads to change then it can be useful, since it is then no longer guilt but the beginning of knowledge. Yet all too often, guilt is just another name for impotence, for defensiveness destructive of communication; it becomes a device to protect ignorance and the continuation of things the way they are, the ultimate protection for changelessness.[38]

It is this conception of killjoy and anger as not merely inhibiting or impeding, but, rather, as the energy that moves, transgresses, and transforms individuals and academic spaces that has benefited many students. Hence, the dissatisfaction and disappointments with White academia contribute to the politicized racialized feminist engagement in envisioning a different site of critical learning, knowledge creation, and the necessary integrity to nurture all students differently based on their intersecting positionalities. The following quote reveals a sociology student's critical reflection on learning processes.

> I think that Benita really brings a lot to the table in terms of her background. Very few teachers are as open to talking about their own race, sexuality, or other positions, but I think that it is really important for students to see this and to learn from it. I don't know why but a lot of students, I think, felt really threatened by Benita coming out as a lesbian of colour in our class and I hear very disrespectful remarks very often about her "agenda" that she was pushing on us.

> But, seriously, good on you Benita for sticking up for yourself! The fact that people are still making idiotic remarks like that demonstrates that there is a

greater need for teachers to be declaring their own biases and positionality. It is not okay that students felt really comfortable talking about patriarchy and racism and privilege from a White, straight professor (first term), but, all of a sudden, felt like it was an "agenda" being pushed on them when they were being taught by a lesbian of colour. The whole thing made me feel really sick.

(Student W)

What emerges from this chapter is an intersectional analysis of the feminist killjoy who interrupts national happiness within White academic institutions of a White settler society by threatening the naturalized field of whiteness. This chapter also demonstrates what Hage has articulated as the discourse of Anglo decline and displacement, which draws on the *worrying nationalist* who is deeply invested in discourses of White nation fantasy exhibiting White supremacy.[39] Similarly, worrying nationalists feared racialized women's presence and leadership within White academia. This fear of displacement by the Other reproduces stranger danger discourses of national anxieties and responses of essentialism, exclusion, and racialization.

The loss of White entitlement by predominately White students translates into the loss of spatial, symbolic, political, and affective entitlement. Spatial entitlement reflects the politics of spatial belonging and gate-keeping in the construction and reinforcement of White academia. It is the site of colonial contact zones and encounters that grants insider or outsider status to differently positioned national subjects. Affective entitlement is embedded in emotions of belonging and attachment that secure the field of whiteness and its consistent craving for happiness. Hence, the displacement of affective entitlement produces affective anxieties not only because of the loss of joy and comfort, but also the experience of symbolic, spatial, and political invasion upon the classroom and nation by the racialized feminist killjoy. Furthermore, the killjoy becomes a symbol that directly threatens the nation-builders and gate-keepers of the White settler society—its space, politics, symbols, and affects. As unhappiness grows, politics of national belonging and citizenship come into question. For example, who is the right national scholar to teach Canadian society within White academia?

Encroachments upon national subjects' entitlements by the stranger or Other produced colonial anxieties and fears of disentitlement and loss of happiness. Struggles and anxieties emerged for students as they experienced the loss of different and intersecting modalities of entitlement in the form of displacement, particularly as their privileges were challenged. My racialized, politicized, queer body troubles such academic spaces as it is a body out of place that speaks, contests, and unsettles hierarchies of power and also creates colonial discomforts and unhappiness.

Notes

1 I use the term "Indigenous" here to refer to First Nations, Metis, Inuit, and Aboriginal communities and peoples. I explicitly use the term "Indigenous peoples" to demonstrate their active presence and connection globally not only as those who have experienced dispossession through colonization and imperialism, but also as those who possess multiplicity of traditional and ancestral knowledges. Indigenous peoples of Canada are the original inhabitants whose identities are deeply connected spiritually and politically to the land. It is on this basis that Indigenous peoples are committed to uphold their inherent sovereign rights to self-government and self-determination. See Patricia Monture-Angus, *Journeying Forward: Dreaming First Nations' Independence* (Halifax, Nova Scotia, Canada: Fernwood Publishing, 1999).

2 Sara Ahmed, "Embodying Diversity: Problems and Paradoxes for Black Feminists," *Race, Ethnicity and Education, 12*(1), 2009: 41–52; Sara Ahmed, *The Promise of Happiness* (Durham, NC: Duke University Press, 2010).

3 Sherene Razack, "When Place Becomes Race," in *Race, Space, and the Law: Unmapping a White Settler Society*, ed. Sherene Razack (Toronto, Ontario, Canada: Between the Lines, 2002).

4 Ghassan Hage, *White Nation: Fantasies of White Supremacy in a Multicultural Society* (New York, NY: Routledge, 2000), 67.

5 Dara Culhane, *The Pleasure of the Crown: Anthropology, Law and First Nations* (Burnaby, British Columbia, Canada: Talonbooks, 1998), 48.

6 Himani Bannerji, *The Dark Side of the Nation: Essays on Multiculturalism, Nationalism and Gender* (Toronto, Ontario, Canada: Canadian Scholars' Press, 2000), 64.

7 See Benedict Anderson, *Imagined Communities: Reflections on the Origin and Spread of Nationalism* (New York, NY: Verso, 1991).

8 Sara Ahmed, *Strange Encounters: Embodied Others in Post-Coloniality* (New York, NY: Routledge, 2000), 98.

9 Linda Carty, "The Discourse of Empire and the Social Construction of Gender," in *Scratching the Surface: Canadian, Antiracist, Feminist Thought*, eds. Enakshi Dua and Angela Robertson (Toronto, Ontario, Canada: Women's Press, 1999), 36–37.

10 Ibid., 36.

11 See Carty, "The Discourse of Empire"; Cecily Devereux, "New Woman, New World: Maternal Feminism and the New Imperialism in the White Settler Colonies," *Women's Studies International Forum, 22*(2), 1999: 175–184; Mariana Valverde, "'When the Mother of the Race is Free': Race, Reproduction, and Sexuality in First-Wave Feminism," in *Gender Conflicts: New Essays in Women's History*, eds. Franca Iacovetta and Mariana Valverde (Toronto, Ontario, Canada: University of Toronto Press, 1992).

12 Carty, "The Discourse of Empire," 36.

13 Ahmed, *Strange Encounters*, 22.

14 Ibid., 97.

15 Ibid., 22.

16 In "Embodying Diversity," Ahmed suggests that "there is a relationship between the negativity of certain figures and how certain bodies are encountered as being negative" (p. 48).

17 Ahmed's "Embodying Diversity" and *The Promise of Happiness* draw on feminists who have been constructed as "killjoy feminists," such as Audre Lorde, *Sister Outsider: Essays and Speeches* (Freedom, CA: Crossing Press, 1984); bell hooks, *Feminist Theory: From Margin to Center* (Cambridge, MA: South End Press 2000); and Aileen Moreton-Robinson, "Tiddas Talkin' Up to the White Woman: When Huggins et al. Took on Bell," in *Blacklines: Contemporary Critical Writing by Indigenous Australians*, ed. Michelle Grossman (Carlton, Victoria, Australia: Melbourne University Press, 2003).

18 See hooks, *Feminist Theory*; Ahmed, *Strange Encounters*.

19 Ahmed, "Embodying Diversity", 48.
20 Hage, *White Nation*, 56.
21 Ibid., 56.
22 Ibid.
23 Ibid., 57.
24 Ibid.
25 Ibid., 58.
26 Ibid.
27 Ibid., 59.
28 Ibid., 61. Hage's *White Nation*, which focuses on Australia, is extremely useful for this chapter because it exemplifies similar histories with Canada as colonial settler societies.
29 Ibid., 62.
30 Ahmed, "Embodying Diversity," 48.
31 Marilyn Frye, *The Politics of Reality: Essays in Feminist Theory* (Trumansburg, NY: Crossing Press, 1983), 2.
32 Ahmed, *The Promise of Happiness*, 59.
33 Ibid.
34 Ibid., 65.
35 Ibid., 66.
36 Ibid., 56.
37 Audre Lorde, "The Uses of Anger," *Women's Studies Quarterly*, 25(1/2), 1997: 278–285, 280.
38 Ibid., 282.
39 Hage, *White Nation*, 17.

13

RACE IN(OUT)SIDE THE CLASSROOM

On Pedagogy and the Politics of Collegiality

Nana Osei-Kofi

It was in reading *I've Got a Story to Tell: Identity and Place in the Academy* as a graduate student that the idea of theory as liberatory came to have meaning for me.[1] The book is described as follows:

> Through storytelling—multicultural, gendered, and classed—the contributors to this text bring the experience of teachers of color to the center of discourse regarding identity, teaching, the politics of difference, and the creation of spaces and places through which the exercise of agency is made manifest within institutions of higher learning.[2]

Through the narratives of the women and men of color in the chapters of this book, I was able to begin to make sense of my own experiences as a woman of color in U.S. higher education. These narratives give voice to what Chandra Mohanty characterizes as the type of "understanding of experience and of the personal that makes theory possible."[3] The contributors to *I've Got a Story to Tell* bring to life what bell hooks describes as "theory emerg[ing] from the concrete, from ... efforts to make sense of everyday life experiences, from ... efforts to intervene critically in ... [one's] life and the lives of others ... [that which] makes feminist [and antiracist] transformation possible."[4]

Standing on the shoulders of those who have come before me, what I aim to do in this chapter, writing from my current location as an associate professor at a predominantly White institution (PWI), is to grapple with the ways in which the enactment of oppositional pedagogies and the creation of oppositional analytic spaces, by faculty of color at PWIs, shape the contours of our collegial relationships within these institutions. In so doing, I take seriously hooks' assertion that theory can only be "healing, liberatory or revolutionary ... when we ask that it do so and direct our theorizing toward this end."[5] Thus, as I theorize from a place of collective experience, I attempt to engage with how we, as faculty of color, may respond to the realities we face in ways that do not simply place emphasis on surviving what Antonia Darder describes as "conditions of 'collegial adversity.'"[6] Instead, I am interested in "how we make [our]sel[ves] anew."[7] That is to say, I am interested in advancing a discourse that grapples with how we not only resist, but also engage in truly counterhegemonic work that advances radical structural change in an era of neoliberalism, and that is premised on rethinking the world, on a belief in the possibility of another world.[8]

I come to this work as a woman of color with experience teaching in different capacities at four PWIs. Currently, I am in the School of Education at Iowa State University, where I direct a social justice studies graduate certificate program and also hold an affiliate appointment in women's and gender studies. I also come to this work as a "criticalist," as an education theorist whose work centers social and cultural criticism for the purpose of social transformation. My work is deeply influenced by a broad range of education and feminist scholars, from Henry Giroux and Antonia Darder to Chandra Mohanty, Jacqui Alexander, and bell hooks. Engaging oppositional pedagogies and creating oppositional analytic spaces was modeled for me as a graduate student by radical faculty of color, and, although I also saw the sometimes detrimental consequences of this, even for tenured faculty, it has always been clear to me that *this* is my work.[9]

Teaching as a Criticalist of Color

Teaching against the grain brings with it a number of different responses from faculty colleagues. One of the first things I recall as a new, untenured, race, class, and gender scholar at a PWI was the flood of requests to guest lecture in classes taught by my new colleagues. My initial response was positive. I was happy and eager to have the opportunity to share my work, and often I was encouraged by the positive responses I received. What I soon learned, however, is that not all opportunities to guest lecture are the same. When I visited classes taught by colleagues who shared my research interests, I like to think that we modeled the best of co-teaching. Through our lively discussions moving back and forth, agreeing and disagreeing, honing in on nuances, considering different arguments, bringing varied bodies of literature to the discussion, we attempted to capture for students the richness and complexity of the issues at stake, while also modeling how students as emerging scholars may enter the conversation. In other situations, however, I became a check mark, an embodiment of change that merely functioned as a tool of the status quo. As long as I could cover issues of race, class, and gender in a guest lecture each semester, the diversity box could be checked with ease, and "business as usual" remained intact. Tokenism in these instances functioned as a way of maintaining the status quo; a tokenism that was not simply about written texts and course content, but also about my presence as embodied racialized and gendered text.[10]

As I have thought about this over the years, there are no easy answers. Resisting "business as usual" as an untenured assistant professor comes with great risk of retaliation from more established colleagues.[11] Meanwhile, although the opportunity to expose students to material that they may otherwise never encounter can open up spaces of possibility, this comes with the realization that tokenism "instrumentalize[s] and commodif[ies] people of color within education,"[12] and that tokenism, by definition, will never foster lasting structural change. Yet, to work for the changes we envision, we must be at the table.

As students have become familiar with my work, my classes have grown in size and have come to include students from a wide range of disciplines and fields of study. This has meant that, over time, a growing number of students have attempted to transfer knowledge acquired in my classes to other classes, where critical discussions of race, class, gender, and sexuality have historically been absent. Unfortunately, all too frequently, these actions—which, to me, represent the deep intellectual engagement we all hopefully want from emerging scholars— have been perceived as challenging the authority of faculty members in other classes. As a result, colleagues have expressed concern that my pedagogy and course content gives birth to "troublemakers." Creating a space for difficult academic engagement, challenging the politics of knowledge, and aiding graduate students in finding their voices as scholar/activists is seen as cause for concern because it rocks the boat and exposes an anti-intellectual stance that is all too common in the academy today.

These experiences, to me, are part and parcel of the many ways in which the work of faculty of color is delegitimized in the academy; of what Darder describes as "unspoken competition over ideas, which unfortunately is indirectly waged through the mentorship of students—making scholarship an issue of personal loyalties, rather than of the larger intellectual and practical concerns of emancipation."[13] I have had both majority and minoritized students recount how some of my colleagues have discouraged them from taking courses with me; these students are advised that the material they will learn in my classes will be of no benefit to them professionally and that it will hurt them to take courses such as these. They are warned of the danger in forever being associated with critical discourses on race, class, gender, sexuality, and social justice in education. Most students interested in my classes understand the issues enough to see how problematic these perspectives are, but, at the same time, there are students who are legitimately concerned when told that their academic and professional goals may be hampered by being associated with critical discourses, especially when these students are of color and aware of the realities of structural racism in higher education. These acts by colleagues reflect, in effect, what Alicia Chavira-Prado describes as "the use of students as instruments of domination."[14] In using students as pawns to delegitimize critical teaching, progressive faculty of color are disciplined for failing to "know their place" as cultural representatives, rather than knowledge producers.[15]

The Politics of Collegiality

As I consider my relationships with colleagues as a function of my classroom practices, it seems to me they exist within a space where, on the one hand, I have incredible experiences with like-minded colleagues in which we share both class content as well as pedagogical approaches. We come together to discuss our successes and failures in responding to student resistance to difficult subject matter, in person, over the phone, and on email, and we support one another in our commitments to be effective teachers and to make a difference through our teaching. The overwhelming majority of these experiences, but not all, are with women, people of color, and gay, lesbian, bisexual, transgender, or queer (GLBTQ)-identified colleagues, and always with faculty who come to the conversation with a significant level of consciousness surrounding oppression. On the other hand, I have colleagues who respond to what I do and who I am with ignorance. Drawing on the work of Marilyn Frye and others, what I am referring to is not ignorance as a passive state of not knowing, or as accidental.[16] Instead, it is an ignorance that is consistent with Frye's suggestion that the active pursuit of ignorance (that is, *to ignore*) by dominant groups, supported by institutional structures, reinforces the privilege held by these groups. This privileged perspective defines what I do as being outside of the mainstream, as separatist, irrelevant to the "average" (read: White, middle-class, heterosexual, able-bodied, Christian, and, preferably, male) scholar in the field, and thus best ignored and kept at bay, except when useful to market an image of diversity. Ignorance also manifests by putting forth majority faculty or "more 'acceptable' people of color . . . to neutralize" that which is seen as too radical."[17] I have often thought that there is *some* potential for radicalizing action when majority faculty members are put forth as the true knowers of the "Other" simply because of their skin color and, often, gender. When they are colleagues who actually do antiracist and antisexist work, I believe there are strategic opportunities to make racism and sexism transparent. Unfortunately, however, as Darder points out, "even esteemed progressive colleagues can become more concerned about not tainting their reputation, in order to preserve the power or influence they feel they've garnered along the way."[18]

As I reflect on my experiences and those of other faculty of color, it is true that there are different approaches that I think of as "approaches of survival" to addressing that which comes with engaging racism and other forms of oppression in classrooms at PWIs as a person of color, all of which are well rehearsed in the literature.[19] For example, to mediate being positioned as responsible for certain content within departments, we can push for professional development to help faculty who uphold the status quo to understand the significance of issues of social justice to the content they teach, and introduce them to the current scholarship on these issues within their specific disciplines and fields of study. Today, when I am asked to guest lecture, I always ask first to see what students are reading in the class on the subject matter I am asked to discuss, to make sure that what I bring to the table will not simply be an "add on."

We can be transparent with students about the ways in which others may position them as a response to the choices they make in relation to their academic pursuits. For many of my students, when they sign up for mainstream classes, they make sure that they are not the only student in the class with exposure to critical content. I also make time outside the regular course schedule for students pursuing work outside the mainstream, the majority of whom are members of minoritized groups, to look critically at what this means for them as graduate students and as emerging scholars, and how they might best navigate these realities.

We can also work to educate students about the ways in which biases shape how many of them view minoritized faculty and faculty whose work is outside of the mainstream. Some of my experiences I share with students concerning this issue include the many times I have been in professional settings where students assume that I am a graduate student, or automatically call me by my first name, in instances where they address my White male colleagues by title and last name. I also discuss the ways in which students often equate scholars like myself, who stray from the canon, as lacking in knowledge and appropriate grounding in the literature. Although minoritized students are, at times, more aware of prejudice, I have found that, as a function of academic socialization, it is not unusual for both majority students and minoritized students to hold these types of biases.

In my experience, the isolation and de-legitimization of one's work that is all too common among faculty of color can, in part, be mediated through good mentoring, community building with like-minded scholars, both within and outside our home institutions, and, as Audre Lorde counsels, by being clear in our pursuits about when, where, and in what ways alliances and solidarity are possible and when and where they are not.[20]

For me, community building has been one of my greatest sources of strength. I have wonderful friends from graduate school and we have supported one another as we moved into and through faculty life. I have also found that, even in the most conservative spaces in academe, there are always pockets of progressive scholars. These are the people who sustain me on a day-to-day basis. A year after earning my PhD, I became involved with the Future of Minority Studies project (FMS) funded by the Mellon Foundation, and the scholars I met through this project, both senior and junior, have guided me directly and indirectly, intellectually and practically. The women of color I spend time with every year at the National Women's Studies Association conference, many of whom are also part of FMS, feed my academic soul. It is through communities such as these that we find new ways to respond to marginalization, legitimization, racism, and sexism, in our everyday. As an example, one of the lessons I have learned from colleagues in spaces such as this is that teaching about race and racism successfully in PWIs often necessitates beginning by engaging students with other forms of injustice to which they can more readily relate. For me, when working with predominately White and religiously conservative students in rural environments, this has often meant using the literature on liberation theology as an entry point for discussing the realities of oppression. Through liberation theology, I have been able to foster dialogue and analysis of how class is manifest in rural communities today, which is something with which many of my students typically have personal experience. Our discussions of class have, in turn, opened up a space for an understanding of race and racism within a larger context of social injustice. Ultimately, this approach has also contributed to students' comprehension of how social context shapes the contours of oppression.

The most important lesson I have learned through my experiences as a woman of color in the academy is that the many manifestations of oppression must be engaged at the systemic level for there to be any hope of lasting change. Mohanty suggests, and I agree, that a failure to do so means participating in the "individualization of power hierarchies and of structures of discrimination."[21] A number of years ago, I was part of a group of minoritized faculty who fought for raises in salary on the basis of equity. We recognized that the issue was both historic and structural, and that it was therefore important for us to stand together in solidarity as we engaged with this struggle. However, the advice we received from influential, senior, White male colleagues was that we should negotiate our salaries individually because that "is the way things are done," and salaries, we were told, at the end of the day, are based on individual merit. Moreover, these individuals articulated the inequities we challenged as simply resulting from an oversight by the individual responsible for salary allocations. This way of framing issues of inequity, void of a systemic perspective, which is all too common when minoritized groups raise concerns, is of great danger to the struggle for change, as it erases historical and structural realities and posits the *individual* as the source of oppression, the experience of injustice as *individual*, and a shift in the *individual* as the key to change. In this problematic view, the suggestion is that all that is necessary to address social and economic injustice perpetrated against groups of people based on race, gender, and class through historically specific processes and systems are attitudinal and behavior changes.[22]

In my insistence on the need for structural engagement, I do not mean to imply that efforts such as the provision of good mentoring, clear guidelines for promotion and tenure, some forms of what we know as "diversity training," and bridge programs for graduate students of color to transition to faculty life are not of value. They are indeed both important and often necessary for survival.[23] What I am submitting, however, is that, if we never go beyond what dominates the "faculty of color success literature," then it suggests that what is at stake is simply the need to improve programmatic efforts, build understanding, and find more effective methods of communication, rather than a struggle over power relations and the need to engage with a history of domination, exploitation, and structural inequity.[24] To use Ann Russo's words, "It is not simply a matter of ideology, ideas, stereotypes, images, and/or misguided perceptions. It is about power and control, be it in terms of money, construction of ideology, or control over organizational agenda."[25] To focus *only* on ways to achieve inclusion within the current structure, without any demands for structural change, is to concede to a colonial system of education that was never intended to include all.[26] Hence, to challenge the present hegemony is not enough.

We need to survive *and* we need to oppose oppressive academic structures. At the same time, we also need to be able to reimagine our world, to reimagine education, to reimagine the academy, and to create spaces in the present that embody, in every way possible, this vision of liberation.[27] As I think of this, to nurture my own sense of possibility in my efforts to work collaboratively with colleagues to create material and intellectual spaces of liberation, I draw inspiration from bold contemporary movements for radical change, such as the Boggs Center's efforts to reimagine community and education in Detroit and beyond, the prison abolition movement's demand for the elimination of the prison system, and the many youth-led groups struggling for the rights of undocumented immigrants. These efforts remind me of what is possible by coming together to do the work that must be done, no matter the struggle.

When I look to the history of the rights of labor, civil rights, women's rights, and GLBTQ rights in the United States, I am reminded of the possibility of change through struggle, and what has been achieved. Simultaneously, this realization brings with it a sobering declaration of the work that remains to be done. For me, this is a poignant reminder that to labor in the academy for radical change, short-term strategies must stem from a longer-term vision. A longer-term vision is essential in order to be able to determine whether short-term strategies are contributing to the type of educational system and society those of us who see a need for change envision.[28] I view short-term strategies as part of what I do when I create assignments where students are required to work collaboratively to identify and work toward creating tangible and sustainable change in real-life situations of injustice in the environments in which they find themselves. To me, this is part of creating a space for students to reimagine the world and take action to bring about change. This is a process through which collaboratively identifying oppressive conditions in environments of which students are a part often fosters a new consciousness among those who, based on their lived experiences, enter into the work without seeing a need to reimagine the world. For students of privilege, issues of injustice are made concrete through their own research and analysis, making oppressive conditions much more difficult to ignore, compared to when seen as only being a part of that which is discussed in the literature, separate from these students' realities. By connecting these short-term strategies to a longer-term vision of an educational system and a society that is just in structure and form, I am able to look critically at whether my efforts as an educator committed to social change transcend the classroom.

I believe what we do to work for change must be done in collectivity in order to challenge the ways in which "in this era of neoliberalism we have all learned how to imagine ourselves primarily as individuals."[29] The "we" I am referring to here is a "we" inclusive of all who view themselves as part of the struggle for a liberatory academy. To challenge and to resist the status quo of unequal power relations in the American academy, I contend that we must place power at the center of our analysis and our actions. One of the ways we can do this is to heed Lila Abu-Lughod's suggestion, drawing on Foucault, that "we . . . use resistance as a *diagnostic* of power."[30] This suggests that, by heightening our attention to the different ways in which faculty of color practice resistance in their everyday, we can better understand "the complex interworkings of historically changing structures of power";[31] interworkings or axes of power that must be made transparent as part of resisting and challenging hegemony.[32] A practice of everyday resistance that I have seen quite frequently is faculty of color choosing not to participate in faculty meetings on a regular basis because, when they do attend, they are treated as invisible. By refusing to participate, whether consciously or not, these are acts of resistance to the dominant institutional narrative of racial harmony, equal participation, and shared governance; acts of resistance that illuminate structures of power.

To practice resistance, we must also nurture communities of resistance, material and metaphorical, politically rooted communities where critical scholarship, teaching, and learning can take place, where historically and theoretically grounded analysis of power and privilege can thrive, where solidarity, support, healing, and transformation can come to life.[33] I know, for me, without these types of experiences of community, however irregular or sometimes flawed, I would not be in the academy today.

The Struggle for Change

In the words of Frederick Douglass, "power concedes nothing without a demand. It never did and it never will."[34] That which is oppositional in the academy today exists as a result of struggle, as a result of demands for changes to an institution historically created to serve the interests of White, propertied men. The establishment of ethnic studies and women's studies, the presence of women, people of color, and the working class in higher education today are all functions of collective demands for change. Hence, the history of educational struggles in the United States lends credence to Andrea Smith's suggestion that, while the system can handle a large number of academics working separately for change, it is when thousands come together and act collectively that we can challenge the system.[35] I have too many examples of colleagues who have offered brilliant analyses and critiques of institutional racism, sexism, and homophobia that are routinely dismissed by those in power as isolated provocateurs without credibility.

In sharing this, I am not arguing against speaking out; I am, however, suggesting that there are strategic reasons tied to the outcomes sought that should encourage careful collective planning of how dissent is expressed, in what context, to what audience, and by whom.

As we move collectively to imagine alternatives, to think of new worlds, it is imperative that we understand the academy as part of the larger political economy. To think of higher education anew requires that we understand and make transparent the ways in which "educational, cultural, social, and economic policy and practices are connected to the multiple relations of exploitation and domination—and to struggles against such relations—in the larger society."[36] As I have discussed elsewhere, "this means that, in looking at the United States, it is necessary to recognize capitalism as the overarching structural force in society."[37] When, for example, courses in Black studies or queer studies are canceled for failing to meet institutional enrollment targets, it is important to see not only how these areas of study are devalued as a function of racist and homophobic values and beliefs, but also the ways in which these values and beliefs intersect with neoliberal ideals to dismantle oppositional spaces in the academy. Moreover, attention to political economy also illuminates how the connections between conditions within the academy and those within the larger society, particularly in terms of the creation of wealth for a small group in society, drive decision-making in all spheres at the expense of the welfare of the majority.

Furthermore, thinking of the academy anew demands that we critically examine our own deployment of power. It is imperative that we consciously resist the uncritical reproduction of existing forms of hierarchical relations. In my own experience, there are many times I have chosen not to take part in organized efforts to struggle for change, not because I did not believe in the issue, but because, as a woman of color, the structure and decision-making used by those involved often were no different than the structures that brought the contested issues being confronted into being. What this illuminates is hooks' assertion that "fundamental to the process of decentering the oppressive other and claiming our right to subjectivity is the insistence that we must determine how we will be and not rely on colonizing responses to determine our legitimacy."[38] The reality and effectiveness of people power, the power of everyday people who come together in struggle, has always been part of significant progressive social change and possibility for change. And this is no less true today than it has been in the past. The circumstances may look different and our approaches must be responsive to the present context. What is fundamental, however, is that we must believe in the possibility of change.

Notes

1 Sandra Jackson and José Solís Jordán, eds., *I've Got a Story to Tell: Identity and Place in the Academy* (New York, NY: Peter Lang, 1999). For a discussion of theory as liberatory

see: bell hooks, *Teaching to Transgress: Education as the Practice of Freedom* (New York, NY: Routledge, 1994), 59–75.

2 Jackson and Jordán, *I've Got a Story to Tell*, 1.

3 Chandra Talpade Mohanty, *Feminism Without Borders: Decolonizing Theory, Practicing Solidarity* (Durham, NC: Duke University Press, 2003), 191.

4 hooks, *Teaching to Transgress*, 70.

5 Ibid., 61.

6 Antonia Darder, *A Dissident Voice: Essays on Culture, Pedagogy and Power* (New York, NY: Peter Lang, 2011), 84.

7 bell hooks, *Yearning: Race, Gender, and Cultural Politics* (Boston, MA: South End Press, 1990), 15.

8 Nana Osei-Kofi, "Junior Faculty of Color in the Corporate University: Implications of Neoliberalism and Neoconservatism on Research, Teaching, and Service," *Critical Studies in Education*, *53*(2), 2012: 229–244, 240.

9 See Darder, *A Dissident Voice*, x–xx.

10 Bryant K. Alexander, "Embracing the Teachable Moment: The Black Gay Body in the Classroom as Embodied Text," in *Black Queer Studies*, eds. E. Patrick Johnson and Mae G. Henderson (Durham, NC: Duke University Press, 2005), 249–265: 250.

11 Juan Muñoz, Rosario Jasis, Patricia Young, and Peter McLaren, "The Hidden Curriculum of Domestication," *The Urban Review*, *36*(3), 2004: 169–187, 169.

12 Darder, *A Dissident Voice*, 85.

13 Ibid.

14 Alicia Chavira-Prado, "Ni Eres Ni Te Pareces: Academia a Rapture and Alienation," in *I've Got a Story to Tell: Identity and Place in the Academy*, eds. Sandra Jackson and José Solís Jordán (New York, NY: Peter Lang, 1999), 135–152: 148.

15 Juanita Johnson-Bailey and Ronald M. Cervero, "Different Worlds and Divergent Paths: Academic Careers Defined by Race and Gender," *Harvard Educational Review*, *78*(2), Summer 2008: 311–332, 321.

16 Marilyn Frye, *The Politics of Reality: Essays in Feminist Theory* (Freedom, CA: Crossing Press, 1983), 118. See also Susan Sullivan and Nancy Tuana, eds., *Race and Epistemologies of Ignorance* (Albany, NY: State University of New York Press, 2007) and Erik Malewski and Nathalia E. Jaramillo, eds., *Epistemologies of Ignorance in Education* (Charlotte, NC: Information Age Publishing, 2011).

17 Darder, *A Dissident Voice*, 85.

18 Ibid., 458.

19 See, for example, JoAnn Moody, *Faculty Diversity: Problems and Solutions* (New York, NY: Routledge, 2004); Caroline Sotello Viernes Turner and Samuel L. Myers, Jr., *Faculty of Color in Academe: Bittersweet Success* (Boston, MA: Allyn and Bacon, 2000); Gregory A. Diggs et al., "Smiling Faces and Colored Spaces: The Experiences of Faculty of Color Pursuing Tenure in the Academy," *The Urban Review*, *41*(4), 2009: 312–333; and Mildred García, *Succeeding in an Academic Career: A Guide for Faculty of Color* (Westport, CT: Greenwood Press, 2000).

20 Audre Lorde, *Sister Outsider: Essays and Speeches* (Freedom, CA: Crossing Press, 1984), 142.

21 Chandra Talpade Mohanty, "On Race and Voice: Challenges for Liberal Education in the 1990s," *Cultural Critique*, *14*, Winter 1989: 179–208, 190.

22 Ibid.

23 Andrea Smith, "Native Studies and Critical Pedagogy: Beyond the Academic-Industrial Complex," in *Activist Scholarship: Antiracism, Feminism, and Social Change*, eds. Julia Sudbury and Margo Okazawa-Rey (Boulder, CO: Paradigm Publishers, 2009), 37–54: 52.

24 Mohanty, *Cultural Critique*, 184.

25 Ann Russo, "'We Cannot Live Without Our Lives': White Women, Antiracism, and Feminism," in *Third World Women and the Politics of Feminism*, eds. Chandra Talpade Mohanty, Ann Russo, and Lourdes Torres (Bloomington: Indiana University Press, 1991), 297–313: 306.

26 Smith, *Native Studies and Critical Pedagogy*, 40.

27 Grace Lee Boggs and Angela Davis, "On Revolution: A Conversation Between Grace Lee Boggs and Angela Davis" (Center for Race & Gender, University of California, Berkeley, March 2, 2012).

28 Smith, *Native Studies and Critical Pedagogy*, 52.

29 Boggs and Davis, "On Revolution."

30 Lila Abu-Lughod, "The Romance of Resistance: Tracing Transformations of Power Through Bedouin Women," *American Ethnologist*, 17, 1990: 41–55, 42.

31 Ibid., 53.

32 Mohanty, *Cultural Critique*, 207.

33 Boggs and Davis, "On Revolution."

34 Frederick Douglass, *Two Speeches by Frederick Douglass: one on West India emancipation, delivered at Canandaigua, Aug. 4th, and the other on the Dred Scott decision, delivered in New York, on the occasion of the anniversary of the American Abolition Society, May 1857* (Rochester, NY: C. P. Dewey, printer, 1857), 22.

35 Smith, *Native Studies and Critical Pedagogy*, 41.

36 Michael Apple, "On the Tasks of the Critical Educational Scholar/Activist," in *Bridging the Gap Between Theory and Practice in Educational Research*, eds. Rachelle Winkle-Wagner, Cheryl A. Hunter, and Debora Hinderliter Ortloff (New York, NY: Palgrave Macmillan, 2009), 21–34: 31.

37 Nana Osei-Kofi, "The Art of Teaching Intersectionality," in *Cultivating Social Justice Teachers: How Teacher Educators Have Helped Students Overcome Cognitive Bottlenecks and Learn Critical Social Justice Concepts*, eds. Paul C. Gorski, Kristien Zenkov, Nana Osei-Kofi, and Jeff Sapp (Sterling, VA: Stylus, 2013), 14.

38 hooks, *Yearnings*, 22.

14

IMMERSION DIVERSITY

Teaching Tourism, Travel Writing, and Race From the Inside Out

Meta G. Carstarphen

Introduction: Race, Travel, and Text

According to the United Nations World Tourism Organization, global international tourist arrivals grew in 2012 over the previous year by 4%, for a total of 1.035 billion travelers, with no slowdown in sight.[1] Tourism is big business and growing. And, according to these 2012 figures, there were more than 1 billion of us traveling in some form of tourism.

Traveling for pleasure, adventure, and leisure is as commonplace today as it was once rare. In the 18th century, for instance, the concept of the "grand tour," or travel to expand one's horizons both geographically and intellectually, launched the tradition of modern travel. Initially, travel was an enterprise restricted, most often, to English and European men of wealth. Socially celebrated literary accounts, such as Thomas Nugent's 1749 essay, "The Grand Tour," helped establish this compelling rationale.[2] A century later, written accounts from well-heeled Anglo-women helped usher in new voices and perspectives on travel, giving feminine perspectives to the discovery of new knowledge.[3]

In today's media landscape, new media discourses help define the travel experience for emerging generations. From newspaper features, to niche magazines, to dedicated cable channels, the proliferation of travel media reflects a hard-to-satiate desire to leave home and parachute in along the fringes of other neighborhoods. But travel and writing are intimately connected, and both draw meaning from their interconnectedness. For example, eclectic forms of writing—including maritime journals, inscription on monuments, letters, and journals—help inform our earliest understandings of early world travelers and their interpretations of new worlds.[4] We read these texts and glean from them understandings of environments and people, revealed through the concrete descriptions they inscribe. But the relationship between writing and travel is not always about the tangible experience. Writing can be, as Gregory Clark suggests, a way through which our students "might learn to read and write as if they were embedded in an expansive social space where they must confront and account for relationships of agency, obligation, and interdependence."[5] If, as Clark suggests, writing is travel, then the resulting texts must become the markers of our journeys; evidence of our having "been there."

But where is "there," exactly? In our classrooms multiplied across all disciplines and locales, we ask our students to write to predictable margins. They write through the lens of research we assign to them, or investigations we design for them, or through the limits of their own personal experiences. Within these parameters, it is a challenging enterprise to invite students to explore race as a component of their and others' experiences. Writing race, then, as a form of travel limits us to the roads we may have already traveled.

But, while the safe and placid journey of some forms of travel can inform experience, I look to another view of travel as a confounding experience. Lawrence Mewshaw expands upon this as he heralds, especially, the experience of travel that willfully takes him beyond his personal comfort zone and into spaces where he relinquishes any "delusions that I'm in control."[6] What this suggests is the power of writing itself can be a dynamic space, not dependent upon fixed definitions or patterned exchanges, but, rather, as an opportunity for a communicative act that is as potentially unpredictable as life itself. And in this space, identity—including race—can become revealed for its contextual and impermanent characteristics.

This chapter discusses an approach to teaching race through travel. Specifically, through a class I created in travel writing, I invite students to grapple with ideas about race and identity as part of their acquisition of career-oriented, professional skills in media and mass communication. But it is in the pursuit of those skills—including the need to interview strangers and accurately represent their ideas—that the notion of what it means to be "raced" becomes powerfully salient.

Where Everybody Knows Your Name

I teach at a predominately, and historically, White university that is recognized as the flagship institution for the state. Our student population is probably not unlike those at similar academic hubs across the country: largely regional, comfortable with the environs yet wildly curious about the new adventures that surround them. But there is an insularity that can sometimes emanate from comfort. Even though many White students have ventured from smaller towns to come to our university, many of them have never left the comfort of state borders in their lives. Others may be well traveled, in the sense that they have been part of church mission trips, family reunions, and vacation cruises. Still, all of us share the cultural narratives about travel and leisure that are virtually inescapable from our imaginations and experiences, unless we make a concerted effort to travel outside of the dominant themes.

To help combat such narrowness, this university instituted a robust travel-study program. Under this umbrella, White students could explore new worlds while continuing their progression as university students. Such duality offered possibilities of making concrete the binary of being[7] that persons of color can often feel. It struck me that the travel/study enterprise was potentially an analogy writ large about what it means to be raced. Placing students in new surroundings allowed our mentees to experience themselves as both U.S. citizens and residents of another culture; as both part of the university cohort at home and a foreign student elsewhere. It was in this context that I imagined a variation on a travel/study program of study that conceptualized these implicit differences as explicit features of a travel/study program.

On campus, there is a context of familiarity, where race seems both invisible and urgent. Race is invisible as a topic, or even a subtopic, in most of the classes these students take. And yet, in most of the daily topics presented to them in the media they consume, there are open references to race as themes of conflict, novelty, or sensationalism. While our students are surrounded by these depictions, they lack a scholarly context in which to explore the meaning of these instances.

A recent study examines the role of "color" words in our perceptions of race, contending that the very language we use, forcing a binary between "Black" and "White," continues to encourage racial tension.[8] The study's authors add that longstanding associations of "Black" with negative images, alongside the positive associations of the word "White," indicate that "labels and language can contribute to and reinforce the ways people think about and relate to different social groups."[9]

Starting points for these discussions must begin with a definition of "race." A robust body of literature has characterized race as a social construction; that is, an outgrowth of societal parameters, as opposed to biological or scientific data. Yet, I believe that, even as students instinctively understand that the biology of racial difference is a pseudo-science, they struggle to understand how that false reality can still be used to define lived experiences. Bonilla-Silva perhaps has the best answer in his definition of what it means to be "raced." He contends that race is a social construction that, as a social category, operates with the force of social reality.[10]

In other words, race can be experienced with the force of reality, even though we may be able to agree that race should not have the power to completely define an individual's experience in society. Still, the "social construction" of race is exactly what my strategy of immersion diversity rests upon. If I can place students in another social context, I can perhaps challenge them to define race and racial identity in a different way.

We're Not in Kansas Anymore, Toto

Travel in any form or context is inherently about place. The most interesting questions emanating from a study of place, though, include the ways in which any given location changes people, or, in reverse, how locale becomes marked by its people. Geography and identity are intertwined in a special rhetoric of location and the desire to be transformed by it. To craft a class that would embody the experience and exploration of race would rest upon my selecting the right place. For me, that place is Puerto Rico.

One online travel guide describes Puerto Rico as a land of "endless sand, swashbuckling history lessons and widely diverse tropical terrain."[11] Wrapped in nearly euphoric language, the Puerto Rico of the travel guides seems mythic in its idyllic constructions. It is an island nation embraced by the arms of the Atlantic Ocean, on one side, and by the Caribbean Sea on the other side. And on its official, and well-developed tourism site, the island's history looms long and deep.[12] With an insider's pride, this website captures a distinctive history that acknowledges Indigenous roots that date back to 2000 B.C., long before the 1493 date credited as Christopher Columbus's "discovery" of it. Still, over the centuries since the Spanish conquest, Puerto Rico's people evolved from the historic amalgamation of three main identity roots: Taino Indians, Spanish colonizers, and the Africans, both free and enslaved, that accompanied them.

Modern Puerto Rico, of course, is home to far more ancestries than these today. But the "*tres raices*" ("three races" or "three roots") formulation of African, Indigenous, and Spanish makes a topology of the Puerto Rican culture and a metaphor for the cultural roots. In her book *Boricua Pop: Puerto Ricans and the Latinization of American Culture*, Frances Negrón-Muntaner argues that the Puerto Rico of our imagination is as much a product of media misrepresentations as the powerful lure of myth and culture.[13] These myths, she maintains, are grounded in depictions of Puerto Ricans as exotic, dangerous, and disposable.[14]

Many of those depictions, from sultry sensuality to picturesque beaches, are part of the persistent iconography of travel to the Caribbean. We have all seen the commercials, and they are seductive. With playful, upbeat music in the background, we see smiling couples frolicking on beaches and lounging by pools on gated properties. And, as if in supporting roles, we see the ever-smiling, ever-accommodating brown-skinned staff, hovering nearby, waiting to serve.

And, while these images are beguiling, as they are intended to be, they actually run counter to the notion of travel as a means of exploring place. What knowledge can be gained within the antiseptic confines of a resort environment? Don't get me wrong—I am not against vacations. But, in the context of a travel-study class, I can resist making the experience of the traveler more dominant than the inherent meaning of the lives of the "traveled to" by placing students in close relationship to the land, its people, and the culture.

Immersion diversity is my strategy for creating contexts where the White students engage in a "transactional" learning position as a member of our class on the road. All of us—instructors included—become active students of the moments presented to us through our direct associations and encounters. The expectations of journalism and mass communication disciplines—whether they express themselves in journalism, video documentary, or in strategically communicated promotional messages—are for public expressions. Since the class is open to all majors, I recognize that some students will not pursue formal careers in media and mass communication. However, what matters is that, in the assignments crafted and the expectations expressed, all students know that they are bound and accountable to one another, to the instructors, and to their subjects by a high level of authenticity. Through a model of transactional diversity that I've established, we move through a process of three broad stages: engagement, action through interaction, and transaction.[15]

Authenticity: What Does It Look Like?

Once students disembark from the long flight from Oklahoma to Puerto Rico, they are immediately surrounded by the island's humidity, its rhythms and smells, and the syncopated sounds of the Spanish language. Our first stage— engagement—continues from pre-departure activities, readings, and conversations about what to expect in Puerto Rico. This engagement necessarily includes research, and, as such, it is a familiar academic tool. In our case, we have specifically studied subjects that seem, at first, disconnected from a modern tourism experi- ence: Indigenous presence in the Americas, European colonization, and the introduction of African slavery. We read historic travel writings that describe these events, and compare perspectives. We have considered the voices of female travel writers and the voices of people of color, who used the language of their captors to describe their own struggles and triumphs. We have asked ourselves what the differences are between the accounts of a James Hakewill compared to an Olaudah Equiano; between a Mary Prince and a Lady Mary Wortley Montagu.

These are challenging, but necessary, ideas to incorporate as part of our engagement phase. Once we land, I encourage my students to see our Puerto Rican hosts through the lens of these combinations, and it gives them a different way of deciphering the visual code of race. Indeed, our pending conversations and encounters with Puertorriqueños will reinforce this new code through the visual imprint of their own relationships with one another across color lines, as well as the vibrancy of the *tres raices* concept in the historic and cultural discussions we will receive. These three races—Indian, African, and Spanish—become introduced to the students as groups responsible for the foundational cultural attributes of Puerto Rico, something for which their recent historical focus prepares them.

I structure the class with day-long study trips outside of a traditional classroom environment. I have deliberately de-centered myself and other instructors accompanying me from the focus of these experiences for the students. Instead, I am in partnership with a native lecturer, José. We meet his family and friends as we also take notes from his lectures on our tour bus, which he drives. At every site we visit, the students learn to connect with other native guides, whose pride and knowledge of their island goes beneath the surface facts for each location. Although I could arrange visits to the same places myself, or have a rotating list of drivers and guides, I stay in relationship with José and his company. He is what I call our "transfluencer"—someone who can both translate (literally and figuratively) the cultural experiences before us, as well as influentially create a more intimate kind of access for my group of public communicators. We have, for instance, been in the home of renowned artist Samuel Lind, and been introduced to an 80-year-old cigar maker named Ramona.

Our transition to the next phase—action through interaction—begins as the students become acclimated to being *not* in control. As *norteamericanos*, we learn that our history and our experiences are not the defining paradigm. We live and travel in a space where European accomplishments are not the universal standards by which to mark our collective global narratives. As such, we become the "Others" whose ways of knowing the world are at the margins, not the center, of experience and cognition. This has profound implications for the journalistic paradigm from which students will undertake research. They are not the experts, but the novices who nevertheless embrace an intense learning curve in order to become knowledgeable in a deep and meaningful way about their topics. And, to sort these out, the students must ask questions. They conduct interviews in direct conversation *with* the Other, as opposed to participating in interviews *about* the Other as seen and interpreted by people like them. This is a profound experience for them, as they acquire the poise and cultural competence to make these connections. They see, by example, that people can confront a difficult history of conflict, war, and exploitation and emerge from that history with a sense of pride that incorporates the contributions of all. They learn to disrupt the racial code of color as well. As Puerto Ricans meet the students, the islanders reflect diversities back to them, by asking about the students' European, African, and Indian roots. On more than one occasion, students have been accurately pegged as "Irish" or "Italian" or "German" in ways that reflected their family backgrounds, but represented very different ways in which they were accustomed to thinking of themselves at home. So, at a fundamental level, White students lose control over their familiar identities and are renamed according to a new topology that sees the nuances of whiteness. Similarly, students with darker skin tones, as well as students of color, find that some residents immediately speak to them in Spanish, mistaking them for native residents.

This new, renegotiated relationship between our students and our Puerto Rican hosts represents a different level of parity. We are not the inapproachable tourists who can only engage with islanders as paid servants. We are not a cloistered student class, held captive by an academic understanding, no matter how sympathetic, of the people, culture, and history before us. At the same time, we are not equals, because we are visitors and will leave after a specified time. All of these realities, though, become part of our transactional, and final, stage of the class experience. In the process of using travel, and writing, as part of the learning experience in a differently constructed social reality, the students con-clude their classwork with their public communication work. Our medium of choice is a class blog, where students record and share their experiences for open audiences at http://commculturepr.blogspot.com/.

They share their perspectives about identity in ways that are both open and subtle. And, as authors with a newfound agency about the social contexts of identity and culture, they get to choose how and when to write about race. As part of their acquisition of new skills, the students learn some of the techniques and tactics used in writing feature stories and essays. I look for evidence that they have broken away from a familiar travel trope of awe, wonder, and the process of "Othering" in travel writing. Instead, I hope for a personal engagement with their topic that reflects a transactional view of a cultural experience full of complexity and shared storytelling. In this construct, I believe our student writers should be comparably revealing of their own identities, even as they explore others. They should be willing to be vulnerable, as they ask others to be so. However, without a process of dislocation, I find that White students will find it difficult to understand that their uncertainties have value.

Conclusion: Race In and Out of the Classroom

Travel can be a powerful experience, and can operate as a very compelling construct for exploring topics of identity and race with students. For scholars of color who teach at predominately White universities populated by a majority of White students, using immersion diversity strategies can open up new spaces of instruction. We find ourselves part of many disciplines and hired by our respective academic institutions to teach canonical knowledge. Yet, we do White students a disservice if we cannot inform their understanding of core concepts and shared histories through the critical lens of racial constructions. To help them do this, students should be brought into meaningful transactional relationships. If they cannot travel across water, perhaps they can travel across campus for collaborative work with ethnic studies departments, fraternities and sororities of color, or even established community groups.

No group of students who participate in my immersion diversity class is ever the same, and the experiences seen through their eyes remain as fresh to me as for them. The students leave with academic credits and experiences that are certainly comparable to any they could participate in on campus. But, as they move through future courses, careers, and social relationships, my hope is that they run to, not away, from the sometimes elaborate meaning of race and identity.

Notes

1 See Marcelo Risi, "International Tourism to Continue Robust Growth in 2013," United Nations World Tourism Organization, Press Release, February 4, 2013, http://media.unwto.org/en/press-release/2013-01-28/international-tourism-continue-robust-growth-2013.

2 Nugent's extended work describes recommended travel itineraries for would-be travelers. His preface, referred to here, offers a philosophical defense of such travel. See Thomas Nugent, "The Grand Tour: Containing an Exact Description of Most of the Cities, Towns, and Remarkable Places of Europe, Together with a Distinct Account of the Post-Roads and Stages . . .," in *Travel Writing, 1700–1830: An Anthology*, eds. Elizabeth A. Bohls and Ian Duncan (Oxford, England: Oxford University Press, 2005; first published, London, England: S. Birt, D. Browne, A. Millar, and G. Hawkins, 1749), chap. 2, 14–18.

3 See Bohls and Duncan, *Travel Writing*, for work by such early, White, female travel writers as Ann Radcliffe and Lady Mary Wortley Montagu.

4 See Bohls and Duncan, *Travel Writing*.

5 See Gregory Clark, "Writing as Travel, or Rhetoric on the Road," *College Composition and Communication*, 49(1), February 1998: 9–23, quote on p. 23.

6 See Michael Mewshaw, "Travel, Travel Writing, and the Literature of Travel," *South Central Review*, 22(2), Summer 2005: 2–10, quote on p. 9.

7 See Meta G. Carstarphen and John P. Sanchez, "The Binary of Meaning: Native/American Indian Media in the 21st Century," *Howard Journal of Communications*, 21(4), October–December 2010: 319–327, which explores comparable identity constructions for African Americans and Native Americans.

8 See Aaron Smith-McLallen, Blair T. Johnson, John F. Dovidio, and Adam R. Pearson, "Black and White: The Role of Color Bias in Implicit Race Bias," *Social Cognition*, 24(1), 2006: 46–73.

9 Ibid., 71.

10 See Eduardo Bonilla-Silva, *Racism Without Racists: Color-Blind Racism and the Persistence of Racial Inequality in Contemporary America*, 3rd ed. (Lanham, MD: Rowman & Littlefield, 2010).

11 See the travel publisher Lonely Planet's online guide to Puerto Rico, http://www.lonelyplanet.com/puerto-rico.

12 See the Puerto Rico Tourism Company's online guide, "History of Puerto Rico," http://www.seepuertorico.com.

13 Frances Negrón-Muntaner, *Boricua Pop: Puerto Ricans and the Latinization of American Culture* (New York, NY: New York University Press, 2004).

14 Ibid.

15 See Meta G. Carstarphen, "Artful Diversity: 3 Guiding Principles," *Public Relations Tactics*, February 28, 2013, http://www.prsa.org/Intelligence/Tactics/Articles/view/10098/1074/Artful_diversity_3_guiding_principles.

15

PEDAGOGICAL CHALLENGES OF "TEACHING THE GLOBAL"

Race, Nation, and Transnational Feminist Praxis

Sanjukta Mukherjee

"[We], as teachers of difference and as *different* teachers, cannot escape the entanglement of local ruptures through a global worldview ... the immediacy of local politics and culture must be kept in dialectical tension with the politics 'out there.'"[1] [my emphasis]

"Three Pillars of White Supremacy. This framework does not assume that racism and White supremacy is enacted in a singular fashion; rather, White supremacy is constituted by separate and distinct, but still interrelated, logics. Envision three pillars, one labeled Slavery/Capitalism, another labeled Genocide/Capitalism, and the last one labeled Orientalism/War, as well as arrows connecting each of the pillars together."[2]

One sunny afternoon in May 2011, I was on my way to teach an introductory women's and gender studies class on transnational feminism. I had been mulling over the geopolitical drama about the capture and assassination of Osama bin Laden being played out on every news channel, national and international, over the preceding week. It was a coincidence that, this week, we were going to discuss feminist critiques of nation, militarization, and war. 9/11 happened barely a month after I had moved from India to the United States for a doctoral degree in geography.[3] It was a time of intense turmoil, personally and politically, as I was adjusting to a new country, a new university and academic culture, and, most importantly, a host of new identities ascribed to me—"foreign student," "Indian," "South Asian," "resident alien," "immigrant," "woman of color." All these new identities emerged amidst an increasing fervor of patriotism and hyper-nationalism within the United States. As usual, before delving into the topic of the day, I asked the students what international news story they had been following that week. Almost everyone started talking about Osama bin Laden's death. Some students were curious yet bewildered by the covert military operation in Pakistan; two students expressed relief because, now that the "terrorist" was dead, they would be able to avoid long lines at airport security; and others mentioned the complicated, insufficient, and often contradictory versions of the reports in different national and international news media. One student questioned how this would impact President Barack Obama's re-election campaign, and yet another commented on how there was no real "proof" that bin Laden was actually dead. I asked the students what they thought about the critiques of war and militarization by feminists they had read for class that day. Their reading assignment was an article by Nadia Ela on Islamophobia in which she showed how Muslim women are constructed as "victims of their culture" (and thus in need of saving, arguably justifying the U.S. invasion of Afghanistan), but allowed to speak out in public against their oppression in the United States, while Muslim men are constructed as "violent, potential threats," and increasingly face myriad forms of surveillance. They also read an article by Minnie Bruce Pratt in which she examines the increasing rates of domestic violence amongst Iraq war veterans and their families in North Carolina, linking the war "out there" with real material effects within the U.S.A. One of the older students, a self-identified White feminist, remarked rather aggressively to me, "Does that mean you agree with what Osama bin Laden did to the American people on September 11?" In the midst of the sudden palpable tension around me, I was completely taken aback by the personal attack and did not know how to respond. At that moment, I became blatantly aware of being the "Other" in the U.S. academy—not just a woman of color but an *immigrant* woman of color, one who is not a U.S. citizen and who, supposedly, does not empathize with the national tragedy of 9/11. I took a few deep breaths, letting the silence reverberate around me, noticing that several students had lowered their heads and were avoiding eye contact with me. At the same time, I could feel their eyes on me, waiting to see how I would respond. Looking around the class, I realized that, apart from the student who had asked me the question, the majority of the students were 18 and 19 year olds, with no memory of 9/11. Based on my interactions with them over the past six weeks of the quarter, I knew that they got most of their information about 9/11 and other international issues from mainstream media and the CIA's *World Factbook*.

This episode raised some important pedagogical and epistemological questions for me. Had I been a U.S.-born woman of color, with U.S. citizenship, would I have been asked the same question? What are the implications of such an episode occurring in a class dedicated to transnational feminism? What does this say about women's studies as a discipline, especially how it has constructed the "Third World"?[4] How do power relations structured by race, class, gender, sexuality, and nation operate in the classroom between and amongst teachers and students? Have other immigrant women faculty from the global south faced similar situations? What specific pedagogical strategies have they drawn on to negotiate being marked by gender, race, and nation in particular ways while simultaneously teaching about colonialism, imperialism, capitalism, and patriarchy?

Piya Chatterjee has provided an excellent analysis of her experiences of teaching cultural anthropology at University of California, Riverside, as an immigrant woman of color from India and Nigeria.[5] Describing the hostility she faced from some of her students when she criticized the colonial and imperial gazes through which "Other" bodies are usually seen, Chatterjee argues that:

> What, how and who we are as instructors and students deeply inflects the apprehension and comprehension of our engagement with difference. That engagement contains, by the very nature of the pedagogical critique, conflict and resistance in ways that can be profoundly problematic not only for students but also for teachers whose speaking authority may be mediated by race, ethnicity, national origin, class and sexual orientation.[6]

Thus, the teacher is not always in a position of power vis-à-vis students and neither is the classroom always a safe space for students and people of color. Often, the classroom is a space of discomfort, a space where long-held beliefs, privileges, and marginalizations are named, analyzed, and challenged. Neither faculty nor students enter the classroom or the academy with their identities (be it gender, race, class, or sexuality, among others) fixed. Rather, these are re-/constructed, negotiated, and always struggled over through the everyday practices and interactions in the various institutional spaces of the university.

In this chapter, I draw on the experiences of teaching transnational feminism in the undergraduate classroom to reflect on how immigrant, female faculty of color navigate specific pedagogical challenges in the United States. I combine my experiences as a teacher with different student responses to the course material and personal conversations with colleagues regarding pedagogy. I argue that discourses of nation, nationalism, and citizenship always mediate how immigrant feminists of color from the global south experience race and racism in the U.S. classroom. A climate of increasing corporatization, militarization, and hypernationalism following 9/11 poses new pedagogical challenges as transnational feminists attempt to draw attention to the interconnections between the global and local, and culture and economy.

There is a long and well-documented history of how the academy marginalizes women and men of color in the United States based on race, class, gender, and sexuality,[7] and the particular challenges faced by faculty of color in predominantly White classrooms.[8] Scholars have provided significant insights into how affirmative action policies, diversity issues, liberal notions of inclusion and multiculturalism have redefined curricula in colleges and universities.[9] Some of these debates have explored the connection between education reforms, especially increasing privatization and its implications for economic and social justice.[10] Other scholars have analyzed how race, nation, citizenship, immigration, and gender are implicated in the manner in which universities are increasingly linked to a global world order.[11] Mohanty illuminates the critical pedagogical challenges during the current project of empire, which manifests in particular "accelerated forms" of militarization, corporatization, and hypernationalism in the post-9/11 transnational world.[12] She argues, "Imperialism, militarization and globalization all traffic in women's bodies, women's labor and ideologies of masculinity/femininity, heteronormativity, racism and nationalism to consolidate and reproduce power and domination."[13] The university and the academic industry are not separate from the social, economic, and geopolitical transformations taking place locally and globally, but are deeply implicated in it. Indeed, Anu Aneja explains that a new anxiety about "Otherness" has accompanied nationalistic preoccupation with security and is plaguing U.S. colleges and universities, even those that once encapsulated a liberal, multicultural, and plural, albeit tokenistic, celebration of difference.[14]

I taught my first women's and gender studies course on transnational feminism at DePaul University in the fall of 2010. Although no stranger to feminist theory and politics, my prior pedagogical practices were focused within the disciplinary boundaries of human geography.[15] This introductory undergraduate course, titled Women's Studies in Transnational Context, is a core requirement for students who are women's and gender studies majors and minors, but it also fulfills one of the liberal studies competencies at DePaul. Hence, while some students who typically take this course are already interested in feminist scholarship, others need it to fulfill their general education requirements. Transnational feminist interventions have been critical within the field of feminist scholarship in the past two decades. They challenge the uniform category of the "woman" and universal notions of "global sisterhood." Instead, they emphasize the ways in which gender-based inequalities are always mediated by other aspects of identity, such as race, class, sexuality, nation, religion, disability, age, and others. Transnational feminism has thus confronted liberal White feminists' tendency to homogenize all "Third World women" as victims assuming easy solidarity around similar oppressions. It highlights the importance of historical and cultural specificities, which create similarities *and* differences, between and amongst women (and men) who are located differently within local and global gender hierarchies. Moreover, within an increasingly globalized world economy, transnational feminism has shown how contemporary capitalism, imperialism, militarism, and racism feed off of one another. It is thus not enough to mobilize against gender injustice alone, but, rather, work across, beyond, and between borders for feminist solidarities that are anticapitalist, anti-imperialist, and antiracist.[16]

As an immigrant woman and faculty of color, teaching transnational feminism in the U.S. classroom has posed particular challenges. For example, when I am critical of U.S. military regimes and cultures within and beyond the borders of the country, I may come across as "un-American." When I teach about feminist critiques of neoliberal globalization, such as the gendered and racialized impacts of cheap garment assembly plants in the U.S.A.–Mexico border towns and the attendant uneven development in Mexico, often I have to navigate polarized and Eurocentric debates on tradition versus modernity and economic "progress." Specific pedagogical practices within the classroom thus re-inscribe racial difference, between and amongst student and teacher, in particular ways.

On one hand, this chapter is about my own experiences of race as an immigrant woman faculty of color. On the other hand, it is about processes of imperialism and colonialism, how knowledge about the racialized "Other" is created, consumed, and challenged within the United States in general and within the discipline of women's studies in particular. The chapter sheds light on what it means to embody racial difference while simultaneously teaching about race. It raises questions about agency and authorial voice, and reflects on particular strategies and teaching tools in the classroom. I believe that this will be useful for anyone interested in critical pedagogies, transnational feminism, and social justice. Through this intervention, I emphasize that race and experiences of racism must be examined beyond the Black/White binary in the United States and demonstrate that gender, class, and nation/-ality mediate the manner in which junior faculty of color, born and brought up outside of America, experience race in the classroom. It also contributes to feminist critiques of objectivity and notions of partiality and situatedness of knowledge by demonstrating that students' comprehension and acceptance of race and racial issues are inextricably linked to how they perceive the teacher within particular social, political, and historical contexts.

Locating Myself and My Institutional Space

In this section, I locate myself and my role as a teacher within the U.S. academy in general, and DePaul University in particular. I do this in relation to the broader transformations happening in the U.S. academy, especially within the context of increasing corporatization, militarization, and internationalization. These changes impact pedagogical practices in the classroom and expose particular contradictions of teaching in a globalized world.

DePaul University, located in the heart of the city of Chicago, is among the largest private Catholic universities in the country. It has about 25,000 students, which include large numbers of transfer students and first-generation college students. Also, as tuition is high, most of the students work alongside attending school. This makes the classroom a dynamic space, as students bring with them interesting life experiences. However, it also poses challenges, because many students have other demands on their time and struggle to find balance between work and school. Although DePaul is located in Chicago, which has large communities of im-/migrants and people of color, many born outside of the United States, the university is a predominantly White space. According to 2011/2012 statistics recorded on the university's website, minority students accounted for

32% of enrollment in fall 2011. While the proportion of international students (i.e., nonresident aliens) recorded in fall 2012 is relatively small (i.e., 2.2 %), trends show that this is the highest since 1995. In terms of full-time faculty, 65.6% are recorded as White, 18.3 % as minority, and 6.7% as nonresident alien. The gender ratio among full-time faculty reflects that the nonresident women of color are the least represented and account for only 5% of the total.[17] These figures will be useful for understanding how immigrant women faculty are positioned within the institutional spaces of the U.S. academy, not just in relation to race but also in relation to nationality and citizenship.

Similar to many other universities in the United States, DePaul has also focused on internationalizing its curriculum since 2006. According to its "Vision 2018" strategic plan, which was launched last year, the university aims to deepen its connections locally, globally, and internationally. The main goals include nurturing a diverse student body, building and retaining diverse faculty, and preparing students to become "responsible global citizens."[18] It is within this climate of internationalization that I was hired in the Women's and Gender Studies program (which has since transitioned to a department) in 2010 to teach international political economy, gender and development, and transnational feminism. As a privileged (middle-class, upper caste) woman of color from India, with a doctoral degree from the United States, and influenced by transnational and postcolonial feminisms, my political, intellectual, and pedagogical commitments are rooted in anti-oppression and social justice work. These academic interests are also very personal and part of my everyday experience of living in the diaspora. Like many other postcolonial feminists who live and work in the heart of empire, I have had to resist being a "native informant," on one hand, and the "model minority," on the other.[19] It has been difficult, for example, to negotiate my identity as a "Third World" woman yet simultaneously challenge discourses essentializing *all* women from the global south, on one hand, and recognize the U.S.-led political, military, and economic hegemony that continues to disempower nations and peoples who were once colonized, on the other. Now, as a teacher within the U.S. academy, I feel compelled to highlight the myriad forms of ongoing resistance against U.S.-led economic, military, and political power within, across, and outside its borders.

DePaul's Women's and Gender Studies department has a strong commitment to the interconnectedness of local, global, and transnational feminist theories and social movements. Transnational feminism has also gained visibility within feminist scholarship in the United States over the past decade. Indeed, "transnational" has become a kind of buzzword within the academy, as scholars navigate the material, ideological, and political implications of border crossings in a seemingly borderless world. I wonder whether this "transnational turn" within the field of women's studies has made it easier for such interdisciplinary programs to gain legitimacy within institutionalized spaces of the academy, not least because of the ongoing internationalization efforts in the United States. At the same time, the transnational turn also makes women's studies more suspect, given its critical stance on many of the ongoing political and economic crises locally, nationally, and globally. Nevertheless, our program transitioned to departmental status fairly easily last year, unlike the struggles encountered by many similar programs in the 1980s and 1990s. I want to differentiate here between "transnational," which is often mistakenly equated with global or international, and "transnational feminism." So, while internationalizing efforts may make the transnational turn of women's and gender studies more attractive to the university, it does not follow that the university is always implicated in transnational feminist projects. Indeed, many scholars have been particularly critical of the inherent corporate bias in internationalizing initiatives.[20] These internationalizing efforts, geared toward building ties with universities abroad and encouraging international student enrollments and exchanges, have often had immigrant faculty of color, with closer ties to their home countries, at the helm. The immigrant faculty of color has thus become more visible in the institutional spaces as a result—but mostly as experts on their home countries (the "native informant") "out there" (i.e., outside the United States). This has positioned other faculty of color within the United States, recruited under national discourses of multiculturalism, differently, and often creating tensions and conflicts of interests between them.[21] The implication of this divide on knowledge production is critical because it not only creates artificial boundaries between what is considered a national versus an international issue, a domestic or a foreign policy issue, a global or a local issue, but it also limits the authorial voice of faculty located differently from intervening in critical debates. But such tensions amongst scholars of color are not limited within the academy. In fact, the Indigenous, feminist scholar and activist Andrea Smith has described several scenarios where organizing efforts amongst women of color in the U.S. had to grapple with different and complex articulations of race and nationality

> A group of women of color came together to organize. An argument ensues about whether or not Arab women should be included. Some argue that Arab women are 'White' since they have been classified as such in the U.S. census. Another argument erupts over whether or not Latinas qualify as 'women of color,' since some may be classified as 'White' in their Latin American countries of origin and/or 'pass' as White in the United States.[22]

Smith contends that the main problem is the manner in which "women of color" and "people of color" politics has been framed in the United States around a discourse of "shared victimhood," within both academic and activist communities.[23] But, as the quote at the beginning of this chapter suggests, different communities of color are *differently* positioned in relation to the three pillars of White supremacy, and, as such, may be simultaneously complicit in oppression of other marginalized peoples. This means that nation and citizenship places immigrant women faculty of color in a different, and, indeed, a subservient, position in relation to the state and the academy vis-à-vis faculty of color born and raised in the United States. Given the long history of U.S. economic and military intervention in the global south, Smith's Orientalism/War and Slavery/Capitalism pillars of White supremacy[24] can help explain why immigrant faculty of color may feel alienated within mainstream internationalization discourses in the U.S. academy. Racial and ethnic identities, however, get even more complicated for mixed race/multiracial faculty with dual citizenship and multiple ties to different nations and communities. But, in all of these cases, it becomes clear that legitimacy of the nation–state through citizenship status brings with it both advantages and disadvantages for people of color in the U.S., and positions immigrant people without citizenship differently in relation to nation/nationalism.

Scholars like Mohanty argue that increasing corporatization of the academy has replaced a social justice commitment to dismantling structural inequalities with a "management" of race, class, gender, and sexual identities.[25] While this management style maintains discourses of multiculturalism, in practice, it recolonizes and marginalizes communities along multiple axes of difference. So, instead of challenging the structural violence of racism, hetero-/sexism, and classism, the liberal celebration of "diversity" as cultural consumption (i.e., ethnic food, music, fashion, people) perpetuates hegemonic inequalities. But, neither discourses of multiculturalism nor those of internationalization were evoked during the recent closure and funding cuts in ethnic studies programs in academic institutions in Arizona. Instead, such racialized practices are framed under discourses of national security, in the aftermath of strict immigration law enforcement, increased securitization, militarization of the United States–Mexico border and surveillance of the Hispanic community. It is ironic that, while ethnic studies courses have been targeted because they seemingly harbor racial disharmony and undermine dominant notions of U.S. democracy, increasing financial and infrastructural support has been given towards language and area study courses on the Middle East and other predominantly Muslim countries, given the current project of U.S. empire and its "war on terror."

Doing Transnational Feminism: The Classroom as a Contested Space

In this section, I examine the particular challenges and rewards of teaching transnational feminism. I demonstrate that my students' responses to some of the course topics are tangled in complex ways to their responses to me as an immigrant woman faculty of color and how "Third World" women have been constructed in Western (read: U.S.) contexts. Over the past two years, I have taught several sections of an introductory undergraduate class in transnational feminism offered by the department of Women's and Gender Studies.[26] Typically, I have about 25 students, with a mix of White students, students of color, and multiracial/mixed race students.[27] However, in all the sections I have taught,

I encountered many Latina students based in the United States with close ties to Mexico, but only three international students.[28] As mentioned before, while some of the students were interested in feminist politics and take the course as a requirement for their majors or minors in Women's and Gender Studies, others take this class to fulfill general education requirements at DePaul. Nevertheless, transnational feminism was very new to most of my students because, even for those who had taken other courses in women's and gender studies, they were focused mostly on U.S.-based feminist movements and/or did not center around questions of economic development, geopolitics, and imperialism.

The main objective of my course is to demonstrate how deploying a "transnational lens" provides new possibilities and challenges to the field of women's and gender studies and to the project of gender justice. This entails decentering dominant discourses and paradigms that have foregrounded liberal *White*, middle-class, U.S. women as *the* pioneers of feminist struggles. The course is thus grounded in examining the influences and disjunctures between multiple U.S.-based feminist movements and those in other parts of the world. I use an interdisciplinary and intersectional approach to understand the multiple hierarchies of oppression structured by race, class, ethnicity, gender, sexuality, nation/ality, age, religion, and so on. The course thus highlights, for example, the ways in which imperialism, colonialism, capitalism, and patriarchy are intertwined. Hence, one of the main components of this course is to emphasize the "interconnections" between systemic/structural/ global processes and local specificities, histories, and social relations.

The course is taught over a period of ten weeks and the class meets twice a week. Because this is an introductory class, I introduce students to some key debates and themes integral to transnational feminism. For two reasons I always begin the course with an examination of colonialism, empire, and historical constructions of gender and sexuality. First, it demonstrates that transnationalism is *not* an entirely new phenomenon, but is in fact rooted in colonial processes. Second, it situates colonial conquests as both racialized and gendered projects. Other topics I cover include neoliberal globalization, "Third World" development, global cities, diaspora, body politics, nation, militarization and war, and feminist debates on universal human rights. Student work is assessed on the basis of class participation in discussion, different kinds of written (e.g., position papers, essays, and focused reading assignments) and oral assignments. Students are required to keep up to date with current affairs, paying particular attention to news stories that make national and international headlines. After the first two times of teaching this course, I realized that students depend on mainstream U.S.-based media outlets for their news stories. I thus highlighted the importance of exploring alternative media outlets, especially independent news channels and blogs, and encouraged students to follow news stories from media based outside the United States and Europe.

In the two subsections that follow, I analyze key themes and patterns that emerged in my classes, pointing to particular rewards and challenges of introducing students to transnational feminism. Similar to other scholars engaged in critical pedagogies, my teaching philosophy is based on dismantling exclusionary practices of racism, sexism, classism, and ableism in dominant society. I am also committed to challenging the hegemonic notion of the teacher as the sole authority figure and producer of knowledge and students as passive consumers and recipients of knowledge.[29] Feminist scholars have long advocated the partiality and situatedness of knowledge, challenging notions of objectivity.[30] While I work hard to create an enabling environment that allows students to engage with one another and draw on their own life experiences, the classroom remains a contested space. As many scholars of color practicing critical antiracist, feminist pedagogies suggest, the classroom is not always a safe or comfortable space, especially when safety and comfort is equated with complicity with existing structures of power and privilege.

Making Connections: Global–Local/U.S.–Them and "Cultural Clash"

On the first day of class, I introduce students to a song by the Palestinian American poet, author, and activist Suheir Hammad, titled "Of Refuge and Language." She wrote this poem in response to the devastation in the aftermath of Hurricane Katrina in New Orleans in 2005. As a teaching tool, the powerful imagery of the YouTube video and the lyrics of the song is a critique of the U.S. government's neglect and slow response to the disaster that mainly affected the poorest African Americans in New Orleans. But, more importantly, the song also convincingly connects the poor, African American victims of the storm and the deplorable conditions of the overcrowded football stadium, where they were evacuated, to the living conditions of other marginalized, displaced, and disenfranchised peoples outside the political boundaries of the United States who have been often derogatorily referred to as "refugees."

> Before the hurricane
> No tents were prepared for the fleeing
> Because Americans do not live in tents
> Tents are for Haiti for Bosnia for Rwanda
> Refugees are the rest of the world[31]

Hammad emphasizes that inequality, malnutrition, and poverty are not just "Third World" issues, and nor are the poor, marginalized, hungry, and vulnerable refugees located only in far-flung foreign countries.

> "Do not look away
> The rest of the world lives here too, In America"[32]

Most of the students in my classes are unfamiliar with Hammad's work. The images they see in the video may be familiar to some, reflecting the predominantly poor, starving, conflict-ridden people of the "Third World," yet the lyrics simultaneously allude to real processes of colonization, imperialism, militarization, and globalization, which connect marginalized peoples within and outside the borders of the United States.

After listening to the song, I ask students to analyze the video. I am mostly greeted by silence. It is almost as if students are awestruck by the juxtaposition of Americans (albeit mainly African Americans) to starving children from Africa or refugees from Haiti. Rarely have they seen such images next to one another. Sometimes, students remark that the images were "powerful," "disturbing," or "reflected racial discrimination in New Orleans," but students have rarely ever connected the "foreign, Third World" countries and their "oppressed peoples" to race-, class-, and gender-based oppression within the U.S. However, I do remember one of my international students, from South Asia, approaching me excitedly after class to tell me that she was a fan of Suheir Hammad and was very encouraged to see "critiques of Western constructions of the Third World in a class." After a couple of quarters, I decided to include a second video clip in my introductory class, a pop-music video titled "Man Ke Manjeere," which is sung by the Indian singer Shubha Mudgal. The song is inspired by the story of Shameem Pathan, a Muslim woman from Ahmedabad, India. She escaped from domestic violence, braved discrimination, and embarked on a career driving a mini-van to support herself and her child. The video not only challenges constructions of "Third World" women as passive victims, but also demonstrates how women are working together for gender justice, thus challenging U.S.-centric notions of feminism. Students always have lots of questions for me when they see this video: "Do women in Indian culture still have to give dowry for their weddings?", "Why are arranged marriages still popular?", "Is domestic violence linked to religion and family values?", "Is there a law against domestic violence?" I realized very quickly that, because I am Indian, my knowledge of the subject and authorial voice in speaking about it in the classroom are always valued and acknowledged. In conversations with my Lebanese-American colleague Dr. Laila Farah, who teaches another section of this class, I learned that student responses to this video were less focused on India, but more on the oppression of Arab women in the Middle East—despite the fact that they do not figure anywhere in the clip. As other scholars have argued, one of the challenges of being considered a "native informant" is that one becomes representative of the entire community and is often expected to be able to make "authentic truth claims" across wide segments of its diverse populations. While I, too, grappled with this issue in the classroom, I was also able to draw attention to the various feminist struggles in India around domestic violence, which had been unfamiliar to students in the past.

Similar to Michiko Hase's experience of teaching global gender issues to predominantly White American students, although more than a decade later, my White students also continue to be more interested in "exotic" issues, such as female genital circumcision (FGC) in Africa and dowry deaths in India.[33] This was evident from the very first day of classes, as I looked through the notecards that I had passed around in which students list the expectations they have from the course, including the themes they want to learn about. I was not entirely surprised by this because antiracist feminists like Angela Davis and Nawal El Saadawi have long critiqued the myopic focus of White, U.S. liberal feminist interests in cultural issues, such as female circumcision in Africa and the Middle East, while ignoring other, systemic issues such as poverty, environmental degradation, war, and economic globalization.[34] To challenge exoticization of racially "Othered" women and the "rescue narratives" of White, liberal feminists' agenda to "save" them, I show a documentary called *The Shape of Water* by feminist scholar and filmmaker Kum-Kum Bhavnani.[35] The film focuses on complex lived experiences of, and alternative strategies by, women from different parts of the developing world in response to economic dependencies to the West, environmental degradation, war and militarization, and patriarchal cultural traditions. The documentary is grounded in the stories and struggles of five women. It captures their engagement in (a) rainforest preservation techniques as rubber-tappers in the Brazilian rainforest; (b) the workings of SEWA, a large trade union of women in India; (c) challenging female genital cutting in collaboration with women from different walks of life in Senegal; (d) Women in Black, a women's peace vigil opposing the Israeli occupation in Palestine, and (e) cooperative farming as seed keepers in the Himalayan foothills to promote economic independence and biodiversity.

Here is a snippet of the dialogues and questions that ensued after students watched this film in class:

> STUDENT ONE: Being from America, it was horrifying to see the brutal practice of female genital mutilation that is still practiced in Africa. I had to look away during the scene where they were showing the archaic-looking instruments used for the procedure.
>
> STUDENT TWO: I was glad to see that there is resistance to this practice by women in Africa though.
>
> STUDENT ONE: But, it must be hard to resist when this practice is so important for their culture.
>
> SM (INSTRUCTOR): Is everything in one's culture always good? Can you think of cultural practices of your own that are problematic?
>
> STUDENT ONE: Gender roles that stereotype women as homemakers or thinking women need to be docile and well behaved all the time. I have Italian heritage, but my family is all American now, so am not really rooted in Italian culture. I have actually grown up in a pretty liberal

environment—my parents never differentiated between my brother and me growing up.

STUDENT THREE: I am Latino and, in our culture, women are very strong, but are also expected to be "womanly"; you know, like dressed in feminine clothing, be well groomed—it is hard to manage both, especially for working women.

STUDENT FOUR: In the African American community, as a woman, I have to always prove that I am serious about having a career instead of following my mother's footsteps by marrying young and having a large family.

SM: Do you see any similarities between female genital circumcision and the forms of gender-based oppression you are facing?

I am greeted by silence for a while. None of the students respond. Clearly, despite being able to recognize gender-based oppression in their own lives, they still think that FGC in Africa is not comparable—perhaps it is more "brutal" than the indirect pressures of conforming to gender roles they face. While there were other issues captured in the film, almost always the first responses are to the FGC stories. It is also interesting that, while the women of color identify their culture in relation to race or ethnicity, the White student defines herself as "American"— with no particular cultural marker. Antiracist feminists and critical whiteness studies scholars have critiqued this as the racial privilege of not recognizing whiteness as a site of racialization in predominantly White cultures.

As an addendum to the film and discussion on FGC, students read articles by Isabelle Gunning and Ben Barker-Benfield. Barker-Benfield historically traces the practice of clitoridectomy, or female circumcision, in late nineteenth-century America, which reveals early gynecology's attempt to cure women of "unruly or unfeminine" behavior in an attempt to control them.[36] He uses the example of poor, Irish, female migrants being chosen as candidates for experimentation on genital circumcision to demonstrate the oppressive history of race and class in early gynecology in the United States. Gunning's essay uses Alice Walker and Pratibha Parmar's controversial film *Warrior Marks* (1993) to critique how even "First World feminists of color," with the best of intentions, tend to exoticize FGC, failing to contextualize it within the complexities of its own culture, homogenizing all of Africa and its diverse communities into one predominant cultural practice.[37]

The tone of the discussion on FGC always shifts after students read these essays. Here are some quotes from reading responses and class discussion:

"I would have never thought to connect FGC with other practices like cosmetic surgeries or reconstructive surgeries in the West. Somehow, FGC seemed more dangerous and life threatening to me. I guess I did not know a lot about FGC itself. I never knew that it is not practiced everywhere in Africa, or that African women themselves were against this practice. I am still not sure whether, as a White woman from the United States, I can help spread awareness about this issue without sounding like I am criticizing African culture?"

"I now remember [that], in the film we watched, one of the senior women who was well respected in her own village acknowledged the dangers of this practice, but she did not want to give it up because it was her livelihood. But another woman in her village, who did not want to circumcise her daughter, was trying to convince her to give it up. Gunning is suggesting that we collaborate with those people who are already working to stop FGC in their own communities and countries . . . it will not sound as if we are criticizing their culture if it comes from their own people, will it?"

"I was so surprised to hear that genital cutting was also practiced in the West amongst White women, often to control them. Why does no one talk about this? Why is FGC always constructed as part of an African or Islamic culture? Actually, for the first time, I am thinking about this practice or similar practices in the West. I am Jewish and male circumcision is a common practice in my family, but we never talk about it in the same way!"

"I find it hard to discuss these issues in class because I feel I don't know enough about it. It seems like such a 'savage' practice, or that is how it is talked about in the Western media. Do you think the media is to blame, though, more than the racist views of people? I mean, I did not know, for example, that dowry deaths in India is a kind of domestic violence. It is always presented as something unique to Indian culture. Would you, coming from India, consider me a racist?"

It is always challenging to navigate the "West" versus "East" cultural clash-type debates in the classroom, when it is obvious the students often see me as representing the "Other" culture. As the fourth quote suggests, it is almost as if the student is apprehensive about offending me, trying to make it clear that she is not racist and that it is the "Western media" that is responsible for her lack of information. On the other hand, though, as the other quotes demonstrate, students also begin to question long-held racialized notions about FGC and the dangers of homogenizing notions of culture. At the end of the term, one of the African American students wrote her final paper comparing cosmetic surgeries and reconstructive surgeries amongst intersex people in the United States with female genital circumcision in Senegal, highlighting the historical and cultural similarities and differences in how patriarchy operates to control gendered and racialized bodies. Teaching this course has been the most rewarding in moments like these!

Globalization and the Economy

As the previous section illustrates, students in my transnational feminism course have been drawn to culturally "exotic issues" of Third World feminism, while, at the same time, they struggle to grasp how cultural inferiority or "backwardness" is invoked to justify colonial and imperial projects. This section highlights that, although, initially, students were unwilling and unable to engage feminist critiques of globalization—particularly, the negative impacts of the World Bank, IMF, and U.S.-based World Trade Organization's policies on the global south, and especially poor women of color—linking these processes to consumption practices in the United States made it easier for students to comprehend.

Similar to Hase, I too use an exercise tracing where products consumed in the U.S. are made.[38] In an assignment called "Globalization and You," students are asked to read the labels of things they own, such as clothing, electronics, stationery, food items, and anything else in their homes or dorms, and then fill out a world map tracing where they are made. In another version of this assignment, I ask students to read the tags on each other's shirts or jackets and list where they are made. Students are always excited to do this assignment. It is a fun and interactive exercise that helps grab the attention of most students because it points to something they have not considered seriously.[39] Students list countries such as Mexico, Malaysia, Vietnam, and Bangladesh for clothing; China and Hong Kong for electronics. Listing the names of different countries allows students to recognize patterns that reflect what Joseph Stiglitz has called the "race to the bottom"—how countries of the global south try to emerge from colonial economic dependencies, competing with one another to lower labor and environmental standards so as to attract multinational corporations. This has resulted in free trade zones in many countries, such as Mexico, Malaysia, Vietnam, and Bangladesh. Some students came across places they had never heard of, such as Macao or Mauritius. Others expressed shock when they come across products made in Romania or Albania in Europe. One student asked me, "But Europe is not in the developing world, why does it support sweatshops?" Another student, wearing an Old Navy shirt, asked me, "My shirt is made in U.S.A.; does that mean there are sweatshops here, too?" These questions enable me to highlight the unevenness of economic globalization and the fact that it impacts people's lives both within and outside of the United States.

I usually pair this assignment with a lecture on the economic history of the developing world, situating how many of the previously prosperous regions of the global south became embroiled in poverty through colonial extractive industries and postcolonial dependencies. A student of color majoring in women's and gender studies once remarked that she was surprised that there was "so much economics in my classes!" She did not expect a course on feminism to engage the economy. I noticed a pattern during this lecture. When I teach about the impact of British colonialism, particularly on India, students are quite receptive. However, when I teach about more contemporary neoliberal policies of the U.S. institutions and corporations impacting countries of the global south, students born and brought up in the United States—both White students and students of color—are less receptive, and indeed, at times, resistant and defensive. Many students also struggle to connect economic globalization to the wide variety of "consumer choice" in the United States. Or that these same processes also impact the poor and women and men of color within the U.S., those who are at the lowest rung of the labor market and work in "feminized" and "racialized" occupations—the cleaners, janitors, food service folks, migrant workers, day laborers, and even public sector workers in child care, education, and nursing. Having said this, though, I noticed that some of my Latina/-o and African American students from, or linked to, working-class communities, and White students involved in social service work are more sensitized about these issues. In fact, I often depend on, encourage, and appreciate their direct interventions in the classroom in response to their less-aware peers on these critical, albeit controversial, issues. Many of these students of color who are personally or professionally linked to communities that have been detrimentally affected by increasing privatization and attendant funding cuts in public services in the United States thus add valuable insights, enabling collective and collaborative knowledge production in the classroom.

Part of the problem as Mohanty identifies in an interview with Dua and Trotz is that, historically, women's studies as a field and feminist departments in the United States have not engaged closely with anticapitalist and antiglobalization movements.[40] So, while it is easier for U.S.-based students[41] to grapple with British colonial practices from which they are spatially and historically distanced, it is much more difficult to come to terms with contemporary forms of neocolonial and imperial economic processes linked to the expansion of U.S. corporate power. I remember one White student wrote in her position paper that it is "very hard for her to accept that her country is implicated in exploitative practices abroad, not just in history (like colonial slave trade) but even now through economic sanctions and development policies." This is another example of the critical role nation, nationalism, and citizenship play in the classroom, influencing student comprehension and apprehension of colonialism and imperialism. On the judicious advice of a colleague who teaches globalization, although in a geography department, I screened the film *Life and Debt* (2003) the second time I offered this course. It enabled students to link colonialism and the economics of empire by examining processes of globalization in the Caribbean island of Jamaica. The film carefully analyzes contemporary Jamaica's tourist economy, dependency on the IMF and World Bank, and increasing poverty and violence with its history of British colonialism, post-independence struggles of industrialization, political instability, and financial crisis.

The topic of globalization and the economy also generates questions such as whether it is better for "Third World" women to have some work to earn their livelihoods instead of starving to death. Or whether "ethical consumption" practices such as buying local and supporting fair trade can be used to counter the race to the bottom? While these are important questions, they are also problematic. The first one is based in Western liberal notions that there is no alternative to capitalism, which normalizes such extreme choices as either exploitative underpaid work or starvation. Second, although it is heartening to hear students discuss ethical consumption, they often struggle to consider any form of collective struggle as a viable challenge to globalization. Many of these students are unaware of the mass antiglobalization protests against the WTO and World Economic Forum in Seattle in 1999. Moreover, they get most of their information from mainstream corporate media, which is notorious for downplaying these resistance movements or portraying them as violent, criminal, or anarchist responses. However, student preoccupation with individual instead of collective resistance may change, given the recent efforts of the Occupy Movement.[42]

Conclusion

Based on my experiences of teaching transnational feminism in a predominantly White university in the United States between 2010 and 2012, this chapter demonstrates how experiences of race and racism for immigrant women faculty of color are always mediated by nation, nationalism, and citizenship. Immigrant faculty of color, who are always bodily marked by difference, are, on one hand, uniquely positioned to illustrate the particular ways in which imperialism, racism, militarism, neoliberal capitalism, and patriarchy are intertwined. Yet, on the other hand, their particular embodiment of difference and critical pedagogical interventions expose them to student resistance and hostility, especially from but not limited to White students.

The students attending the above-detailed course struggled to understand the interconnectedness of local and global issues, one of the key tenets of transnational feminism. I noticed that, while they gravitated to "cultural" concerns that exoticized Third World women and their issues, most of them were more resistant to engage critiques of hegemonic economic policies of the United States and Western financial institutions such as the World Bank and IMF. My Indian origin, one of the countries of the global south where the majority of the people have been negatively impacted by some of these economic policies, made it tricky for me, as an immigrant, female faculty of color, to raise these issues in class. While I could draw on my personal and research experiences on India to give relevant examples, which the students appreciated, I also frequently became the authentic "native informant." My authorial voice was most valued while I was teaching about "native" issues impacting the developing world, but less valued when I raised questions about the role of the United States or the West in ongoing neocolonial and imperial projects. Teaching a comparative women's studies and anthropology class on international and U.S. women, Chatterjee observed that,

"When the teacher herself is from the Third World, her comments might be perceived as some authentic representation of the cultural specificities introduced."[43] The danger this poses is derived from the fact that, "The specific difference (of personality, posture, behavior) of one woman of color stands in for the difference of the whole collective, and a collective voice is assumed in place of an individual voice."[44] So, like Chatterjee, I have found the need to emphasize to my White students and students of color that I am both insider/outsider to India and the United States and that my knowledge is always situated in relation to the privileges and challenges of living in the diaspora. I, too, have to constantly learn how to articulate and teach these issues in relation to my particular local, cultural and national, political contexts.

Similarly, student resistance or hostility to my critiques of economic globalization or war and militarism reflect that being embodied as a migrant feminist of color without U.S. citizenship places me in a particularly precarious position. Transnational feminist critiques need to thus ground notions of difference related to nation/nationalism and citizenship in women's studies classrooms. Mohanty argues that particular genealogies of nationalism need to be examined more critically in American women's studies.[45] While feminist scholarship has been attentive to questions of the intersectionality of gender, race, class, and sexuality, the category of the nation has been relatively under-theorized in feminist work on the United States. She calls for a decentering of U.S. feminist scholarship and praxis, which has "always encoded stories of North America as central to its knowledge production. In fact, it is in times of crisis, in times of war, that these stories of the nation get mobilized, and are therefore patently visible for all to see."[46]

Mohanty helped me understand and contextualize the episode I used to begin this chapter.[47] In the aftermath of U.S.-led "war on terror" and Osama bin Laden's capture and assassination, my critique of militarism led to a hostile response from a White student in the classroom: "Does that mean you agree with what Osama bin Laden did to the American people on September 11?" Although initially quite shocked by this personal attack, I realized my student's position resonated popular rhetoric about the "war on terror" manufactured by the Bush administration and mainstream media, where either you condoned the war or you were considered un-American, un-patriotic, or, worse, aligning with the potential "terrorists." I responded to this question by assuring the White student that while I did not support what happened on 9/11, I was also opposed to the U.S. wars in Iraq and Afghanistan. Most students were not aware that the CIA had armed and supported bin Laden to fight the Russians in Afghanistan during the Cold War. After briefly giving them a historical background of this, I suggested that interesting insights could have been gained had Osama bin Laden been brought to trial in an international court of law. I emphasized that 9/11 needs to be contextualized and connected with the historical intervention of U.S. financial and military institutions in the global south. While the U.S. was reeling from the attacks on its own soil, which is certainly understandable, CIA-backed insurgencies had been instrumental in military coups across Latin America, Central America, Argentina, Iran, and parts of Africa. I use a transnational feminist lens to link such geopolitical and "foreign" policy matters, seemingly distant from "domestic" issues, to understand the negative impacts of privatization of public services, deregulation of the financial sectors, and the current economic crisis in the United States.

However, these narratives of student resistance also need to be assessed in relation to the general trend toward internationalization and "corporate multiculturalism"[48] in the U.S. academy. This kind of multiculturalism and liberal celebration of "difference" is a market-driven process, linked to privatization of higher education, which, as Mohanty has argued, can perpetuate race-, gender-, and class-based inequalities.[49] Internationalization of curricula has meant initiating programs and campuses abroad and increasing numbers of international students because of the revenue they generate. Often, the increasing presence of international students in the United States has led colleges and universities to hold conferences and training sessions that enable international students to adjust to U.S. academic culture. Far less attention and support is invested on how foreign-born immigrant faculty experience race and racial difference in the U.S. classroom. I often run into other immigrant faculty of color who face similar pedagogical challenges, but there is very limited scope and institutional space to seriously discuss particular teaching strategies and tools that have been used successfully in the classroom. I think it is imperative that we, as faculty of color, create and foster crosscultural and interdisciplinary dialogues about these pedagogical issues within the academy.

This chapter, on one hand, has allowed me to reflect upon the particular rewards and challenges of teaching transnational feminism as an immigrant woman of color in a predominantly White classroom in the United States. On the other hand, the chapter functions as an important attempt to dialectically link these experiences, both the challenges and the rewards, to more structural and political processes that raise issues of knowledge production, agency, institutional authority, and specific pedagogical strategies in relation to "teaching the global."

Acknowledgements

I thank Ann Russo, Laila Farah, and Karen McNamara for reading previous drafts of this essay and providing valuable feedback. I am also grateful to Chandra Talpade Mohanty for referring me to Anu Aneja's work. Finally, I thank Piya Chatterjee for her insights on pedagogy, which also inspired part of the title "teaching the global".

Notes

1 Piya Chatterjee, "Encountering 'Third World Women': Rac(e)ing the Global in a U.S. Classroom," *Pedagogy: Critical Approaches to Teaching Literature, Language, Composition and Culture*, 2(1), 2002, 79–108: 81, 104.

2 Andrea Smith, "Heteropatriarchy and the Three Pillars of White Supremacy: Rethinking Women of Color Organizing," in *Color of Violence: the Incite! Anthology* (Cambridge, MA: South End Press, 2006), 66–73: 66.

3 By "9/11," I am referring to the attacks on the World Trade Center and the Pentagon on September 11, 2001.

4 Although a controversial term, I use "Third World" to denote, first, countries that are not a part of the industrial capitalist first world or the former Soviet second world, and, second, those countries that have an economic history of social and sectoral disarticulation due to the manner in which they have been integrated into the global capitalist economy under colonial and neocolonial forces. In *Feminism Without Borders: Decolonizing Theory, Practicing Solidarity* (Durham, NC: Duke University Press, 2003: 44) Chandra Talpade Mohanty further explains that, "In the postindustrial world, systemic socioeconomic and ideological processes position the peoples of Africa, Asia, Latin America, and the Middle East, as well as 'minority' populations (people of color) in the United States and Europe, in similar relationships to the state."

5 Chatterjee, "Encountering 'Third World Women.'"

6 Chatterjee, "Encountering 'Third World Women,'" 80.

7 Suzanne Bryson and Mary de Castell, *Radical In(ter)ventions: Identity, Politics, and Difference/s in Educational Praxis* (Albany, NY: State University of New York Press, 1997).

8 bell hooks, *Teaching to Transgress: Education as the Practice of Freedom* (New York, NY: Routledge, 1994); George Yancy, *Look, a White!: Philosophical Essays on Whiteness* (Philadelphia, PA: Temple University Press, 2012).

9 Chandra Talpade Mohanty, "On Race and Voice: Challenges for Liberal Education in the 1990s," in *Between Borders: Pedagogy and the Politics of Cultural Studies*, eds. Henry A. Giroux and Peter McLaren (New York, NY: Routledge, 1994), 145–166; Leslie G. Eyre and Linda Roman, *Dangerous Territories: Struggles for Difference and Equality in Education* (New York, NY: Routledge, 1997); Giroux and McLaren, *Between Borders*.

10 Pauline Lipman, *High Stakes Education: Inequality, Globalization, and Urban School Reform* (New York, NY: Routledge, 2004); Peter McLaren and Nathalia E. Jaramillo, *Pedagogy and Praxis in the Age of Empire: Towards a New Humanism* (Rotterdam, Netherlands: Sense Publishers, 2007).

11 Himani Bannerji, "Re:Turning the Gaze," in *Thinking Through: Essays on Feminism, Marxism, and Anti-racism* (Toronto, Ontario, Canada: Women's Press, 1995).

12 Chandra Talpade Mohanty, "US Empire and the Project of Women's Studies: Stories of Citizenship, Complicity and Dissent," *Gender, Place and Culture*, 13(1), 2006: 7–20.

13 Mohanty, "US Empire and the Project of Women's Studies," 9.

14 Anu Aneja, "Of Masks and Masquerades: Performing the Collegial Dance," *Symploke*, 13(1), 2006: 144–151.

15 Within the broad interdisciplinary field of human geography, feminist geography is an established subfield. Although feminist geographers have been long influenced by the wide array of feminist scholarship in the humanities and social sciences, my experience with students in women's and gender studies at DePaul University revealed that they are not familiar with feminist geography.

16 M. Jacqui Alexander and Chandra Talpade Mohanty, *Feminist Genealogies, Colonial Legacies, Democratic Futures* (New York, NY: Routledge, 1996); Mohanty, *Feminism Without Borders*.

17 In the faculty statistics, 9.4% is recorded as unknown. See http://oipr.depaul.edu/factfile/newfactfile.asp?year=2011&sec=7&IsDrop=True.

18 "Vision 2018: Dedication to Excellence, Commitment to Community" strategic plan document (Chicago, IL: DePaul University, 2012).

19 Kimine Mayuzumi, "'In between' Asia and the West: Asian women faculty in the transnational context," *Race, Ethnicity and Education, 11*(2), July 2008: 167–182.

20 Jan Currie, "Globalization as an Analytical Concept and Local Policy Response," in *Universities and Globalization: Critical Perspectives*, eds. Jan Currie and Janice Angela Newson (Thousand Oaks, CA: Sage Publications, 1998).

21 I owe particular thanks to Ann Russo for pointing me to this tension between multiculturalism and internationalization that has pitted different women and academics of color against each other in the United States.

22 Smith, "Heteropatriarchy and The Three Pillars of White Supremacy," 66.

23 Ibid.

24 Smith, "Heteropatriarchy and The Three Pillars of White Supremacy."

25 Mohanty, *Feminism Without Borders*, 178.

26 I have also taught transnational feminism as a graduate seminar, but, in this essay, I restrict myself to the experiences from the undergraduate classroom.

27 I want to highlight that, in my courses, I always ask students to identify themselves (usually at the beginning of the quarter, but sometimes also during the course of the quarter); that is, how they want to be recognized/addressed and/or how they see themselves in relation to race, ethnicity, class, gender, sexuality, nationality, and so on.

28 Out of these, two students self-identified as woman of color from the "Third World" and the other student identified herself as a White, antiracist feminist who had lived in Africa and Europe.

29 Giroux and McLaren, *Between Borders*; Homa Hoodfar, "Feminist Anthropology and Critical Pedagogy: The Anthropology of Classrooms' Excluded Voices," *Canadian Journal of Education/Revue canadienne de l'éducation, 17*(3), 1992: 303–320.

30 Sandra Harding, "Feminism, Science, and the Anti-Enlightenment Critiques," in *Women, Knowledge, and Reality: Explorations in Feminist Philosophy*, eds. Ann Garry and Marilyn Pearsall (New York, NY: Routledge, 1996), 298–320.

31 Suheir Hammad, "Refugees," in *Whose World Is This?*, comp. K-Salaam and Beatnick (Jamaica, NY: VP Records, 2008).

32 See Hammad, "Refugees." Although officially produced in 2008 in MP3 form, I used a 2007 version of this poem distributed as a YouTube video through Make It Plain Productions, http://www.youtube.com/watch?v=Fun5BV8fFdI.

33 Michiko Hase, "Student Resistance and Nationalism in the Classroom: Some Reflections on Globalizing the Curriculum," *Feminist Teacher, 13*(2), 2001: 90–107.

34 Angela Y. Davis, "Women in Egypt: A Personal View," in *Women, Culture and Politics*, Angela Davis (New York, NY: Vintage Books, 1990), 116–154; Nawal El Saadawi, *The Hidden Face of Eve: Women in the Arab World* (London, England: Zed Books, 1985).

35 I thank Laila Farah for alerting me to the role of art and media as tools of transnational feminist praxis. Indeed, I depend heavily on music, videos, films, poetry, and various forms of visual and performance art as important pedagogical tools, especially in the introductory classes. See the documentary film *The Shape of Water*, Kum-Kum Bhavnani (Santa Barbara, CA: Kum-Kum Bhavnani, 2006).

36 Ben Barker-Benfield, "Sexual Surgery in Late-Nineteenth-Century America," in *An Introduction to Women's Studies: Gender in a Transnational World*, eds. Inderpal Grewal and Caren Kaplan (Boston, MA: McGraw Hill Higher Education, 2002).

37 Isabelle R. Gunning, "Cutting through the Obfuscation: Female Genital Surgeries in Neoimperial Culture," in *Talking Visions: Multicultural Feminism in a Transnational Age*, ed. Ella Shohat (Cambridge, MA: MIT Press, 2001), 203–224.

38 Hase, "Student Resistance and Nationalism in the Classroom."

39 Although I must highlight that some students are more aware than others, especially those who have been engaged in activist organizations or student movements protesting sweatshops (such as the campaigns of United Students Against Sweatshops (USAS)), which have become popular and quite successful in some U.S. campuses recently.

40 Enakshi Dua and Alissa Trotz, "Transnational Pedagogy: Doing Political Work in Women's Studies: An Interview with Chandra Talpade Mohanty," *Atlantis*, 26(2), 2002: 66–77, quote on pp. 67–68.

41 I do not intend to homogenize all students in the U.S. classroom. But, the point I am making is that while most students acknowledge race and ethnicity as a marker of their own identity within the borders of the country, they find it much harder to understand the geopolitical role of the U.S.A. in the broader project of empire in the global economy.

42 In fact, this movement is a great example of a transnational social justice mobilization because it was directly influenced by the mass mobilizations across North Africa and the Middle East since December 2010 and January 2011, popularly called "the Arab Spring." Asmaa Mahfouz, the Egyptian female activist whose video blog on different social media outlets is credited with helping to spark the protests in Tahrir Square, visited Occupy Wall Street in October 2011.

43 Chatterjee, "Encountering the 'Third World Woman,'" 102.

44 Ibid.

45 Mohanty, "US Empire and the Project of Women's Studies."

46 Ibid., 15.

47 Mohanty, "US Empire and the project of Women's Studies."

48 Heidi J. Nast and Laura Pulido, "Resisting Corporate Multiculturalism: Mapping Faculty Initiatives and Institutional-Student Harassment in the Classroom," *The Professional Geographer*, 52(4), 2000: 722–737.

49 Mohanty, *Feminism Without Borders*.

16

TEACHING INDIGENOUS CLASSES IN NON-INDIGENOUS CLASSROOMS

Joe Watkins

Introduction

The creation of ethnic studies classes in the 1960s and 1970s was heralded as an opportunity for "an increase of students of color, faculty of color, a more comprehensive curriculum that spoke the concerns and needs of marginalized communities of color."[1] With this rise in the number of students and faculty of color came a corresponding need to provide alternative instruction that emphasized the contributions of nonwhite Americans to the shared culture-history of the American population. However, did that struggle create the classroom we had hoped to create?

I am an associate professor in the Native American Studies program at the University of Oklahoma—and I am also a member of the Choctaw Nation of Oklahoma, an American Indian tribe. My training is within anthropology, with an emphasis in archaeology, and I have always had to balance my ethnic background against my academic field of study, while, at the same time, balancing my academic field of study against my ethnic background. It is not easy being one of the few American Indian archaeologists with a PhD (perhaps still less than 25!) since both the academy and my ethnic group believe I cannot be one and the other at the same time. Many American Indians believe that being an archaeologist is the same as being a disrespectful grave-digging atheist; many archaeologists do not believe I can "objectively" do archaeology because they believe I have misplaced loyalties to my ethnic group. Such issues also appear within the university classrooms where I teach.

What are "Indigenous Classes" and "Non-Indigenous Classrooms"?

The title of this chapter presents two extremely important concepts to the overall discussion related to trying to explore race within predominantly White classrooms. I conceptualize "Indigenous classes" to be classes that offer Indigenous perspectives on particular topics or disciplines. In this regard, I use "Indigenous" as a generic term to describe those populations that existed within a region prior to its colonization.[2] In this regard, teaching Native American studies classes in a university setting is more often than not a presentation of alternative perspectives on mainstream topics as a means of increasing "diversity" within predominantly White institutions, and in my university institution in particular. The classrooms often comprise students from mixed backgrounds and heritages who have alternative means of comprehending and examining the academic material; even in situations where Native American students might be the numerical majority, it is important to realize that these are still "non-indigenous classrooms."

The MERLOT Pedagogy website[3] offers suggestions for teaching in diverse and multicultural classrooms, and many of the suggestions it offers would help to create more open learning environments. However, the Western academic structure of the "professor" as leader and the student as "follower" is, in many ways, anathema to many non-Western styles of learning.

The Socratic method of teaching, for example, is a form of inquiry and debate between individuals with opposing viewpoints based on asking and answering questions to stimulate critical thinking and to illuminate ideas. It is a dialectical method, often involving an oppositional discussion in which the defense of one point of view is pitted against the defense of another; one participant may lead another to contradict himself/herself in some way, thus strengthening the inquirer's own point. However, in some cultures, it is considered rude and disrespectful to question the "expert"; and some instructors teach particularly broad and complex ideas and expect questions to be asked during office hours and not within the classroom itself. These learning and teaching styles are often deeply embedded within cultural mores that many do not understand or even realize exist.

I have had classes mixed with American Indian and non-Indian students and have seen the difference in the way each group approaches discussion points. The non-Indian students will generally be more open about questioning ideas and controversial points, while, in general, the American Indian students will listen quietly, either nodding in agreement or casting their eyes downward with slight shakes of the head to indicate disagreement. These movements are so subtle they are often missed, and, to most instructors, they might not even register as worthy of note. Many tribal cultures often discourage public disagreement and, instead, search for consensus, and so calling attention to flaws is not always something American Indian students feel comfortable doing. By asking leading questions as a means of drawing out alternative perspectives, I am better able to alleviate some student discomfort, but the hesitancy to draw negative attention to a classmate still can cause discomfort. Often, too, the instructor can deflect some of the hesitancy by reminding students that discussion and disagreement are okay, and that, *in the academic culture*, discussion is accepted and encouraged.

Additionally, conversation with Native American students often must be initiated by the instructor, or students must be expressly invited into conversation. While most students seem hesitant to engage professors in conversation, Native American students more often defer to rank and privilege and must be "invited" to speak. Direct conversations are difficult and often become circuitous until the point is reached. In many ways, these cultural issues conflict with what is expected of students in Western classrooms, where vocality and argumentation might be considered the norm.

These are the areas where an Indigenous instructor can be caught in the gulf between Western academic expectations and non-Western cultural understandings. Western academic cultures require us to test for *comprehension* but not for *understanding*, whereas non-Western cultures require that we strive for *understanding* but not necessarily *comprehension*. As an Indigenous professor, the gulf can often seem un-crossable, but the drive to try to build bridges is insurmountable.

Barriers to Communication

With the increasing number of representatives of students from varying cultures, the need to understand the ways that culture influences the process of learning is paramount. Students learn not only in terms of commonly recognized individual learning styles, such as "visual," "auditory," or "tactile," but also in ways that are subtle and discrete. For example, while an individual might be an auditory learner (gathers and processes information primarily through oral lectures), that student's culture might prevent him or her from asking questions for clarification—it might be perceived that to ask questions might somehow insult the instructor's ability to present the information clearly for the student's benefit. The student's culture, therefore, would prevent questioning, and the lack of understanding would then be placed on the student, not on the instructor. In this way, students whose cultures discourage asking questions out of fear of insulting the instructor often come to see themselves as unworthy, stupid, or lacking.

Culture Matters,[4] a publication of the U.S. Peace Corps, is an indispensable book for helping instructors better understand the variety of ways people process information and interact with others. The various exercises also help people understand the ways in which individual communication styles might not work in all circumstances. Also, the exercises provide helpful suggestions for how to provide alternate means of presenting information, communicating with others, and understanding the general perceptions others may have of the information being presented.

I try to have at least one lecture about communication styles within every class I teach, especially as it relates to Native American issues within the academy. Often, those lectures constitute the first time students in the classroom are taught about such things, and I can see the light go on in some of the students' eyes as they recognize themselves and their families in the descriptions. There are also lots of head nodding about high context and low context situations and direct–indirect communication. Such information helps students understand the ways that they can better communicate not only with instructors but with other students as well, and it also helps them understand some of the barriers to communication they might experience in the academy.

Other situations exist where actions common to the dominant American culture can be problematic to student–teacher interaction. In my personal dealings with members of some American Indian groups in southwestern Oklahoma, I have noticed and been told that tribal members are often taught *NOT* to look into another person's eyes, since such action can be deemed as an effort to determine whether or not the person is telling the truth or lying. They instead are counseled to look slightly beyond the person's eyes, such as at a person's ears or lips, only occasionally glancing in the eyes to encourage conversation. In American culture, however, such an act of evading the gaze is sometimes interpreted to be the hallmark of someone trying to evade the truth, rather than a sign of respect for the other. Instructors who come from an informed background can recognize such actions for the cultural sensitivity it represents; those who are unaware often struggle trying to decode the meanings or simply misinterpret the cultural significance of the behavior.

American Indian graduate students often get pegged as unprepared by non-Native instructors because of the students' tendency *not* to speak up in class, even in seminars where speaking and discussing other authors' works is required. Again, the cultural tendency against speaking out (and thereby drawing attention to oneself) is often at the root of such "inaction," even when the student might know the answer and knows the reading material well. It was difficult for me, as a graduate student, to openly critique a respected author's work, as this would imply that I knew more than the author. Also, it would imply that the instructor's interpretation was faulty. Yet, after nearly failing out of my first semester, I learned that it was acceptable (and indeed required) within the graduate school classroom culture to question the "experts," something that would not have been acceptable in my home.

Challenges to Teaching

There are obviously numerous challenges to teaching about racial topics within classrooms of mixed ethnicities. I use "ethnicity/ethnic" rather than "race/racial" because, as an anthropologist, I know that "race," as a genetic or biological concept, does not exist. What is generally used to define a person's "race" is the outward (phenotypical) appearance that the general public uses as shorthand for identification or placement of a person's ethnicity.[5]

However, regardless of what we may know academically and scientifically, there are issues associated with teaching classes that examine experiences of specific ethnic groups in the American historic, economic, and cultural milieus. Students do not come to us with a clean slate; they bring with them the sum total of life experiences that they and their families have had to go through. They then use these experiences to filter their knowledge and their relationships with others in such a way that it can become difficult for them to see alternative ways of viewing a subject or idea.

"Race" as Safety Net

Ethnic students sometimes enroll in and attend classes that relate to their ethnicity as a means of seeking a haven from the outside (White) world. Perhaps, in these students' minds, hanging out with other like-minded (and similar in appearance) students will make it easier for them to fit in at a predominantly White university. Some American Indian students enroll in our classes expecting to learn how "to be Indian," while others enroll thinking they already know all the answers ("I'm Indian and so this will be an easy grade"). In this way, the student's "race" becomes a safety net, allowing him or her to continue to exist with self-perceived peers. While the social aspects of the group can be a major factor in retention and graduation, it can also lead to reinforcement of the "us–them" divide that already permeates the university community, particularly in terms of a "White–Other" divide.

"Race" as Divisor

In his book *The Magic Children*,[6] Roger Echo-Hawk discusses his journey from being a "professional Indian" to giving up "race" and trying to create a world without it. His journey took him through the stages of being "Indian" to being "Pawnee" to being just plain Roger Echo-Hawk. "Echo-Hawk," Carol Ellick writes, "has inserted the word 'race' into contexts with what I hope is an effort to provoke thinking."[7] And such provocation flows from his works, especially in relation to American Indian studies programs. Echo-Hawk writes: "History tries to tell us that racism is the typical noxious byproduct of the zealous doing of race. So it seems useful to suspect that even a cursory examination of racial Indianhood will reveal that socially empowered Red Pride racialism is just as racist as socially empowered White Pride racialism."[8] Later still in his book, he writes: "We have an urgent need for conscientious specialists in 'Indian studies' to lead the way in reconfiguring the study of racial Indianhood in light of the realities of race."[9]

Echo-Hawk's statements lie at the heart of Native American studies, as well as, to an extent, the other ethnic studies programs that exist in American colleges and universities. If we, as "specialists in 'Indian studies,'" inadvertently or purposefully instruct our students to believe that there is a biological "something" that creates an "Indian," then we are truly doing a disservice to them. It is imperative that we stress the fact that the "Indian" of "Indian studies" is comprised of a series of shared historical, social, and cultural events through time and geography that have impacted (and continue to impact) communities of people whose ancestors inhabited this continent prior to the coming of the non-Native, White groups.

Sometimes, this is a difficult point to make to Native American students, but one that is well worth the effort. It is important that all students feel welcome, even though some are not Indian "by blood" or by tribal membership. I try to enforce the idea that "Indianness" is not a matter of blood by using the example of Cynthia Ann Parker, who was captured by the Comanche Indians in 1836 at the age of eight. Cynthia Ann "became" Comanche, in spite of her German American ancestry, and even tried to return to the Comanche after she was "rescued" and returned to her non-Indian White family in 1860. Still, in spite of this, there are those students who feel non-Indians should not have a place in the program.

At my university, many non-Indians, especially Whites, enroll in Native American studies classes because the classes fulfill requirements for graduation. Many of these White students, however, come to the classes with a background informed by misconceptions, half truths, or downright politically biased information. In this regard, the classes can serve either as an academic "wake-up call" or they can be perceived as a "politically correct" way of appeasing "White guilt," in much the same way that affirmative action programs have been called "reverse discrimination."[10] Even including such articles as Peggy McIntosh's "White Privilege: Unpacking the Invisible Backpack"[11] in general course readings can be interpreted as being openly antagonistic by some White students.

Too often, underlying stereotypes are at the center of such issues. Negative stereotypes about American Indian casinos create misperceptions of widespread wealth among ALL American Indian people, free education for American Indian students, and the widespread belief that American Indians do not need to work because of tribal support. Laying those stereotypes to rest begins by opening them up to the light. Some students are hesitant to admit to the stereotypes they have, and so placing the discussion in a somewhat neutral light ("What stereotypical comments have you *heard* about American Indians?" or "What stereotypes do you think *others* have about American Indians?") makes it easier for students to discuss them without appearing to be the ones who have misguided perspectives/perceptions.

Occasionally, some students will not believe that White privilege exists. In instances where such deeply held beliefs occur, I have found it educational to ask students to come up with five privileges *they believe* other ethnic groups have that the group to which they belong does not. Classroom discussions based on these lists bring out lively interactions between the students, and often lead to introspection. One caveat is important to consider: Some people will never see such privilege, whether it exists or not, and it is not our job as teachers to *make* them believe it exists, but it is clearly important that they are at least exposed to the idea of its existence.

The purpose of Native American studies classes (and other ethnic studies classes as well) is to inform the general public/larger community about the perspectives of various subcultural groups that can be applied to a variety of academic disciplines—not to teach anyone "how to be Indian" or to take a stand against one cultural group or another. Such classes are not about forms of hegemonic assimilation or driven by an intrinsic antagonism. While it should be emphasized that the particular perspectives of the group being studied should be the primary ones informing discussions, it is also important that students realize that discussion of other opinions on topics should be encouraged. As with any university setting, the free exchange of ideas should be the primary focus of classroom spaces.

Suggestions for Exploring Teaching Methods

While it is often necessary to experiment with different ways of presenting information to students, it is also necessary to find culturally relevant ways of presenting the information, especially if the information is perceived to be in conflict with those cultural perspectives.

I teach a course called Indigenous Archaeology at both the graduate and undergraduate levels. Preconceived notions of the archaeologist as a "grave-robber" influence many American Indian perspectives, creating conflicting ideas of archaeology as a sacrilegious action that has impacted, and continues to impact, American Indian culture disproportionately. Still, more than 130 American Indian tribal nations formally have taken over some aspects of federal historic preservation programs from the state government, including archaeological ones, as a means of better controlling the impact of federally funded or licensed projects on American Indian land and the heritage therein.

But students often feel conflicted about various aspects of the academic discipline, especially as it relates to the early history of the North American continent. I have written about a situation in a class I taught where all the students were Native American,[12] as it relates to conflicting histories and origins. Here, I will only summarize that situation. At issue was the archaeological proposal that the earliest habitation of North America was about 15,000 years ago, which can be seen to be in direct conflict with the idea that American Indians "have always been here." I used the opportunity to talk about the scientific method, hypothesis testing, observation, and so forth, rather than enter into a debate about the probability that a separate species of humans evolved in the Old and the New World.

But the discussion about human migration into North America is not just an academic one. Vine Deloria, Jr., wrote about the political implications of the scientific theory of migration: "By making us immigrants to North America, they [scientists] are able to deny the fact that we were the full, complete, and total owners of this continent. They are able to see us simply as earlier interlopers and therefore throw back at us the accusation that we had simply *found* North America a little earlier than they had."[13] Adding this perspective to the discussion, we were able to focus on the *sociopolitical* aspects of the scientific method as well as the academic ones. By melding the social with the academic, those students were better able to comprehend the sorts of issues that can occur within university settings. The example also served to open up discussion on issues that arose when the perspectives of the dominant culture conflicted with those of a minority one. And so, rather than saying, "Science is right; Indians are wrong," it became an opportunity rather than a confrontation over belief systems.

More difficulty arises, however, when one teaches Native American studies classes that have mixed Native and non-Native (White) students. More often than not, the non-Natives are the ones who are hesitant to discuss especially potent issues, for fear of being labeled "wrong" or "racist." In such circumstances, it is important, at the beginning of the semester, to explicitly state ground rules— polite conversation, respectful listening, quiet reflection, informed discussion, and acceptance of disagreement. I find it eases discomfort to openly lay out these ground rules early on, so that people can interact freely without fear of reprisal, verbal out-breaks, or hurtful retorts. Still, the first few discussions are always challenging. Even if Native students make up a numerical majority, it takes time for them to become comfortable in offering their perspectives; it also takes time for non-minority White students to feel comfortable offering their perspectives in a class where they might be the "academic minority."

I have found that one of the best methods of bridging the dynamic tensions in classrooms is through humor—often self-depreciating, but occasionally openly "critical." In classrooms with a large number of Native American students, I find it easier to joke about myself as a way of letting students realize I am a bit "looser" in classroom decorum, even as I let them know about the other ground rules about classroom behavior. But, while I let the students know I am quick to laugh at myself, it is also important that they understand the same guidelines about respect apply.

I have also observed that students will use humor as a means of "social control," much like many traditional societies do. For example, in situations where many of the Native students know each other academically and socially, often comments are laced with innuendo and satire. Student comments such as, "Dang, I thought you were using the whole book," lets everyone know he or she felt the presentation was text heavy without having to directly criticize the presenter. Other comments enforce the notion that "many a true word is spoken in jest," and the students find ways of making others feel more comfortable with the critical evaluation of the student's presentation.

Being a Stronger Instructor

Sometimes, it might be more difficult when students and instructors share ethnic identity; no one wants to believe the instructor is easier or harder on one person because of ethnic identity. But I do believe that, sometimes, the students might get the mistaken idea that the misbalance of ethnic identity can create issues: either they don't have to worry about things because "the instructor and I are both Indian," that they can't get a fair grade because "the instructor is Indian and I'm not," or that "the other student got a good grade because the instructor is Indian and so is the student." It is perhaps most difficult to remain neutral in all regards—positively and negatively—when it comes to grading and classwork.

I find that good rubrics are essential to maintaining fair grading systems. It is easier for students to see what I expect at certain grade levels—at least within a minimal structure—and easier for myself, as well, to be able to remove many subjective aspects of grading. In addition, the rubrics offer implicit suggestions for structuring papers, presentations, and other assignments.

I also try to minimize the "all-or-nothing" approach regarding assignments. I break the assignments up into logical steps, with points given during the class for each one. For instance, I require the students to turn in a written sentence giving their proposed paper topic, an outline of the paper, a "draft" final, and then the final paper. By requiring the four parts of the paper process and giving points for each, the students are not relying on one grading event. Students earn points by completing the logical steps toward writing research (or term) papers. This serves to get students used to the academic process of paper writing and publishing, but also alleviates some of the end-of-term procrastination. By requiring the "draft" final two-thirds of the way through the academic term, I can read, review, and comment on the paper so that the final paper is stronger and better written. This exposes the students to the editorial process as well, so that they do not simply write the paper and forget about it, but, rather, are charged with reviewing editorial comments, accepting (or rejecting) those comments and acting on them, and then finalizing and submitting the revised paper.

When You Have to Get Tough

Given the method of instruction common on most of today's college and university campuses, it is necessary to find ways to bring students into the conversations of the classroom, even when they are uncomfortable contributing. While formal presentations are always important as a means of creating student self-confidence and comfort standing in front of classes, I often try to ask students "What do *you* think this means?" or other open-ended questions, rather than hunting for specific right/wrong answers. In this manner, the students become more comfortable offering their own ideas about particular issues, while, at the same time, feeling involved in their own learning journey. This process often creates some issues when asking such questions to specific individuals as it tends to draw attention to them, but, by the end of the term, most students are comfortable with this means of generating critical discussion.

I realize teaching is not a popularity contest, even though student evaluations often make it seem as if it is, but I find it difficult to read evaluations that make it appear the student was disappointed in the class. I entered teaching late in my career—having begun teaching at the university level in 2003 at the University of New Mexico—and wanted to be the type of teacher that I appreciated. But perhaps I have become a bit too lax, as I have not been one to be too strict about some of the deadlines I impose on my students. Many of our Native American students are nontraditional or returning students, and they often let their outside obligations take precedence over their personal learning journeys. Even though we understand how their family obligations often seem to conflict with their academic ones, we have to act decisively as student excuses get more numerous and scholarly production declines.

How do we balance the needs of the student with the requirements of a good education? I can't give a student a passing grade just for "trying" to do something; that student has to give me something to grade. But some students seem to feel entitled to receive a degree because they "paid" tuition and fees for the classes they took. I would rather not give "incompletes" without some strong mitigating circumstances because I do not believe it is fair for someone to have additional time to finish a class while others turn in their assignments on time and accept the grades they earn.

Ultimately, we have to get tough and ask students to leave the program as we come to realize that they cannot live up to our requirements for graduation. We want our students to succeed and give them numerous chances to do so, but there are some who cannot complete minimal requirements, cannot communicate through the written word, or cannot commit enough to complete classes on a timely basis. We must not look at these students as *our* failures, but we do owe it to them to help them move on into an area where they *can* succeed.

Politics and Academics: Educate or Advocate?

One of the most difficult things to accomplish is becoming an "objective" presenter of information in such a way that doesn't preclude learning or preclude informed examination of the topics. Students can perceive instructors who push topics too far in one direction or another as an advocator first and an educator second. Is our role as ethnic studies instructors to present "objective" facts, or is it to use those facts to create discussions that illustrate the issues ethnic groups face within the dominant White American society so that the students are better able to recognize them, and, hopefully, act on them in the future? In our program, I believe it is our role to present an American Indian perspective first, since the perspectives of the dominant White culture are generally embedded within most of the other university classes. This mission should not be seen to be advocating one hegemonic position over another, but as an attempt at educating the students about alternative perspectives and the ability to offer critique of those perspectives where necessary.

This is, to me, what is most disturbing about the passage of Arizona HB 2281 in 2010. In April 2010, a measure known as House Bill 2281 was brought before and passed by the Arizona State Legislature. On May 11, 2010, Arizona Governor Jan Brewer signed the new bill into law. The law prohibits any public school district from offering in its program of instruction any course and class that specifically administers classroom instruction based solely from an ethnic perspective; promotes the overthrow of the United States government; forwards resentment toward a race or class of people; is comprised primarily for pupils of a particular ethnic group; or that advocates ethnic solidarity instead of individualism. The bill professes to be one that draws students together and lessens the racial distinctions that exist in the classroom, but it has come under fire as being culturally insensitive.

The law politicizes the teaching of alternative perspectives as it tries to prevent the political inculcation of students by a singular perspective, yet it continues to enforce the dominant White version of history. The purpose of ethnic studies classes in secondary school is to "urge all students to think deeply about the diverse cultural and ethnic makeup of the world and to become sensitive to this diversity in social relations."[14] We should not advocate any perspective solely on the basis of an ethnic or racial position, but we cannot shirk our responsibilities to offer that perspective to those who wish to better understand it.

Concluding Comments

The structure and purpose of the university classroom is certainly under fire today. More and more state legislatures are cutting funding while, at the same time, others, such as the state of Texas legislature, are trying to run the university along a business model[15] as a means of ensuring "accountability." Will ethnic studies classes survive such an onslaught? Is the Arizona action the precursor of the future?

I was talking with a student after a tribal historic preservation class where I had spent the majority of the period talking about American Indian and non-Indian perspectives and ways of consulting as part of the historic preservation process. The student, a young woman with a communications degree, said, "I couldn't understand why you were teaching Indians how to consult with Indians until I remembered 'Oh yeah, not everyone here is Indian.'" It is important that we not forget that our classes are ways for us to expose to everyone what it means to have a minority perspective informed from an ethnic background—our students will only benefit from such an offering, and our future leaders *need* to be aware of those perspectives.

Notes

1 National Association for Ethic Studies, "About," http://www.ethnicstudies.org/about/naes-history.
2 Joe Watkins, "Through Wary Eyes: Indigenous Perspectives on Archaeology," *Annual Review of Anthropology, 34*(1), 2005, 429–449.
3 MERLOT (Multimedia Educational Resource for Learning and Online Teaching) Pedagogy Portal, http://pedagogy.merlot.org.
4 *Culture Matters: The Peace Corps Cross-Cultural Workbook*, Peace Corps Information Collection and Exchange (Washington, D.C.: US Peace Corps Information Collection and Exchange, n.d.).
5 American Anthropological Association, "Response to OMB Directive 15: Race and Ethnic Standards for Federal Statistics and Administrative Reporting," September 1997, http://www.aaanet.org/gvt/ombdraft.htm; "Statement on 'Race,'" May 17, 1998, http://www.aaanet.org/stmts/racepp.htm.
6 Roger C. Echo-Hawk, *The Magic Children: Racial Identity at the End of the Age of Race* (Walnut Creek, CA: Left Coast Press, 2010).
7 Carol Ellick, "Close Your Eyes and Then Listen to Their Words," *Current Anthropology, 52*(5), 2011, 759–761.
8 Echo-Hawk, *The Magic Children*, 64.
9 Echo-Hawk, *The Magic Children*, 166.
10 NBCNews.com, "Does Affirmative Action Punish Whites?" April 28, 2009, http://www.msnbc.msn.com/id/30462129/ns/us_news-life/t/does-affirmative-action-punish-whites; Chris Truitt, "Affirmative Action or Reverse Discrimination?" (n.d.), http://www.christruitt.com/archives/affirmative_action.php; Fred L. Pincus, "The Social Construction of Reverse Discrimination: The Impact of Affirmative Action on 'Whites,'" *Journal of Intergroup Relations, 28*(4), Winter 2001/2002, 33–44.
11 Peggy McIntosh, "White Privilege: Unpacking the Invisible Backpack," 1989, http://www.uakron.edu/dotAsset/1662103.pdf, accessed June 29, 2012.
12 Joe Watkins, "Communicating Archaeology: Words to the Wise," *Journal of Social Archaeology, 6*(1), 2006: 100–118, 106–107.
13 Vine Deloria, Jr., *Red Earth, White Lies: Native Americans and the Myth of Scientific Fact* (New York, NY: Scribner and Sons, 1995), 84, emphasis in original.
14 Julian Kunnie, "Apartheid in Arizona? HB 2281 and Arizona's Denial of Human Rights of Peoples of Color," *The Black Scholar, 40*(4), Winter 2010: 16–26, 20.
15 Thomas K. Lindsay, "The Texas Model of Higher Education Reform," HuffPost Education blog, July 3, 2012, http://www.huffingtonpost.com/thomas-lindsay-phd/texas-education-reform_b_1646482.html.

AFTERWORD

Teaching Whiteness to White Students

Maria del Guadalupe Davidson

In moments of solitude, when I sit down with my computer and my thoughts in order to grapple with the complexities of race, there is a certain mindset that comes over me. The written word allows me to be bold and provocative. Yet, though I find writing about race to be liberating, my mindset toward *teaching* courses that explore race is exactly the opposite: I never find it easy. To be clear, it is not difficult to engage with students about issues such as affirmative action or the connection between race, gender, and poverty. Such topics are familiar enough that the lines of discussions about them are already drawn out and tend to follow established patterns. While they are rarely unnerving, one topic, in particular, causes butterflies to form in my stomach, and often leads me to re-read my notes over and over again: this is the topic of *whiteness*. Teaching, not writing, about whiteness is, for me, a soul-shaking experience; one that is nerve-racking, but powerful.

One important point to note from the outset is that teaching about whiteness does not only have a bearing on White students in the classroom. To be clear, it is not just White people who may advocate for and participate in whiteness. This means that nonwhites can act in ways that reinforce the assumptions of whiteness; they, too, can say and do things to support its supremacy. Examples of this include the desire for straight hair, light skin, and the belief that Black American English is inferior to White American ("standard") English.[1] bell hooks echoes this point in her article "Representing Whiteness in the Black Imagination," in which she observes: "Now, many Black people live in the 'bush of ghosts' and do not know themselves separate from Whiteness, do not know this thing we call 'difference.'"[2] Whiteness and other forms of historical oppression, as hooks goes on to explain, "force black folks to internalize negative perceptions of Blackness," and one of the ways in which Blacks and other nonwhites reveal that they have "succumbed" to whiteness is by enacting White ways of being.[3] As a result, in many cases, in teaching about whiteness, professors do not only have to expose the implications of whiteness to White students but to the nonwhite students in the classroom as well. For the nonwhite students can also have incorporated the negative assumptions and beliefs of whiteness in similar ways as White students. And, even if nonwhite students have not incorporated these negative assumptions and beliefs, whiteness still can have a significant impact on their lives, knowingly or not.

How, then, does this realization about whiteness shape my role as a teacher? To answer this question, let me begin with an admission about my own apprehensions when it comes to teaching about whiteness. On the one hand, I recognize the danger that whiteness presents to Black and "brown" bodies. On the other hand, I recognize that many of my students are White, and I have the same concern for them as with any other student. I do not want to hurt their hearts, I don't want to make them feel bad or guilty, and I am reluctant to drop the heavy weight of the history of whiteness on them. As a result, the challenge is to strike the right balance; that is, to get them to recognize the reality of whiteness, but, at the same time, to do so in a way that doesn't do them harm.

My initial approach to this might be called an *Avenue* Q-ing of the teaching moment. By this, I mean that I signal to my White students through words and gestures: "Don't take what I'm saying too much to heart or be weighted down by too much guilt, because really everyone's a little bit racist [*wink-wink*]." This takes some of the edge off of a difficult and potentially dangerous topic. But, by trying to soften the impact, am I failing my responsibility to educate my White students by making them confront unsettling realities? Am I engaging in bad faith by avoiding my own responsibility to speak the truth and to confront injustice? In so doing, am I playing into the very same White structure that I set out to critique? These questions come back again and again when I teach about whiteness. These are never just intellectual questions that are abstracted from real life. Instead, they are personal issues that always point back to me. This is why I never find it easy to teach about whiteness; this is why it is so often soul shaking to me.

What follows are some pedagogical reflections based on my experiences of teaching whiteness. They describe the process by which I lead students from an intellectual understanding of the concept of whiteness to the ultimate self-reflection that I hope to produce within them. The aim is to show how to strike a comfortable balance between the dangerous extremes mentioned above when teaching about whiteness.

The Concept of Whiteness

In *Displacing Whiteness*, Ruth Frankenberg describes whiteness as "the unmarked marker" and as an "empty signifier."[4] This means that whiteness identifies or "marks" others, while, at the same time, remaining unmarked or often impervious to interpretation by White people. Richard Dyer describes this phenomenon of whiteness aptly when he writes:"This property of whiteness, to be everything and nothing, is the source of its representational power."[5] I explain to my students that leaving whiteness unmarked places the nonwhite person in the position of being "different" in relationship to whiteness. Whiteness thereby comes to represent the norm, and, therefore, those bodies outside of the norm are measured against the standard of whiteness. Yet, there are two important points to make about whiteness: first, it is constructed as much as any other social category; second, it is wholly meaningless outside of a relational–oppositional context.

In his formative essay "The Struggle to Define and Reinvent Whiteness," Joe Kincheloe engagingly explains the genesis of the category of whiteness. Kincheloe's article, though challenging, provides students with a critical and historical foundation for understanding whiteness. He insightfully traces the category of whiteness back to the European Enlightenment and "the notion of rationality" embodied (or, rather, disembodied) within the "construction of the transcendental White, male, rational subject who operated at the recesses of power while concurrently giving every indication that he had escaped the confines of time and space."[6] The faculty of reason thus becomes the primary indicator of whiteness and of humanity. It is through this "rationalistic womb" that, according to Kincheloe, "whiteness begins to establish itself as norm that represents an authoritative, delimited, and hierarchical mode of thought."[7] Kincheloe examines how whiteness came to be associated with other positive traits, such as "orderliness" and "self-control." Since whiteness is a relational category, it could only establish itself in opposition to another category. Thus, "nonwhiteness" came to characterize the negative/opposite terms: "chaos, irrationality, violence, and the breakdown of self-regulation."[8]

The Reality of Whiteness

The above, albeit brief discussion, provides students with a framework for understanding the history of the concept of whiteness. This initial approach offers, for White students in particular, an opportunity to conceptualize whiteness without yet implicating them in it. Grounding the origins of whiteness within the context of the European Enlightenment enables White students to distance themselves from the past and to conceptualize their whiteness as inconsequential. At some point, however, I think that professors have to move beyond this initially safe, academic, theoretical approach to teaching whiteness to discussing the real, contemporary impact that whiteness has had (and continues to have) on people of color throughout the world. So, for example, one historical impact that I typically use to explain the corrosive and hegemonic influence that whiteness has had on people of color is the colonization of the latter vis-à-vis their territory and culture. This process of colonization, I explain, has been carried out mostly by White, Western Europeans. Kincheloe explains that since nonwhites were perceived by Western Europeans "as irrational and thus inferior in their status as human beings, they had no claim to the same rights as Europeans—hence, White racism and colonialism were morally justified around the conflation of whiteness and reason."[9]

Here, we come to see that the colonization of people of color (e.g., Africans, Asians, Native Americans) was directly related to the concept of whiteness. White people came to define themselves in terms of their superiority and "colonized people's deviation from the norm of rationality, thus making colonization a relational response to inequality."[10] Through this linkage, it is fair to say that many of my White students begin to comprehend how whiteness has been historically destructive. *Yet*, are they able to see that whiteness is not a thing of the past and that it is not merely an academic discussion? Are they able to see that it relates to them personally and that many of them are the beneficiaries of whiteness? Are they able to see, in turn, that the problems faced by many nonwhite communities are the direct result of whiteness?

At this point in the discussion, most White students are able to understand the concept of whiteness and see it at work in history or in other (foreign) places. However, they are able to do this at a safe distance. So, although many of them acknowledge their European ancestry, they do not see the connection between themselves and some "distant" European past ("I've never been there"). They have White American ancestry, but they do not connect themselves to the history of Black enslavement, Native American removal, or Japanese internment ("I didn't enslave anyone, take anyone's land, or imprison anyone"). They have seen brutal images from Reconstruction, segregation, and the Civil Rights Movement, but they are not implicated by any of it ("I didn't lynch Black people, deny anyone service, or order water cannons to be turned on any crowd"). This is the part of teaching whiteness where my soul begins to shake. An instructional shift takes place here, where we transition from looking at whiteness from the outside to bringing it into the classroom and making it visible here and now.

Most White students are unable to do this on their own. They have developed a thick, self-protective layer that shields them from a history complicated by race and racism. The challenge of the teacher is to break through that layer. One effective way to do this is to insert raw emotion into the discussion. This involves going beyond the comprehension of the concept and history of whiteness; it involves getting White students to *see* that whiteness, especially their own whiteness, is something that they enact and benefit from on a daily basis.

The challenge in teaching whiteness, as noted earlier, is to find a productive way to do so, one that encourages students to engage an inconvenient truth, but does so in a way that is beneficial to students as well. What follows is an account of some of the contours of the discussion that leads students to confront their own whiteness.

Making Whiteness Visible

Let me begin by way of a detour through a description of another classroom. In his introduction to *What White Looks Like: African American Philosophers on the Whiteness Question,* George Yancy describes a scene from a graduate course on African American Literature. Yancy, who was enrolled as a student in the course, explains that he became very disappointed with "superficial readings by the [White] graduate students" of two particular texts—*Narrative of the Life of Fredrick Douglas* and *Incidents in the Life of a Slave Girl.* Yancy's frustration eventually boiled over into justifiable anger, and he responded in a way that, I think, was designed to shake those White graduate students out of their White slumber and their sense of self-protection:

> I would like to know what the rest of you feel about the White racist behavior of the whites in these texts. Do you feel guilty? And how do you feel about the fact that your own whiteness implicates you in a structural White power system from which you are able to gain so many privileges? How do you understand your whiteness vis-à-vis the whites in the texts?[11]

In response to his question, he received a "thoughtful" response from the professor, one "groping" rejoinder, and a reply from a male student that "I need to get back to you on this. I have not given thought to this before."[12]

Yancy's overall frustration at the lack of response to his question is something that carries over into other classes, especially those that engage the concept of whiteness. The other students in the class probably regarded themselves as "good-will whites,"[13] who could not imagine that they could ever lay "an oppressive" hand on anyone. However, as Yancy notes, "they failed to locate their own center of power"[14] within a society framed around whiteness. Hear it from me now: Yancy has put his finger on the pulse of a significant pedagogical problem. I, too, have found that Whites, when confronted with their whiteness, often cope with it through various forms of disassociation in which "other White people are racist—not I." As a result, it is likely that one will find, at best, a weak emotional response in White students to their own history, and little to no response to the ways in which their own whiteness is implicated in the current reality of White supremacy.

While we might share Yancy's frustration with his fellow students, we should also be aware that teachers may also fail to take up these issues. These issues can function as important "teachable moments." This is what someone who teaches whiteness, or teaches about race generally, needs to be able to do.

When a White student or a student like Yancy responds to whiteness with any range of emotions, a professor needs to know how to channel them and to harness them to serve instructional goals. In what follows, I want to share some effective strategies for doing so.

Learning to Sit with Discomfort

I often teach Janine Jones's essay "The Impairment of Empathy in Goodwill Whites for African Americans," in my unit on whiteness, for its salient critique of whiteness. At the end of her essay, Jones poses a provocative question: "What does a heart of whiteness *really* desire?" This question moves the discussion forward, from the task of making whiteness visible to the task of getting students to confront the whiteness in and around them. I help students do this in a couple of ways: first, I expose certain ways in which they are actively but unwittingly engaging in whiteness; second, in order to disrupt the blinding effects of whiteness, I present the concept of awareness developed by Albert Memmi, which I will explain below.

There are a few ways that I demonstrate how students are actively engaged in whiteness. One exercise is based on Peggy Macintosh's "White Privilege: Unpacking the Invisible Knapsack." The students in the classroom then go on a "privilege walk," where nonwhite students talk about being profiled by the police or followed in a store, where students in the room are asked whether they have a family member or friend in the penal system, or where they are asked whether they know someone who has been murdered. These exercises start to shake White students out of their slumber and help them to see some of the privileges of their whiteness. White students begin to realize that some social goods are obtainable simply due to their whiteness, that they don't have to experience some things because of their whiteness, and that there are material benefits that they receive because of their whiteness.

Surprisingly enough, another way to get students to see the impact of whiteness today is through a discussion of crime. I provide several scenarios and then ask students to "race the crime" by indicating whether it was committed by a Black person or a White person. One scenario, for instance, describes a serial killer. I ask: "Who do you think is more likely to be a serial killer, a Black person or a White person?" Most of the students (Black and White) will say that a serial killer is likely to be White. I then ask them to explain why they believe this. Without fail, some brave student will inevitably say something to the effect that to be a serial killer takes a certain amount of planning, being methodical, and intelligence. These characteristics, the student concludes, add up to the person being White. We compare this with other types of crime, and discuss what this implies about the types of crime that Black people commit. The answer to the question is typically the opposite; that is, that Black people commit crimes that are unplanned, not methodical, unintelligent, and perhaps even irrational. I then *remind* them of Kincheloe's argument that aligned the concept of whiteness with rationality. This reiterates the ways in which their perceptions of criminal behavior have been shaped by the concept of whiteness. Moreover, it opens up the possibility that this extends to other aspects of their lives that may also be framed by whiteness.

You can, at this point, feel the discomfort in the room. The key is not to explain the discomfort away or deny it, but (as George Yancy once told me) to allow students to tarry with the discomfort. As an educator, it is important to remember that most students are probably not able or prepared to take responsibility for the whiteness around them or the whiteness that they enact—this may be for a variety of different reasons: lack of maturity, self-denial, lack of comprehension. More importantly (and, for me, this is critical), my class may be the first and perhaps the last place in the university that these students have an opportunity to read or discuss the topic of whiteness.

That said, it seems that a reasonable goal is to challenge students to become *aware of the whiteness around them.* One way to help them see what this involves is to introduce them to Albert Memmi's book *Racism.* There, Memmi raises an important but difficult question: "Are we then all racists for all times?"[15] For his part, Memmi denies that this is the case. However, he does acknowledge that we are always "tempted by racism." For Memmi, there remains in us "a soil prepared to receive and germinate its seeds the minute we let down our guard."[16] Students find this idea to be thought provoking, and it can lead to a productive discussion of what it means to be "tempted by racism," as well as the implications of "letting your guard down." In these discussions, some students point out how we tend to fall back on stereotypes to explain the actions of person who may be different from us; how we might use a word like "ghetto" to describe a Black woman we perceive as "loud"; or, how we make off-the-cuff comments about people of different races and ethnicities. Surprisingly, many students open up about how easy it is to succumb to racist thoughts and actions, especially when they are in what I like to call "racist safe spots" or "PC-free zones"—where they are surrounded by friends, family, or social peer groups in which racist remarks and attitudes are unchecked.

Memmi's response to the temptation of racism is a simple one. Since we are all tempted by racism, we have to be vigilant about our racist proclivities. We cannot close our eyes to this reality; instead, Memmi observes that "only by being fully cognizant of it can we hope to succeed."[17] At this point, I make the case to my students that Memmi's argument about racism, more generally, applies to whiteness. Students have to try to be cognizant of the whiteness in the room and the whiteness that they enact. I tell them that it is only through awareness and the practice of constant vigilance that they can hope to confront, if not eradicate, the impact of whiteness. This, too, may be uncomfortable; nevertheless, it is again in sitting with this discomfort that, perhaps, we may find the resources to disrupt the hegemony of whiteness and blunt its destructive power.

★ ★ ★ ★

For me, co-editing this volume has been an attempt to find strength and peace in my soul. It is my sincere hope that *Exploring Race in Predominantly White*

Classrooms can in some way communicate to scholars, who walk their raced bodies into spaces that are profoundly challenging, that they are not alone and that their experience is a shared one. It is also my hope that scholars find teaching and intellectual resources in this volume as well. The work that you do is important.

Notes

1 In his article "Geneva Smitherman: The Social Ontology of African-American Language, the Power of *Nommo,* and the Dynamics of Resistance and Identity through Language" (*The Journal of Speculative Philosophy,* 18(4), 2004: 273–299), George Yancy presents what I consider to be one of the best articles ever written on philosophy and language. See also *Reframing the Practice of Philosophy: Bodies of Color, Bodies of Knowledge,* ed. George Yancy (Albany, NY: State University of New York Press, 2012), chap. 15.
2 bell hooks, "Representing Whiteness in the Black Imagination," in *Displacing Whiteness: Essays in Social and Cultural Criticism,* ed. Ruth Frankenberg (Durham, NC: Duke University Press, 1997), 166.
3 Ibid.
4 Frankenberg, *Displacing Whiteness,* 15.
5 Richard Dyer, *White* (New York, NY: Routledge, 1997), 458.
6 Joe L. Kincheloe, "The Struggle to Define and Reinvent Whiteness: A Pedagogical Analysis," *College Literature,* 26(3), Fall 1999: 162–194, 164.
7 Ibid.
8 Ibid.
9 Ibid., 165.
10 Ibid.
11 George Yancy, "Introduction," in *What White Looks Like: African-American Philosophers on the Whiteness Question,* ed. George Yancy (New York, NY: Routledge, 2004), 4.
12 Yancy, "Introduction," 3.
13 Janine Jones, "The Impairment of Empathy in Goodwill Whites for African Americans," in *What White Looks Like: African-American Philosophers on the Whiteness Question,* ed. George Yancy (New York, NY: Routledge, 2004), 65–86.
14 Yancy, "Introduction," 4.
15 Albert Memmi, *Racism,* trans. Steve Martinot (Minneapolis, MN: University of Minnesota Press, 1999), 23.
16 Ibid.
17 Ibid., 24.

CONTRIBUTORS

Benita Bunjun is a Post Doctoral Fellow at the Centre for the Study of Gender, Social Inequities and Mental Health. One of her current research projects is The Academic Well-Being of Racialized Students. She earned her PhD in Interdisciplinary Studies at the University of British Columbia, Canada. Her doctoral thesis—*The (Un)Making of Home, Entitlement, and Nation: An Intersectional Organizational Study of Power Relations in Vancouver Status of Women, 1971–2008*—contributes to three broad areas: first, nation-building and colonial encounters; second, intersectionality; and, third, social change movements and organizational well-being. Bunjun is the past president of the Canadian Research Institute for the Advancement of Women, where she chaired the Intersectional Feminist Frameworks working group. She is also the past multiyear project coordinator of Vancouver Status of Women's Racialization of Poverty project. Currently, Bunjun teaches in the areas of women's and gender studies and sociology. Her involvement in marginal communities (academic and non-academic) has focused and continues to focus on the intersectional social constructions and relations of the gendered, sexualized, dispossessed, and racialized.

Meta G. Carstarphen, PhD, APR, teaches at the Gaylord College of Journalism and Mass Communication at the University of Oklahoma and serves as Director of the Graduate Program. Her research interests include rhetorical constructions of racial identity, gender portrayals, ethnic representations in media and mass communication history, and the social constructs of strategic communication. With professional experience in public relations and journalism, she has consulted on topics related to community relations, nonprofit public relations, and cross-cultural integrated communication. Awarded the first Gaylord family professorship in 2005, Carstarphen's resulting research explored the narratives, rhetoric, and history of Oklahoma's first American Indian and African American newspapers. Recent books include *Race, Gender, Class, and Media: Studying Mass Communication and Multiculturalism* (co-author, Sharon Bramlett-Solomon; Kendall-Hunt Publishers, 2012) and *American Indians and the Mass Media* (co-editor, John P. Sanchez; University of Oklahoma Press, 2012).

Maria del Guadalupe Davidson is Assistant Professor of Business Communication in the Michael F. Price School of Business, Co-Director at the Center for Social Justice, and an Affiliate Faculty member of the Women's and Gender Studies Program at the University of Oklahoma. She is the author of *The Rhetoric of Race: Toward a Revolutionary Construction of Black Identity* (University of Valencia Press, 2006) and co-editor of two volumes, *Critical Perspectives on bell hooks* (with George Yancy; Routledge, 2009) and *Convergences: Black Feminism and Continental Philosophy* (with Kathryn T. Gines and Donna-Dale L. Marcano; State University of New York Press, 2010). She is currently working on a book about black women and agency.

Kirsten T. Edwards, PhD, is Assistant Professor of Adult and Higher Education in the Department of Educational Leadership and Policy Studies at Jeannine Rainbolt College of Education, University of Oklahoma. Her research merges womanism and womanist theology, curriculum studies, and philosophies of higher education. More specifically, Edwards is interested in the ways that faith, race, gender, class, and culture impact learning, teaching, and knowledge production in university settings. Her publications have additionally considered how identities impact pedagogical approaches in the study of equity, inclusion, and social justice along the educational pipeline. Edwards' research has been published in various peer-reviewed venues, such as the *Journal of Curriculum Theorizing*, the *International Journal of Leadership in Education*, and the *Journal of Curriculum and Pedagogy*. Edwards' honors and awards include being a finalist in the 2012 *International Journal of Leadership in Education*'s Emerging Scholar Manuscript Competition, a Louisiana State University (LSU) Dissertation Year Fellowship recipient, the 2010 LSU Black Faculty and Staff Caucus "Most Outstanding Graduate Student" award recipient, a National Council for Black Studies Summer Institute program participant, and an LSU School of Education "Dissertation of the Year" award winner.

Arnold Farr, Associate Professor of Philosophy at the University of Kentucky (UK), received his PhD in Philosophy from UK in 1996. He became a member of the Department of Philosophy at Saint Joseph's University (SJU) in Philadelphia, Pennsylvania, in August of 1996 and was tenured in 2002. After 12 years at SJU, he was hired by the Department of Philosophy at the College of Arts and Sciences, UK, where he is Director of Graduate Studies. He is also a member of the interdisciplinary Committee on Social Theory at UK. He is the former Co-Chair of the interdisciplinary Africana Studies program in the UK College of Arts and Sciences, and was the first Scholar in Residence for the Martin Luther King, Jr. Centre at UK. Farr's research interests are German idealism, critical theory, Marxism, Africana philosophy, psychoanalysis, postmodernism, and liberation philosophy. He has published numerous articles and book chapters on all of the above topics. Farr is a co-editor and co-author of *Marginal Groups and Mainstream American Culture* (University Press of Kansas, 2000), and, in 2009, his *Critical Theory and Democratic Vision: Herbert Marcuse and Recent Liberation Philosophies* volume was published by Lexington Books. He is currently working on a collection of essays on Herbert Marcuse, a book entitled *Misrecognition, Mimetic Rivalry, and One-Dimensionality:Toward a Critical Theory of Human Conflict and Social Pathologies*, and Marcuse's intellectual biography.

A. Todd Franklin is Professor of Philosophy at Hamilton College, Clinton, New York. He teaches courses on existentialism, Nietzsche, and critical race, gender, and cultural theory, and is a past recipient of Hamilton College's "Class of 1963 Excellence in Teaching Award" (2000). His research focuses on the existential, social, and political implications of various critical and transformative discourses aimed at cultivating individual and collective self-realization. The author of several scholarly works on the social and political import of various forms of existential enlightenment, Franklin is also the co-editor, with Jacqueline Scott, of a volume titled *Critical Affinities: Nietzsche and African American Thought* (State University of New York Press, 2006).

Kathy Glass received her PhD in English from the University of California, San Diego. She is Associate Professor of English and Director of Undergraduate Studies at McAnulty College and Graduate School of Liberal Arts, Duquesne University, in Pittsburgh, Pennsylvania. Her areas of research include African American literature, Black feminist critical theory, American literature, women's studies, American studies, and Black studies. She is the author of *Courting Communities: Black Female Nationalism and "Syncre-Nationalism" in the Nineteenth-Century North* (Routledge, 2006), and "Tending to the Roots:The Sociopolitical Activism of Anna Julia Cooper," *Meridians: Feminism, race, transnationalism, 6*(1), 2005: 23–55. She has also published chapters on critical pedagogy and Black feminist thought.

Clevis Headley received his PhD in Philosophy from the University of Miami, Florida. He is currently Associate Professor of Philosophy at Florida Atlantic University (FAU) and Director of the Ethnic Studies Program in the Dorothy F. Schmidt College of Arts and Letters, FAU, as well as Director of its Master's in Liberal Studies program. In addition, he is a founding member, Vice-President Emeritus, and Co-Director of Publications of the Caribbean Philosophical Association. Headley has published widely in the areas of critical race theory and

Africana philosophy. He has also published in analytic philosophy, focusing specifically on Gottlob Frege.

Clarence Sholé Johnson is Professor of Philosophy at Middle Tennessee State University, where he teaches courses in ethics, epistemology, early modern philosophy, and Africana philosophy. He has published in these areas as well as in social and political philosophy, and his publications include *Cornel West and Philosophy: The Quest for Social Justice* (Routledge, 2003), chapters in a number of philosophy books, entries in a forthcoming *Encyclopedia of African Religions and Philosophy* (edited by V.Y. Mudimbe), and articles in a variety of major scholarly journals such as the *Journal of Social Philosophy*, *Social Philosophy Today*, *Journal of Philosophical Research*, *Dialogue: Canadian Philosophical Review*, *The Southern Journal of Philosophy*, *Southwest Philosophy Review*, and *Metaphilosophy*. Johnson is also a member of the Phi Beta Delta honor society for international scholars, for which he twice served as President of the Beta Omega (Spelman College) Chapter.

Jo-Anne Lee is Associate Professor in the Department of Women's Studies at the University of Victoria in British Columbia, Canada. A sociologist by training, her research focuses on antiracist, decolonizing theory and practice. She has an extensive background in community development and organizing with women and girls in urban settings. She is co-editor, with John S. Lutz, of *Situating "Race" and Racisms in Time, Space, and Theory: Critical Essays for Activists and Scholars*, published by McGill-Queen's University Press in 2005. She also co-edited, with Rita Wong, a special issue of *West Coast Line* titled "Active Geographies: Women and Struggles on the Left Coast", 42(2), 2008, that brought together older and younger grassroots activists from Asian Canadian, Indigenous, and other backgrounds in a multi-genre, multidisciplinary, and multigenerational collection. Her research appears in international journals such as *Gender, Place and Culture: A Journal of Feminist Geography*, *Child and Youth Services*, and *Gender and Education*, as well as in academic presses such as those of the University of Toronto, McGill University, and the University of British Columbia. Lee is at the forefront of establishing antiracist feminist girlhood studies as a new field of scholarship and practice. She is a co-founder and director-at-large of Antidote, a grassroots network and community-based organization for multiracial and Indigenous girls and young women in Victoria, British Columbia, that, in 2009, won the Representative for Children and Youth's "Cultural Heritage and Diversity Award of Excellence" for its pioneering work in addressing youth and diversity. Her path-breaking work in participatory action research uses popular theatre, video documentaries, digital media, and arts-based methods. As past President of the Canadian Research Institute for the Advancement of Women (CRIAW), Canada's only independent national feminist research establishment, Lee helped it adopt more nuanced intersectional approaches in its regional, national, and international work with women.

Zeus Leonardo, Associate Professor, teaches the Language and Literacy, Society and Culture and the Leadership for Educational Equity programs at the Graduate School of Education of the University of California, Berkeley, and is an Affiliated Faculty Member (Education) of the university's interdisciplinary Designated Emphasis in Critical Theory project. He has published several dozen articles and book chapters on critical theories of race, including "The Souls of White Folk: Critical Pedagogy, Whiteness Studies, and Globalization Discourse" (*Race Ethnicity and Education*, 5(1), 2002: 29–50), "Critical Social Theory and Transformative Knowledge: The Functions of Criticism in Quality Education" (*Educational Researcher*, 33(6), 2004: 11–18), and "Pale/ontology: The Conceptual Status of Whiteness in Education" (in Michael W. Apple, Luís Armando Gandin, and Wayne Au (Eds.), *The Routledge International Handbook of Critical Education*, Routledge, 2009). His books include *Race, Whiteness and Education* (Routledge, 2009) and *Race Frameworks: A Multidimensional Theory of Racism and Education* (Teachers College Press, 2013). Leonardo's current research interests involve the study of ideologies and discourses in education. Much of his work is inter-disciplinary and draws insights from sociology, contemporary philosophy, and cultural studies. In particular, he engages critical theories to inform his analysis of the relationship between schooling and social relations, such as race, class, and culture. His research is informed by the premise that educational knowledge should promote the democratization of schools and society.

Sanjukta Mukherjee is an Assistant Professor and Affiliated Faculty Member (Women's and Gender Studies) of the International Studies graduate program of the College of Liberal Arts and Social Sciences at DePaul University, Chicago. Her research and teaching interests lie at the intersection of transnational feminisms, feminist political economy, antiracist anti-imperialist pedagogies, research methods/methodologies, critical development studies and urban geographies. She received a PhD in Geography from Syracuse University, New York, and a postdoctoral fellowship from the University of Toronto's Munk Centre for International Studies (now the Munk School of Global Affairs). Currently, she is working on a book manuscript titled *Producing the IT Miracle: The Neoliberalizing State and Changing Gender and Class Regimes in India*, which examines the socio-spatial implications of Third World states' transition to neoliberalism, particularly in relation to changing gender constructions of labor in hi-tech spaces of production. She has taught courses in subject areas such as transnationalism; globalization and gender; political economy of cities; feminism postcoloniality and development; urban lives—race, class, and gender; and research methods.

Nana Osei-Kofi is Director of the Difference, Power, and Discrimination program and Associate Professor of Women, Gender, and Sexuality Studies at Oregon State University (OSU). Prior to this, she was Associate Professor and Director of the Social Justice Studies Certificate program in the School of Education at Iowa State University. Her scholarship focuses on critical, feminist, and public pedagogies; the politics of American higher education; visual cultural studies; and arts-based inquiry. Journals in which her work has appeared include *Discourse: Studies in the Cultural Politics of Education*, *Equity & Excellence in Education*, and *Race, Ethnicity and Education*. She has served on the editorial board of the *Review of Higher Education* and is currently a member of the editorial board of *Feminist Formations*, and the advisory board of the *Journal of Critical Thought and Praxis*. Osei-Kofi holds an MA in Applied Women's Studies and a PhD in Education from Claremont Graduate University, California.

Antonia Randolph is a lecturer in the Department of Sociology, Social Work, and Anthropology at Christopher Newport University, Virginia. Her research and teaching interests include diversity discourse in education, multicultural capital, non-normative Black masculinity, and the production of misogyny in hip-hop culture. She has been published in *Anthropology and Education Quarterly*, *Youth and Society*, and *Race, Gender, and Class*. In 2013, her book *The Wrong Kind of Different: Challenging the Meaning of Diversity in American Schools* was published by Teachers College Press. Randolph holds a BA in Sociology from Spelman College, Georgia, and a PhD in Sociology from Northwestern University, Illinois.

Joe Watkins is the Supervisory Anthropologist and Chief of the Tribal Relations and American Cultures program at the National Park Service in Washington, D.C. Prior to this, he was an Associate Professor and the Director of the Native American Studies Program at the University of Oklahoma. He is the author of *Indigenous Archaeology: American Indian Values and Scientific Practice* (Alta Mira Press, 2000) and *Sacred Sites and Repatriation* (Chelsea House Publishers, 2006), and a co-author (with Carol J. Ellick) of *The Anthropology Graduate's Guide: From Student to a Career* (Left Coast Press, 2011). Watkins has published numerous articles in a variety of journals, and has been heavily involved in examining the ethics of anthropology's relationships with Indigenous populations worldwide.

Dyan Watson is an Assistant Professor of Education at the Lewis & Clark Graduate School of Education and Counseling in Portland, Oregon, and serves as the social studies coordinator for the secondary program in teacher education. She teaches methods classes for preservice social studies teachers, research methods classes for doctoral students, and researches how race mediates teaching. Her doctoral thesis—*Norming Suburban: How Teachers Describe Teaching in Urban Schools* (Harvard Graduate School of Education, 2007)—was a qualitative study that explored novice teachers' beliefs about teaching in urban schools. She has had articles published in the *Journal of Teacher Education*, *Urban Education*, and *Rethinking Schools*.

Karsonya Wise Whitehead is an Assistant Professor in the Department of Communication and an Affiliate Assistant Professor in African and African American Studies at Loyola University, Maryland. She is a historian who works in the Black documentary tradition. She is the author of two forthcoming books, *Emilie Frances Davis, Her Life, In Her Own Words: 1863–1865* (University of South Carolina Press, 2014) and *The Emancipation Proclamation: Race Relations on the Eve of Reconstruction* (Routledge, 2014). She is also the author of numerous articles, lesson plans, and state curriculums and has received various fellowships and grants to support her work, including, in 2012, a Gilder Lehrman Institute of American History fellowship and, in 2010, a National Endowment for the Humanities Summer Stipend. Whitehead has served as the historical consultant for a series of documentaries on Philadelphia, as guest editor for the 2013 special edition of the Association for the Study of African American Life and History's *Black History Bulletin*, and as historical content editor for Red Lion Press' children's, historical fiction, graphic novel series, which was released in 2010.

George Yancy is Professor of Philosophy at the McAnulty College and Graduate School of Liberal Arts, Duquesne University, in Pennsylvania. He received his BA in Philosophy at the University of Pittsburgh, his first Master's degree from Yale University in Philosophy, and his second Master's degree, in Africana Studies, from New York University, where he received a distinguished fellowship. His PhD (with distinction) is in Philosophy and from Duquesne University. His work focuses primarily in the areas of critical philosophy of race, critical whiteness studies, and philosophy of the Black experience. He has authored, edited, or co-edited 17 books, 39 academic articles, and 32 book chapters. His first authored book received an honorable mention in the Gustavus Myers Center for the Study of Bigotry and Human Rights "outstanding book award" national competition, and three of his edited books have received *Choice* "outstanding academic title" awards. He is Co-Editor of the American Philosophical Association's "APA Newsletter" *Philosophy and the Black Experience*, and is an ex officio member of the APA Committee on Black Philosophers. Yancy has twice won the Duquesne University McAnulty College and Graduate School of Liberal Arts Faculty Award for Excellence in Scholarship. He is currently working on two edited books and a new authored title.

INDEX